LEIBNIZ
LOGICAL PAPERS

LEIBNIZ

LOGICAL PAPERS

A Selection
Translated and Edited
with an Introduction
by
G. H. R. PARKINSON

Senior Lecturer in Philosophy
University of Reading

CLARENDON PRESS
OXFORD
1966

*Oxford University Press, Ely House, London W.*1
GLASGOW NEW YORK TORONTO MELBOURNE WELLINGTON
CAPE TOWN SALISBURY IBADAN NAIROBI LUSAKA ADDIS ABABA
BOMBAY CALCUTTA MADRAS KARACHI LAHORE DACCA
KUALA LUMPUR HONG KONG

Printed in Great Britain at the Pitman Press, Bath

CONTENTS

[1] Italics indicate that the title translated is Leibniz's.

ABBREVIATIONS

1. Leibniz's Works

A   *Gottfried Wilhelm Leibniz: Sämtliche Schriften und Briefe*, Academy Edition (Darmstadt and Berlin, 1923–). References are to series and volume.

C   *Opuscules et Fragments inédits de Leibniz*, edited by L. Couturat (Paris, 1903).

D   *G. G. Leibnitii Opera Omnia*, edited by L. Dutens, 6 vols. (Geneva, 1768).

DM   *Discours de Métaphysique*, edited by H. Lestienne (2nd ed., Paris, 1952).

FC   *Nouvelles Lettres et Opuscules inédits de Leibniz*, edited by Foucher de Careil (Paris, 1857).

G   *Die philosophischen Schriften von Gottfried Wilhelm Leibniz*, edited by C. I. Gerhardt, 7 vols. (Berlin, 1875–90).

G.M.   *Leibnizens mathematische Schriften*, edited by C. I. Gerhardt, 7 vols. (Berlin and Halle, 1849–63).

Grua   *G. W. Leibniz: Textes inédits*, edited by G. Grua (Paris, 1948).

NE   *Nouveaux Essais sur l'entendement humain*. The text is that of *A vi. 6;* references are to book, chapter, and section.

Schmidt   *Gottfried Wilhelm Leibniz: Fragmente zur Logik*, edited and translated by F. Schmidt (Berlin, 1960).

A page reference in brackets, placed after a reference to one of Leibniz's works, indicates the pages of the present volume.

2. Other Works

C.L.   *La Logique de Leibniz*, by L. Couturat (Paris, 1901).

Fischer-Kabitz *Gottfried Wilhelm von Leibniz*, by Kuno Fischer, 5th ed., revised by W. Kabitz (Heidelberg, 1920).

Jungius *Logica Hamburgensis*, by J. Jungius, edited by R. W. Meyer (Hamburg, 1957).

Kauppi   *Über die Leibnizsche Logik*, by R. Kauppi (Helsinki, 1960).

Kneale   *The Development of Logic*, by W. and M. Kneale (Oxford, 1962).

Lewis   *A Survey of Symbolic Logic,* by C. I. Lewis, 2nd ed.
         (New York, 1960).
LR   *Logic and Reality in Leibniz's Metaphysics,* by G. H. R.
         Parkinson (Oxford, 1965).

3. *Other Abbreviations*

L.-   A marginal note by Leibniz.
. . .   A lacuna in the manuscript.
. . . . . . An omission made by the editor.

INTRODUCTION

The importance of Leibniz in the history of logic has been recognized for many years; nevertheless, it is probably true to say that most people know Leibniz's logical papers through what has been written about them, rather than by acquaintance with the works themselves, either in the original or in translations. There are good reasons for this. Although Leibniz published little about logic during his lifetime, he left a great deal of unpublished work, relatively little of which is dated. Subsequent editors have published extensive selections from this material without trying to impose any order on it, with the result that the reader receives a daunting impression of chaotic profusion. This is not to blame these editors, to whom—in particular, to Gerhardt and Couturat—students of Leibniz owe a great deal; it is simply to explain why, with a few exceptions, Leibniz's logical works are usually known by description rather than by acquaintance.

The present book offers translations of a selection of Leibniz's logical papers, ranging from those written in youth to those written in maturity. The works selected are those which the translator believes to be Leibniz's most important in the field of logic; the arrangement is, as far as possible, chronological. A certain amount of explanatory comment is necessary if these works are to be understood, and it will be the function of this introduction to provide such comment.

Gottfried Wilhelm Leibniz was born in Leipzig on 1 July 1646,[1] some two years before the Peace of Westphalia put an end to the Thirty Years War. He studied first at the Nikolaischule in Leipzig, and then at the University, where his father (who died when Leibniz was only six) had been professor of moral philosophy. A brief account of the type of education that Leibniz received will provide a background against which his logical works may be set. This education was narrowly traditional, the tradition being that of German-Protestant Aristotelianism.[2] At

---

[1] 21 June, O.S.

[2] On this tradition, see P. Petersen, *Geschichte der aristotelischen Philosophie im protestantischen Deutschland* (Leipzig, 1921), and D. Mahnke, *Leibnizens Synthese von Universalmathematik und Individualmetaphysik* (Halle, 1925), pp. 81–88. For the type of education that Leibniz received at school, see W. Kabitz, 'Die Bildungsgeschichte des jungen Leibniz', in *Zeitschrift für Geschichte der Erziehung und des Unterrichts*, vol. ii (Berlin,

school, the main emphasis was on divinity; arithmetic was taught only at an elementary level, and geometry was not taught at all. Logic was studied chiefly in the *Compendium Logicae Peripateticae* of Johannes Rhenius, a textbook of Aristotelian logic written, after the manner of Melanchthon's manuals, in question and answer form. Nor were the intellectual horizons of the University of Leipzig, which Leibniz entered in 1661, much wider; here again, the emphasis was on traditional Aristotelian doctrine.[1] Leibniz, however, was able to break out of the narrow limits of the educational system. A precocious student—he taught himself Latin from an illustrated copy of Livy when he was about eight[2]—he was soon given access to his father's library, where he read at will. The books themselves appear to have been in the same Aristotelian tradition as the education that he received at school and university, but they did at least enable him to study the tradition at first hand.[3] An interest in logic soon showed itself; when Leibniz was only thirteen or fourteen he was 'filling sheets of paper with wonderful meditations about logic',[4] and testing his masters with questions about categories.[5]

In view of all this, it is not surprising that in later life Leibniz described himself as 'almost self-taught'[6] in his youth. However,

---

1912); also Fischer-Kabitz, pp. 711–12, and R. W. Meyer, *Leibnitz and the Seventeenth-Century Revolution*, trans. by J. P. Stern (Cambridge, 1952), pp. 85 ff.

[1] Meyer, op. cit., p. 86.

[2] Fischer-Kabitz, p. 711.

[3] Leibniz states that he read Zabarella, Ruvio, and Toletus before he was twelve (*G vii. 126*), but it seems likely that his study of the Scholastics dates from 1661 at the earliest (Fischer-Kabitz, p. 712).

[4] *G vii. 126*. In this passage, Leibniz states that his logical studies, like his study of the Scholastics, began when he was 'not yet twelve', but this again seems to be an exaggeration (Fischer-Kabitz, pp. 33 and 712).

[5] *G vii. 126, 185, 292, 516–17; C 346*. These questions related to what Leibniz later called the idea of an alphabet of human thoughts, an idea which he first published in 1666 (cf. p. xiii below). Leibniz's problem was this: there are, he said, categories for simple terms, i.e. for concepts, by which concepts may be arranged systematically to form propositions—why, then, are there not categories for complex terms (i.e. for propositions), by which truths may be arranged systematically to form deductive arguments? Leibniz noted later that he was then unaware (as were his teachers) of the fact that the systematic arrangement of truths in this way is just what is done in geometry, when propositions are arranged in accordance with their dependence on one another, so that his question was unnecessary. However, in pursuing this problem, it occurred to him that such a systematization would be possible if a better account were first given of the categories of simple terms; a list of such terms would constitute, in Leibniz's later terminology, the 'alphabet of human thoughts'.

[6] *G vii. 185*.

as Leibniz himself said, he owed much to two of his teachers at Leipzig, Adam Scherzer and Jakob Thomasius;[1] nor was his university education confined to the city of his birth. It was probably because he was dissatisfied with the teaching of mathematics at Leipzig that he spent the summer of 1663 at Jena, studying under Erhard Weigel. Weigel was far from being a great, or even a well-informed, mathematician—he seems, for example, to have had no knowledge of such an important recent development as Cartesian geometry.[2] Nevertheless, he was a good teacher, and there is no doubt that he influenced Leibniz.[3] In his *Analysis Aristotelica ex Euclide restituta* (1658), referred to by Leibniz as *Analysis Euclidea*,[4] Weigel criticized the Scholastics for having misunderstood Aristotle's logic. Weigel's view was that Aristotle recognized as valid only mathematical proof, and that his logic should therefore be re-established on a Euclidean basis. More generally, Weigel wanted the whole of philosophy to be given the rigour of a mathematical discipline; in this, he is a precursor of Leibniz's ideas about a Universal Characteristic.[5]

Weigel also stressed the importance of arithmetic, both as a theoretical and as a practical discipline. This idea reappears in the *De Arte Combinatoria*, the work with which Leibniz sought to obtain a position as a teacher in the Philosophical Faculty at Leipzig in 1666.[6] The theme of the treatise, excerpts from which form the first item in the selections translated below, was what would now be called combinations and permutations, and was by no means new; Leibniz could have found such matters discussed in the works of Tartaglia, Buteo (Jean Borrel), Cardan, and Pascal.[7] At the time of writing, however, he had no knowledge of these works, except through references in the *Deliciae Physico-Mathematicae* of Schwenter and Harsdörffer, a popular book of problems published in 1636.[8] As might be expected, the *De Arte Combinatoria* is

---

[1] Fischer-Kabitz, pp. 38, 713.
[2] M. Cantor, *Vorlesungen über Geschichte der Mathematik* (Leipzig, 1898), iii, pp. 36–37.
[3] Cantor's somewhat harsh dismissal of Weigel (ibid.) is based on a one-sided view; a more complete and more attractive picture can be found in Meyer, op. cit., pp. 88–90.
[4] *A vi. 1, 235, 282*; *C 179*. For a discussion of the *Analysis*, see Fischer-Kabitz, pp. 714–15, and W. Kabitz, *Die Philosophie des jungen Leibniz* (Heidelberg, 1909), pp. 9 ff.
[5] See p. xvii below.
[6] Leibniz used only a part of it, known as *Disputatio Arithmetica de Complexionibus*, for the disputation, held on 17 March 1666 (*A vi. 1, xix*).
[7] Cantor, op. cit., iii, p. 38.
[8] *A vi. 1, 173*. Further references to this work in the *De Arte Combinatoria* are in *A vi. 1, 202, 204, 213, 215–18*. Mention may also be made

in many respects immature—the work of a 'young man just out of school', as Leibniz himself later called it.[1] Nevertheless, it is a work of the greatest interest, in that it contains (still not wholly recognized by Leibniz) some of the basic ideas of his logic: namely, that every proposition has a subject and a predicate, that all truths are or are reducible to identical propositions, and that the proposition is best treated intensionally. Leibniz continued to value the work because it touched on an idea whose full importance he says that he grasped only later,[2] the idea of an 'alphabet of human thoughts',[3] and it is this idea which is the central theme of the passages translated here.

In the *De Arte Combinatoria* Leibniz follows the traditional division of logic into two parts: 'inventive logic', or the 'logic of discovery', and the 'logic of judgement', the 'analytic part of logic'.[4] Leibniz claims that the theory of combinations and permutations can throw light on both these parts of logic; indeed, he goes so far as to say that the theory constitutes almost the whole of the logic of discovery.[5] This branch of logic is further divided into two; one part concerns terms, and is called the 'theory of divisions', whilst the other is called the 'theory of propositions', since propositions are its concern.[6]

In the course of showing the relation of combinations and permutations to the theory of division Leibniz considers such problems as the determination of various kinds of mandate, or the number of the Aristotelian elements,[7] and in the middle of this discussion he considers a problem which belongs to the logic of judgement—the determination of the number of valid syllogistic moods.[8] This problem was to exercise Leibniz again,[9] and

here of another influence on the *De Arte Combinatoria*, Johann Heinrich Bisterfeld, whose *Phosphorus Catholicus* is quoted in the work (*A vi. 1, 199*). From Bisterfeld, Leibniz derived some of the basic ideas of his treatise—the ideas of unity in multiplicity, of the divisibility of what is compound into its simple elements, and of its reconstructibility from them (Kabitz, op. cit., pp. 6–8; Mahnke, op. cit., pp. 68, 72. Cf. L. E. Loemker, 'Leibniz and the Herborn Encyclopedists', *Journal of the History of Ideas*, 1961, pp. 323 ff).

[1] *G vii. 186.*
[2] *G vii. 186; C 175.*
[3] *G vii. 11, 185, 199, 292; C 220–1, 430, 435.*
[4] *A vi. 1, 177* (p. 3). For this distinction, cf. Cicero, *Topics*, ii. 6, and Boethius, Second Commentary on the *Isagoge* of Porphyry, i. 2.
[5] *A vi. 1, 177* (p. 3).
[6] Ibid.
[7] *A vi. 1, 177–8.*
[8] *A vi. 1, 179 ff.*
[9] e.g. *C 410 ff.* (pp. 105 ff.).

since his discussion in the *De Arte Combinatoria* is unnecessarily complicated[1] it is not translated here. It is in connexion with the second part of inventive logic, the 'theory of propositions', that Leibniz introduces the idea of an alphabet of human thoughts. He begins by stating a view which is fundamental to his logic, and which he never abandoned: namely, that every proposition has a subject and a predicate.[2] He next proposes, as a task for inventive logic, the problem of determining all the possible predicates of any given subject, and all the possible subjects of any given predicate. To solve this problem, he argues, it is first necessary to show how any term can be analysed.[3] He is clearly using 'term' in the traditional sense of the subject or predicate of a proposition,[4] and the fact that he speaks in this context of an alphabet of human *thoughts* indicates that he regards such terms as concepts. The analysis, then, is one of concepts; stated roughly, Leibniz's view is that every concept is either ultimate and indefinable, or is composed of such concepts. The indefinable concepts are called by Leibniz 'first terms',[5] and a list of these constitutes what he was later to call the 'alphabet of human thoughts', for derivative concepts are formed from first terms in much the same way as words are formed from the letters of the alphabet.[6] Leibniz proposes to regard the first terms as constituting the first of a series of classes; the second class of the series consists of the first terms arranged in groups of two; the third class, of the first terms arranged in groups of three; and so on.[7]

It is unnecessary to discuss in detail here Leibniz's application of this scheme to his problem about subjects and predicates,[8] but it is worth while to note the way in which he uses it to explain predication. He says[9] that the predicates of a given subject are either its first terms, or they are the derived terms 'nearer to' the first terms and of which all the first terms are in the given subject. This can be explained as follows. Suppose that *a*, *b*, and *c* are first terms and that when combined they constitute the term *x*. We may predicate of *x* any one of these first terms—e.g. *a*—or any

---

[1] Leibniz treats singular and indefinite propositions independently of universal and particular propositions, even though he believes (*A vi. 1, 183*) that a singular proposition can be treated as a universal, and an indefinite as a particular proposition.
[2] *A vi. 1, 192* (p. 3).
[3] *A vi. 1, 194* (p. 4).
[4] *A vi. 1, 192* (p. 3); cf. Jungius, p. 67.
[5] *A vi. 1, 195* (p. 4).
[6] *G vii. 292.*
[7] *A vi. 1, 195* (p. 4).
[8] For a discussion of this point, see C.L., pp. 41–44.
[9] *A vi. 1, 195* (p. 5).

combination of these first terms belonging to the second class—
e.g. *ab*. In saying that these derived terms are 'nearer to' first
terms, Leibniz may mean that they are nearer to first terms than
x is, since *x* (which is equivalent to *abc*) belongs to the third class.
Leibniz adds[1] that we may also predicate of a subject its entire
definition; in this case, we may say of *x* that it is *abc*.[2]

This view of predication was of greater importance for Leibniz
than he first realized. The view, it has just been suggested, is that
when for example the term *x* is equivalent to the term *abc*, one may
say of *x* that it is *a*, *b*, *c*, *ab*, *ac*, *bc*, or *abc*. From this it follows that
one may not say of *x* that it is *d*, if *d* is a term which is not equivalent to *a*, *b*, *c*, or any combination of them. This suggests that a
proposition is true when it is of the form '*abc* is *abc*', '*abc* is *bc*',
'*abc* is *c*', etc., which Leibniz was to express later in the form of the
assertion that a true proposition is or is reducible to an identical
proposition.[3] Further, in saying that (for example) *x* is *a* one will
be saying that *a* is *one of* the concepts constituting *x*, or, as Leibniz
was to put it later,[4] one will be saying that the concept of the
predicate, *a*, is *included in* the concept of the subject, *x*. It must be
admitted that this was not Leibniz's express opinion when he
wrote the *De Arte Combinatoria*; on paper, he follows Hobbes by
regarding predication in terms of addition or subtraction, or he
follows Aristotelian and Scholastic tradition by speaking of the
mind 'compounding and dividing'.[5] Yet the more mature views
mentioned above seem clearly implicit, and with them Leibniz's
view that to assert a proposition is to say that one *concept* is

---

[1] *A vi. 1, 196* (p. 5).
[2] A similar account is to be found in one of Leibniz's later works, *De
Synthesi et Analysi Universali*. This was probably written in about 1679
(C.L., pp. 189 n. 1 and 323 n. 1) and refers explicitly to the *De Arte
Combinatoria*. In this work Leibniz again divides primitive terms (which
he calls *summa genera*) into groups of two, three, &c., which are called
respectively genera of the second and third grade, &c. He continues
(*G vii. 293*): 'Given any species, there could be enumerated in order the
propositions which are demonstrable of it—i.e. its predicates, both those
which are wider than it and those which are convertible—of which the
more memorable could be selected. For suppose that there is a species
y, whose concept is *abcd*, and that for *ab* there is substituted *l*; for *ac*, *m*;
for *ad*, *n*; for *bc*, *p*; for *bd*, *q*; and for *cd*, *r*, which are groups of two.
Suppose also that for *abc* there is substituted *s*; for *abd*, *v*; for *acd*, *w*; and
for *bcd*, *x*, which are groups of three. All these will be predicates of *y*, but
the convertible predicates of *y* will be the following only: *ax*, *bw*, *cv*, *ds*,
lr, *mq*, *np*. I have said more about this in my little treatise *Of the Art of
Combination*, which I published when I had scarcely reached manhood.'
[3] On identical propositions, see also p. xxiv below and *LR*, pp. 57 ff.
[4] Cf. pp. xxi, xxiv, xxxii, xxxvii, xxxix.
[5] *A vi. 1, 194* (p. 3).

included in another—that is, his 'intensional' view of the proposition.[1]

To return to the idea of a class of first terms, an 'alphabet of human thoughts': in the *De Arte Combinatoria* Leibniz makes no attempt to list these terms. All that he offers is an analysis of certain mathematical terms, which he himself describes as an 'extemporary essay',[2] starting, not from first terms absolutely, but only from those which are first in mathematics. His analysis has justly been criticized for its crudity,[3] but it is of historical interest and so is translated below.[4] More important in the development of Leibniz's thought is something which he introduces as an appendix to his discussion of first terms. This is the idea of a 'universal writing' or 'universal polygraphy',[5] which will be constructed by giving a separate sign to each of the first terms. Later, and particularly in his letters, Leibniz had much to say about the value of such a writing; in the *De Arte Combinatoria* he is more concise, though none the less bold, claiming that as this writing is learnt 'a fundamental knowledge of all things will be obtained'.[6]

Not only would possession of the alphabet of human thoughts provide us with, as it were, the conceptual atoms from which absolutely all molecular concepts can be formed, but in knowing this alphabet, and in knowing how all derived concepts are to be reduced to it, we should have what Leibniz regards as a powerful instrument of deductive proof. That this is so is implied by his views about such proof. In the *De Arte Combinatoria* he remarks briefly that demonstration has one *locus* or topic, definition.[7] In

---

[1] On this, see p. xxi below. The fact that Leibniz says (*A vi. 1, 196* (p. 5); cf. *G vii. 293*) that in predication 'something wider is predicated of something narrower', except where the whole definition is predicated, might seem to imply that he regards the predicate as a wider *class* in which the subject is included—that is, that he regards the proposition 'extensionally'. But he seems here to be thinking of the proposition in terms of concepts, and in calling a predicate wider than a subject he may simply mean that when a predicate is not a definition of the subject it can be predicated of other terms, as, for example, *a* can be predicated of terms other than *abc*.

[2] *A vi. 1, 199* (p. 6).

[3] 'No more philosophical than a telegraph code': Kneale, p. 326.

[4] *A vi. 1, 199–201* (pp. 6–10).

[5] *A vi. 1, 201–2* (pp. 10–11).

[6] *A vi. 1, 202* (p. 11). On Leibniz's predecessors in this field, see C.L., pp. 51 ff, and J. Cohen, 'On the Project of a Universal Character', *Mind*, 1954, pp. 49 ff.

[7] *A vi. 1, 199* (p. 6). *Loci* are discussed by Leibniz in the nearly contemporary *Nova Methodus Discendae Docendaeque Jurisprudentiae* (1667), in which he says, 'The foundation of "topics" or the art of invention are *loci*, that is, transcendent relations such as whole, cause, matter, similar,

letters and papers written in 1671 and 1672 he explained that
what he meant here was that demonstration was nothing but a
combination of definitions;[1] that all *a priori* propositions simply
assert a definition, or a part of a definition, of what is defined—
'for the same idea can be expressed by various definitions, from
which arises a fertile means of constructing theorems'.[2] An
alphabet of human thoughts, then, will be useful in that it is
reached through giving definitions of terms, and to have these
definitions at hand will make deductive proof easier.

Shortly after the publication of the *De Arte Combinatoria*,
Leibniz turned his back on university life. In 1667 he rejected the
offer of a professorship of law at the University of Altdorf, where
he had obtained the degree of Doctor of Laws,[3] and chose instead
to be nearer to the centres of political power. He began by entering
the service of Johann Christian, Baron of Boineburg, formerly a
minister of the Elector of Mainz, and when Boineburg died in
1672 he accepted, after some hesitation, the post of librarian to the
Duke of Hanover. He served three successive Dukes of Hanover—
Johann Friedrich, Ernst August, and Georg Ludwig—from late in
1676 until his death in 1716. His official duties were various; not
only was he librarian, but he also functioned as a jurist; until 1685
he concerned himself with the working of the Harz silver mines,
and on giving up this post took up another, that of historian of the
House of Brunswick,[4] of which the Dukes of Hanover were members. In the midst of all this activity Leibniz found time to write
books and papers in such varied fields as science, mathematics,
philosophy, and theology, and to carry on a vast correspondence—
he estimated that he wrote over three hundred letters a year.[5] This
great and many-sided activity brought with it its own nemesis;
Leibniz undertook much, but was able to complete comparatively
little, so that he could say with Ovid, 'Inopem me copia fecit'.[6]

&c.' (*A vi. 1, 279*). This does not explain what these *loci* have in common,
but Leibniz probably assumed that the reader would have in mind
passages such as Cicero, *Topics*, ii. 7: 'Just as it is easy to find what is
hidden when the place (*locus*) has been pointed out and noted, so, when
we wish to examine some argument, we ought to know its "places"; for
that is the name which Aristotle gave to the regions (*sedes*), as it were,
from which arguments are brought.'
[1] To Magnus Hesenthaler, 1671: *A ii. 1, 200*. Cf. *A ii. 1, 398*.
[2] For Gallois, 1672: *A ii. 1, 229*. Cf. *A vi. 1, 460–1*; *G vii. 191*.
[3] Fischer-Kabitz, pp. 45–46.
[4] Fischer-Kabitz, p. 182.
[5] G.M., iii. 434.
[6] To Tschirnhaus, March 1694: Gerhardt, *Der Briefwechsel von Gottfried
Wilhelm Leibniz mit Mathematikern* (Berlin, 1899), p. 493.

This is especially the case with his logical works, as can be seen from the fact that, apart from the *De Arte Combinatoria*, none of the works translated here was published by Leibniz.

The sketch of Leibniz's life that has just been given has covered nearly fifty years; it is now time to return to the early years of this period. It was on Boineburg's business that Leibniz visited Paris, where he was to spend four very fruitful years, from March 1672 to September 1676.[1] It has already been mentioned that the mathematical instruction which Leibniz had received in Germany was far from adequate; he himself said that before going to Paris he was 'not even a novice in mathematics'.[2] In Paris, discussions with mathematicians of the calibre of Huygens[3] brought him to a mastery of the subject. However, his increased skill in mathematics does not seem to have borne immediate fruit in the field of logic, in which he appears to have done no work that can be ascribed to the years between 1666 and 1678. He did, however, develop the idea of a universal writing which he had put forward in the *De Arte Combinatoria*.[4] In letters to Gallois, editor of the *Journal des Savants* and secretary of the Académie des Sciences, and to Oldenburg, secretary of the Royal Society,[5] Leibniz describes the advantages which will come from the invention of what he now calls a 'Universal' or 'Real Characteristic', or a 'Universal' or 'Real Language'—the former consisting of written symbols, the latter being essentially the same, except that it is spoken rather than written. Such a language or symbolism, Leibniz claims, will be a guide to experiment;[6] further, the construction of valid deductive arguments will simply be a matter of following the grammar of the language.[7] The symbolism can also be used as a calculus, without paying attention to the meaning of what is written; in this way, as Leibniz says elsewhere,[8] the mind 'will be freed from having to think directly of things themselves, and yet everything will turn out correctly'.

[1] On this stay, see e.g. Fischer-Kabitz, pp. 89–108.
[2] *G vii. 522.*
[3] Cf. Fischer-Kabitz, pp. 102, 736.
[4] There is one paper from this period, indeed, which does not merely develop the *idea* of a universal writing, but seems to have been meant as a specimen of it. It contains a crude symbolization of moral concepts (*C 29–30*), and was perhaps intended for Boineburg.
[5] *A ii. 1, 228–9 (1672), 239–42 (?1673).*
[6] *A ii. 1, 240.*
[7] *A ii. 1, 241.*
[8] *C 256–7*; cf. *A ii. 1, 228.*

It is implied that this symbolism will be based on the alphabet of human thoughts;[1] now it is obvious that, if this alphabet is to be discovered, a great deal of preliminary work must be done. One might perhaps think that what Leibniz needs is some kind of dictionary, to provide him with at any rate a preliminary analysis of concepts. In fact, Leibniz did ask Gallois to provide him with definitions from the dictionary compiled by the Académie Française, saying that these would help him to construct his Characteristic;[2] much later in life, again, and presumably with the same end in view, Leibniz made a number of collections of definitions of terms.[3] It is usually said, however, and not without reason, that Leibniz believed that what must precede the Universal Characteristic is an encyclopaedia.[4] There is no inconsistency here; the encyclopaedia and the definitions of terms were closely linked in Leibniz's mind, no doubt because the factual propositions about (say) some substance which would be contained in the encyclopaedia would eventually figure as part of the definition of that substance. Certainly, one of Leibniz's earliest plans for an encyclopaedia[5] says that it should begin with definitions of some of the more common and important words.

As Leibniz realized, the task was one which would require co-operative effort;[6] it was for this reason that he tried to enlist the support of the secretaries of learned societies, and this was one of the reasons why he was active in promoting the formation of further learned societies.[7] Our concern here, however, is not with Leibniz's encyclopaedia[8] but with his logic—not, that is, with what might be called the vocabulary of his universal language, but with its grammar. In fact, the next passages translated here (No. 2) are grammatical studies. They are short excerpts from three papers;[9] none of these is dated, but they can be assigned

[1] For example, Leibniz looks for definitions of terms to help him in the construction of his symbolism: *A ii. 1, 380, 428*.
[2] Ibid.
[3] Couturat (*C 437–510*) lists five such collections, which date from 1702–4, and reproduces one of them. The items in the first three are arranged in accordance with Dalgarno's *Lexicon Grammatico-Philosophicum*; the last is in alphabetical order.
[4] C.L., p. 117; Kneale, p. 330; cf. *G vii. 187*. Leibniz also says (*A ii. 1, 240*) that to learn his symbolism is to learn an encyclopaedia. This would no doubt be true; but there must first be made, using ordinary language, a compilation and analysis of what is known, before this can be put in systematic and symbolic form.
[5] *A ii. 1, 200* (1671).
[6] *A ii. 1, 242; C 31, 96*.
[7] C.L., pp. 501 ff.
[8] On this, cf. C.L., Chap. 5.
[9] *C 243–5, 286–7, 288–90*.

with reasonable confidence to the year 1678, since they are related by their subject-matter to works known to have been written in that year.[1] In all these papers, Leibniz's main concern is with the construction of a rational language, by the elimination of what is logically unnecessary. He argues, for example, that it is unnecessary to have distinctions of gender, or declensions and conjugations;[2] he argues also that most nouns can be eliminated, being replaced by an adjective governing the word 'entity'.[3] He also has some interesting things to say about Aristotle's definition[4] of a noun as what expresses a thing without time, and of a verb as what indicates time.[5] From the logical standpoint, however, what is most interesting about these papers is Leibniz's analysis of relational propositions.

It is now a commonplace that syllogistic logic, restricted as it is to propositions which are either of the subject-predicate form or are about classes and what they include or have as members, cannot handle deductive arguments which depend upon the logical properties of relations. For example, it is impossible to give a syllogistic proof of a valid argument such as 'Because a horse is an animal, the head of a horse is the head of an animal'.[6] However, it is perhaps not yet a commonplace that this was already known in the seventeenth century; in particular, the Hamburg logician Joachim Jungius (1587–1657) had classified arguments of this type in his *Logica Hamburgensis*.[7] Jungius, whose works were known to and admired by Leibniz,[8] had argued that the scope of logic must be enlarged so that it can account for relational arguments.[9] In the papers under consideration, however, Leibniz says that logic needs supplementation rather than expansion, and that this supplementation must come from 'rational grammar', which will transform relational arguments into forms which traditional logic

---

[1] *Lingua Generalis* (C 277–9, February 1678); *De Grammatica Rationali* (C 280–1, April 1678); *Analysis Linguarum* (C 351–4, September 1678).

[2] C 286 (p. 13); C 290 (p. 16).

[3] C 289 (p. 16). In another paper, Leibniz uses the word 'subject' instead of 'entity', so that 'man' becomes 'human subject, or, subject of humanity' (C 433).

[4] *Poetics*, Chap. 20.

[5] C 286 (p. 14).

[6] This example was given by the nineteenth-century logician de Morgan, quoted by W. S. Jevons, *The Principles of Science* (2nd ed., London, 1877), p. 18.

[7] 1st edition, 1638; 2nd edition, 1681.

[8] Leibniz mentions Jungius in the same breath as Aristotle and Descartes, or Galileo and Kepler (G vii. 186; C 345).

[9] Cf. C 287 (p. 15).

can handle.[1] Leibniz is not wholly explicit, but it seems that he is proposing to argue as follows. Take, for example, the argument 'David is the father of Solomon, therefore Solomon is the son of David', which is based on the relation of paternity.[2] Leibniz seems to mean that we are to analyse both 'David is the father of Solomon' and 'Solomon is the son of David' as 'David is a father, and by that very fact Solomon is a son', so that the argument becomes, 'David is a father, and by that very fact Solomon is a son; therefore David is a father, and by that very fact Solomon is a son'.[3] This, of course, is not a syllogism, but Leibniz would regard it as validated by the principle of identity, 'A is A', which he considered to be a logical principle, and indeed one of 'the two great principles' used in reasoning.[4] It may be objected that Leibniz has not succeeded in analysing relations away, for the terms 'father' and 'son', which occur in the propositions offered as an analysis of the relational argument, are themselves relational terms. However, it is possible that Leibniz did not intend to reduce relational propositions to those of another form, but that his sole concern was to present relational arguments in a guise which would permit them to be handled by the methods of what he regarded as logic;[5] if so, the objection just raised would be irrelevant.

The next two works translated, Nos. 3 and 4, are the second and sixth of a group of papers, numbered from 1 to 6, written in April 1679.[6] Three undated papers are probably to be ascribed to the

[1] C 36, 244 (p. 13), 287 (p. 14), 406.
[2] C 284; NE, 4.17.4. Leibniz, following Jungius, calls this an example of the 'inversion of a relation' (ibid.).
[3] Compare the account of another argument based on the inversion of a relation in C 244 (p. 13); LR, p. 48. The analysis of 'is the father of' is suggested by C 287 (p. 14); another possible analysis (cf. C 245 (p. 13)) would be 'David is a cause in so far as Solomon is an effect'.
[4] G vi. 413. The argument stated above has the form 'A, therefore A', where 'A' stands for a proposition. Leibniz would regard this as a 'hypothetical proposition' (C 262), and as saying that A contains A (C 389 (p. 78)), which in turn is for him the same as saying that A is A (C 365–6 (pp. 55–56)). The fact that relational arguments are validated by the principle of identity, a fundamental principle for Leibniz, may explain why he said later in the Nouveaux Essais (1703–5) that 'asyllogistic' arguments can be proved 'by means of truths on which common syllogisms themselves depend' (NE, 4.17.4; A vi. 6, 479). (For the date of the Nouveaux Essais, see A vi. 6, xxiii–xxvi.)
[5] This is suggested by a letter of 1679 (A ii. 1, 498) in which Leibniz says that his ideal is 'to make all reasonings reducible to a certain and indubitable form'. For a fuller discussion of Leibniz's account of relational arguments, cf. LR, pp. 46–52.
[6] These are: Elementa Characteristicae Universalis (C 42 ff.), Elementa Calculi (C 49 ff.), Calculi Universalis Elementa (C 57 ff.), Calculi Universalis

same period, since the method of symbolization used in them is similar to one of the methods used in the dated group.[1] In all these papers, Leibniz is trying to find a numerical method of representing logical inferences, and they may accordingly be regarded as his first work in the field of symbolic logic. He had already suggested in the *De Arte Combinatoria* a way in which 'first terms' and derivative terms might be represented numerically;[2] now he adopts the principle that the composition of concepts is analogous to arithmetical multiplication, and after assigning certain numbers to 'first' or simple terms, he represents a derivative term by the product of the numbers of the simple terms which compose it.[3]

None of these papers satisfied Leibniz, as he made clear when in 1686 he again tried to give a numerical proof of logical inferences.[4] However, to say nothing of their historical interest, the two papers translated here are worth attention for other reasons. The first, *Elements of a Calculus (Elementa Calculi)*, is interesting for the clear account is gives[5] of that 'intensional' view of the proposition which has already been mentioned,[6] and which is the view usually preferred by Leibniz. According to this view, to assert a subject-predicate proposition is to say that the concept of the subject includes the concept of the predicate; according to the 'extensional' view, on the other hand, to assert a subject-predicate proposition is to say that the subject (whether an individual or a class) is a member of or is included in the predicate, which is a class. For example, on the former view the proposition that every man is a rational animal would be taken as saying that the concept of man includes the concept of rationality; on the latter view, the same proposition would be taken as saying that the class of human beings is included in the class of rational beings. In the *Elementa Calculi* Leibniz distinguishes the two views clearly, and he also makes clear his reason for preferring the conceptual, intensional approach. This is[7] that concepts 'do not

---

Investigationes (C 66 ff.), *Modus examinandi consequentias per numeros* (C 70 ff.), and *Regulae ex quibus de bonitate consequentiarum formisque et modis syllogismorum categoricorum judicari potest, per numeros* (C 77 ff.).
[1] The three are *Calculus Consequentiarum* (C 84 ff.) and two untitled papers (C 89 ff., 245 ff.). In all these, terms are symbolized by a pair of numbers, one positive and one negative, as in C 70 ff. and C 77 ff.
[2] A vi. 1, 195 ff. (pp. 4–5). Cf. p. xiii above.
[3] C 42, 49 (p. 17), 60.
[4] C 386, par. 129 (p. 75). For a critical discussion of these papers, see C.L., pp. 326 ff.; Lewis, pp. 11 ff.; Kauppi, pp. 145 ff.; Kneale, p. 338.
[5] C 51 ff., pars. 7–12 (pp. 18–21).
[6] Cf. p. xv above.
[7] C 53 (p. 20).

depend on the existence of individuals'. What Leibniz means is that a proposition such as 'Every perfectly good man is happy' may be true even if there are no perfectly good men, and his way of allowing for this possibility is to say that the proposition in question asserts something about the concept of the perfectly good man, irrespective of whether this concept has any instances. This is interesting, in that some logicians have been puzzled as to why Leibniz preferred the intensional approach, and have ascribed this preference to his respect for the authority of Aristotle;[1] the present passage suggests that he had another, and better, reason.

The next paper translated, usually abbreviated to *Regulae de bonitate consequentiarum*, uses a symbolism which Leibniz developed in the fifth paper of the series of April 1679;[2] in this symbolism a term is represented, not by one number, but by a pair of numbers, one positive and one negative, with no common divisor. The *Regulae debonitate consequentiarum* has been discussed from the standpoint of modern formal logic by J. Łukasiewicz,[3] who judges that the arithmetical interpretation of the syllogism which it contains is sound. Leibniz, however, abandoned this interpretation, probably because he thought that it could be used to prove a syllogism in the third figure which is in fact invalid, as follows:[4]

Every pious man is happy
$$+10 \quad -3 \qquad +5 \quad -1$$
Some pious man is not wealthy
$$+10 \quad -3 \qquad\qquad +8 \quad -11$$
Therefore some wealthy man is not happy.
$$+8 \quad -11 \qquad\qquad +5 \quad -1$$

These figures satisfy the conditions which Leibniz lays down for the arithmetization of propositions:[5] in the first proposition, $+10$ can be divided by $+5$, and -3 by -1; in the second, $+10$ cannot be divided by $+8$;[6] in the third, $+8$ cannot be divided by $+5$. The syllogism, however, has the mood AOO, which is not valid in the third figure. In traditional terms, the syllogism com-

---

[1] e.g. C.L., p. 438.

[2] *C 70* ff.

[3] *Aristotle's Syllogistic* (Oxford, 1951), pp. 126 ff.

[4] Cf. *C 246*, in which this syllogism is deleted. Leibniz wrote after it, 'This is not valid, because . . .', and then evidently realized that on his interpretation the syllogism was valid (C.L., p. 334).

[5] *C 78–9* (pp. 26–27).

[6] Nor, of course, can -3 be divided by -11; but in Leibniz's symbolism this is not necessary for the representation of a particular negative. All that is required is that of one pair of figures of the same sign, the first figure shall not be divisible by the second (*C 79*).

mits the fallacy of the illicit major, the term 'happy' being undistributed in the major premiss but distributed in the conclusion.

Nos. 5 and 6 of the translations are two related papers, *A Specimen of the Universal Calculus* (*Specimen Calculi Universalis*) and *Addenda to the Specimen of the Universal Calculus* (*Ad Specimen Calculi Universalis Addenda*). The date of these papers cannot be determined exactly, but it seems likely that they were written after the essays of April 1679 and before the *Generales Inquisitiones* of 1686.[1] Neither can be called a finished piece of work; rather, they present us with two, or indeed three, sketches of a calculus. Thus, the *Specimen* begins by presenting a deductive system; two propositions, one categorical and one hypothetical, are declared to be 'true in themselves',[2] and four propositions are proved.[3] Then, however, Leibniz seems to break off, and gives definitions of a number of terms.[4] Why he does this is not made clear; however, he has said earlier in the paper that it is an advantage if many deductions can be made from few assumptions, and (taking up again the idea of an alphabet of human thoughts) that this will be achieved when symbols are assigned to the simplest elements of thought.[5] It may be, then, that the definitions are meant to be at any rate stages on the way towards the discovery of these 'simplest elements'. The *Addenda* presents a more developed logical system than the *Specimen*, but is if anything even more confused in its presentation. Leibniz begins by stating what he later calls[6] five 'principles of the calculus'; these are followed by the deduction of five theorems. Then, in the margin of the manuscript,[7] Leibniz makes a fresh start, giving a more rigorous presentation of the bases of his calculus, in the shape of a postulate, six propositions 'true in themselves', an inference 'true in itself',[8]

---

[1] Couturat (*C.L.*, p. 336) regards the system presented in these papers as more coherent and more developed than the essays of April 1679, and also implies (op. cit., p. 344) that it is less developed than the *Generales Inquisitiones*.
[2] *G vii. 218*, pars. 2 and 3 (p. 33). The hypothetical proposition is called an 'inference'.
[3] Pars. 4, 6, 8, and 9 (pp. 33–35). Not all these propositions follow from the two propositions declared to be 'true in themselves'; what is said in par. 9 rests in part on par. 8, which is proved independently of pars. 2 and 3.
[4] *C 239* ff. (pp. 36 ff.).
[5] *G vii. 219* (p. 33).
[6] *G vii. 224* (p. 42).
[7] *G vii. 223* (p. 42).
[8] In this case, Leibniz's 'inference' is an inference according to modern usage—that is, it is of the form '*p*, therefore *q*'. Contrast n.2 above.

and a restatement of the five 'principles of the calculus' already mentioned. Like the *Specimen*, the *Addenda* concludes with a number of definitions,[1] whose function in the paper is not made clear.

The small number of theorems in each paper is to some extent explained by the fact that the range of the calculus is deliberately limited to a consideration of universal propositions;[2] in the *Specimen*, indeed, Leibniz restricts himself to universal affirmative propositions.[3] In his symbolization, Leibniz abandons for the moment the attempt at representing propositions numerically, and symbolizes 'Every *a* is *b*' as '*a* is *b*'.[4] It will be noticed that in the *Addenda* Leibniz gives as an example of '*a* is *b*' the singular proposition 'God is wise'; however, he is not inconsistent in this, since he had argued in the *De Arte Combinatoria* that a singular proposition can be regarded as a universal proposition.[5]

Despite their limitations, the *Specimen* and *Addenda* contain a number of points of interest. The first is that Leibniz seems here to take up a neutral position with regard to the intensional and extensional points of view. He does not express a preference for either, and in the *Addenda*[6] he says that a certain theorem can be proved either from the assumption that the subject of a proposition is a container and the predicate a content, or that the subject is a content and the predicate a container. The former is naturally taken as a reference to the intensional, the latter to the extensional approach.[7]

The three propositions declared to be 'true in themselves' in the *Specimen*, and the first two such propositions in the *Addenda*,[8] are what Leibniz calls elsewhere 'identical propositions'; in his usage, this term covers propositions of the form '*ab* is *a*' as well as of the form '*a* is *a*'.[9] In the *Specimen*, Leibniz adds that 'a true

---

[1] *G vii. 225* ff. (pp. 43 ff.). Many of the terms defined are common to the two papers—e.g. 'some', 'one', 'several', 'disparate', 'attribute', 'property', 'proper attribute', 'definition', 'defined term'.

[2] *G vii. 218* (p. 33), *223* (p. 41).

[3] *G vii. 219* (p. 34). Mention is made of particular propositions in the *Addenda* (*G vii. 226–7* (pp. 45–46)), but this occurs, not in the proof of a theorem, but in that part of the paper which contains definitions.

[4] *G vii. 218* (p. 33), *223* (p. 42). Leibniz had used letters in the essays of 1679 (e.g. *C 50* (p. 17)); there, however, they are substitutes for numbers, whereas in the *Specimen* and *Addenda* they stand directly for terms.

[5] *A vi. 1, 182–3*; see below, p. liv. The passage in the *Addenda* is *G vii. 224* (p. 42).

[6] *G vii. 223* (p. 42).

[7] Cf. *C 53* (p. 20).

[8] *G vii. 218* (p. 33), *224* (p. 42).

[9] He gives the name 'identical proposition' to propositions of this sort

proposition is one which arises by means of inferences from what is assumed and what is true in itself'.[1] The phrase 'what is assumed' seems, from the sentence which follows, to refer to definitions, and what Leibniz is saying is close to his often-expressed view that every true proposition is either an identical proposition or is reducible to such a proposition by substituting definitions for defined terms.[2] The difference is that Leibniz here regards as primitive, not only identical propositions, but the syllogism in *Barbara*.[3]

After mentioning definitions in the *Specimen* Leibniz remarks[4] that although symbols may be arbitrary, truth is not. This is a renewal of an earlier attack on Hobbes' view that truth arises 'from the human will, and from names or symbols'.[5] The attack is contained in a dialogue written in 1677; in it, Leibniz agrees that thinking and reasoning presuppose a use of symbols, and that the definitions of symbols are arbitrary.[6] But, he continues, Hobbes' conclusion does not follow; for[7] 'although symbols are arbitrary, their use and connexion has something which is not arbitrary, namely a certain symmetry (*proportio*) between symbols and things' and 'it is always true, without any decision (*arbitrio*) on our part, that on the assumption of such and such symbols such and such reasoning will be valid.'

Of the theorems proved in these papers, perhaps the most interesting—and probably the one which interested Leibniz most,

in an unpublished paper, *Calculus Ratiocinator*, regarded by Kauppi as a study for the *Specimen* (Kauppi, pp. 155, 156 n. 3). Cf. *C 11, 272, 369* (p. 59); *NE*, 4.2.1; FC, p. 182; *LR*, p. 57.

[1] *G vii. 219* (p. 33).

[2] A true proposition is or is reducible to an identical proposition: *C 513, 519*; *G vii. 296*. Reduction by substitution of definitions: *A ii. 1, 398*; *A vi. 1, 460–1*; *G ii. 239*; *G vii. 191*; FC, p. 181. In speaking of the reduction of propositions by the substitution of definitions for defined terms, Leibniz is speaking of what would now be called the rule of definitional substitution. It is interesting that in the *Addenda*, *G vii. 224* (p. 42), he also states what would now be called a substitution rule for term variables, which allows him to state that if (e.g.) *ab* is *a* is a theorem, so also is *bc* is *b*, and *bcd* is *bc*.

[3] *G vii. 218* (p. 33); cf. *G vii. 224* (p. 42). It will be noticed that Leibniz reverses the traditional order of the premisses by putting the minor premiss before the major, a practice he defends in *NE*, 4.17.8.

[4] *G vii. 219* (p. 33).

[5] *G vii. 191*. The reference to Hobbes is to *De Corpore*, Bk. 1, Chap. 3, secs. 7–9.

[6] *G vii. 191*.

[7] *G vii. 192–3*.

since he called it a 'fine theorem' (*praeclarum theorema*)—is the
proposition that if *a* is *b* and *d* is *c*, then *ad* will be *bc*[1]. This, as
Bertrand Russell has pointed out,[2] is an analogue of a theorem of
Principia Mathematica which may be rendered as 'If, if *p* then *r*
and if *q* then *s*, then if *p* and *q* then *r* and *s*', where *p, q, r*, and *s* are
variables whose values are statements. A number of the definitions
are also of logical interest. Leibniz offers alternative definitions of
'the same', which are closely related to modern definitions of
identity. The definition given in the *Specimen*, 'Those terms are
"the same" of which one can be substituted in place of the other
without loss of truth', was adopted by Frege as his definition of
identity in the *Foundations of Arithmetic*,[3] whilst the definition in
the *Addenda*, which states that *a* and *b* are 'the same' if every *a* is *b*
and every *b* is *a*, is close to some more recent definitions.[4] Finally,
mention may be made of the analyses, in both the *Specimen* and
Addenda, of the concepts of 'one' and 'several',[5] which are of
interest in view of Russell's claim that Leibniz's logic cannot
account for propositions such as 'There are three men'.[6]

The translations of the *Specimen* and *Addenda* are followed by
General Inquiries about the Analysis of Concepts and of Truths
(*Generales Inquisitiones de Analysi Notionum et Veritatum*). This
paper was written in 1686, the same year as the *Discourse on
Metaphysics*—a work which it complements, in that it develops
the view about truth from which metaphysical conclusions are
derived in the *Discourse*.[7] The theory of truth, however, occupies
only a small part of the *Generales Inquisitiones*, which is in the
main concerned with problems of formal logic. Leibniz was
obviously pleased with the paper, remarking that in it he had
made excellent progress;[8] it is, however, a difficult work, neither

---

[1] *G vii. 223* (p. 41).
[2] Cf. Russell and Whitehead, *Principia Mathematica* *3.47.
[3] Trans. by J. L. Austin (Oxford, 1950), p. 76. Leibniz's definition is in
G vii. 219 (p. 34).
[4] e.g. W. V. Quine, *Mathematical Logic* (Harvard, 1947), p. 136; A.
Tarski, *Introduction to Logic* (2nd ed., New York, 1946), p. 55. For
Leibniz's definition, see *G vii. 225* (p. 43), and compare the definition of
'coincident' in *C 52* (p. 20).
[5] *C 239* (p. 36); *G vii. 225* (p. 44).
[6] Bertrand Russell, *The Philosophy of Leibniz* (2nd ed., London, 1937),
p. 12. Cf. *LR*, pp. 36 ff.
[7] See, in particular, the account of contingent truths given in pars.
60–61 of the *Generales Inquisitiones* (p. 61), which develops the account
given in par. 13 of the *Discourse on Metaphysics*.
[8] *C 356* (p. 47 n.1).

concise nor coherent,[1] in which Leibniz often seems to be groping his way. For this reason, it will be discussed here in greater detail than the other works translated.

It falls into two unequal parts. In the first,[2] Leibniz is in the main concerned with the terms of propositions; in the second, which consists of numbered paragraphs, the logical relations between propositions are discussed.[3] One of the interesting features of the first part is that, without mentioning it explicitly, it takes up again the idea of an alphabet of human thoughts. Almost certainly, however, the idea is present in a modified form. At some stage, Leibniz reached the conclusion that it is not possible for us to reach concepts which are really primitive, i.e. incapable of further analysis. This is made clear in *An Introduction to a Secret Encyclopaedia* (*Introductio ad Encyclopaediam Arcanam*), written probably between 1679 and 1686.[4] Here, after saying that a primitive concept can only be of God, Leibniz continues:[5]

'We do not understand distinctly enough the way in which the natures of things flow from God, nor the ideas of things from the idea of God, in which ultimate analysis, i.e. the adequate knowledge of all things through their causes, would consist.'

---

[1] As will be seen later, it does not present a unified calculus, and not all the issues which are deferred for later consideration are in fact taken up. For example, in *C 361* (pp. 51–52) Leibniz promises a further discussion of the concepts of colour and of extension; but this discussion never takes place.

[2] This part ends at *C 363* (p. 53).

[3] It is not certain that Leibniz initially meant the work to have this form. The title, as Couturat has noted (*C 356*), is an afterthought, and it may be that Leibniz meant at first simply to provide an analysis of terms, i.e. of concepts. The complex classification of terms which occupies the first part of the work is not used in the second, which suggests that Leibniz did not have the second part in mind when writing the first.

[4] Couturat suggests that this was written after the *Consilium de Encyclopaedia Nova* of June 1679 (C.L., pp. 132–3), and Schmidt (p. 503) places it before 1686, on the grounds that its discussion of necessary and contingent truths (*C 513–14*) is not carried on in terms of the analogy between rational and irrational numbers which Leibniz introduced in the *Generales Inquisitiones* (*C 388* (p. 77)). A date before 1684 is suggested by Kauppi (p. 26), who regards the classification of concepts in *C 512* as an earlier form of the account given in the *Meditationes de Cognitione, Veritate et Ideis* of 1684 (*G iv. 422*). But it is not certain that it is an earlier form; it might be a later reference to the same doctrine, like par. 24 of the *Discourse on Metaphysics* (1686).

[5] *C 513*.

The result is that[1]

> 'An analysis of concepts such that we can reach primitive concepts, i.e. those which are conceived in themselves, does not seem to be within human power.'

The complete analysis of concepts, then, is beyond our powers;[2] however, Leibniz still thought it possible and useful to look for concepts which, whether or not they are 'absolutely the first' (*absolute primae*) are at any rate 'first for us' (*secundum nos primae*).[3] To a list of such concepts Leibniz continued to give the name of an 'alphabet of human thoughts'.[4] The concepts which are declared in the *Generales Inquisitiones* to be primitive, or at least to be such that they may be assumed to be primitive,[5] seem to be of this type. The criteria in accordance with which these concepts are to be selected are not stated in the *Generales Inquisitiones*, but are described elsewhere. It has already been mentioned[6] that the alphabet of human thoughts as originally conceived would, in Leibniz's view, have been useful as an instrument of deductive proof, which is regarded by Leibniz as resting on the analysis of concepts. It is evident that deductive proof is also to be borne in mind when selecting concepts which are 'first for us'. This is made clear in the *Introductio ad Encyclopaediam Arcanam*, in which Leibniz, after saying that human beings cannot reach absolutely primitive concepts, remarks that[7]

> 'The analysis of truths is more within human power; for we can prove many truths absolutely and reduce them to primitive indemonstrable truths.'

The point is that, in order to make such a reduction—that is, to reduce some truth to an identical proposition[8]—it is not necessary to analyse the concepts which occur in the proposition which is

---

[1] *C 514*.

[2] Compare the statement in *C 431* that we cannot show how all things flow from God and nothing. This comes from *De Organo sive Arte Magna Cogitandi*, which Couturat relates to the plans for an encyclopaedia put forward by Leibniz in 1679 (C.L., p. 128 n. 2).

[3] *C 220–1*; cf. *G vii. 292–3*.

[4] *C 220–1*; *G vii. 292*. Leibniz was still referring to such an alphabet as late as 1709 (*G iii. 545*).

[5] *C 358* (p. 49), *360* (p. 51).

[6] Cf. p. xv above.

[7] *C 514*. Cf. *G vii. 83*: 'It is very difficult to come to the end of the analysis of things, but it is not so difficult to complete the analysis of the truths which one needs'.

[8] Cf. p. xxiv above, and *C 518*.

to be proved as far as they can be analysed.[1] If, for example, we are asked to prove the proposition 'Every man is rational', and we reduce it to 'Every rational animal is rational', we have done what is required, even if 'rational' and 'animal' are capable of further analysis. This, then, is what Leibniz means when he says that 'for perfect demonstrations of truths, perfect concepts of things [sc. complete analyses of concepts] are not required', and that 'it is sufficient to carry the analysis of ideas as far as the demonstrations of truths require'.[2] The 'alphabet of human thoughts' will now contain the results of such analyses.

Such is the general context in which the list[3] contained in the *Generales Inquisitiones* of 'terms which can be considered as primitive'[4] is very probably to be understood. Its immediate context in the paper is a complex classification of terms. These are first divided into 'integral' and 'partial' terms;[5] the former can be the subject or predicate of a proposition as they stand, whereas the latter, which include terms such as 'the same' and 'similar', need some addition—e.g. 'as A', 'to A'—if they are to be a subject or predicate. Leibniz discusses integral terms first;[6] his classification of these, which also involves a distinction between various types of particles,[7] raises some problems. He describes these terms and particles by the adjectives 'primitive', 'simple', 'derivative', and 'composite'. As might be expected, a 'primitive' term or particle is one which is unanalysable.[8] A 'simple' term or particle is not defined, but it appears from Leibniz's examples that he has in mind a single symbol or word, such as 'A' or 'in'.[9] Terms which are put together without the help of particles, such as the term 'AB', are called 'composite'; those which are put together by means of particles, such as the term 'A in B', are called 'derivative'. Particles can also be composite—for example, 'with-in'—or derivative. Each of the latter consists of a term and a particle, and although Leibniz does not give examples, he may have in mind such expressions as 'in B' or 'with-in B'.

On the basis of these distinctions, Leibniz presents a classification of particles and integral terms which can be shown clearly in

[1] *G vii. 84.*
[2] *C 220, 431.*
[3] *C 360–1* (pp. 51–52).
[4] *C 358* (p. 49).
[5] *C 357* (p. 47).
[6] Ibid.
[7] *C 358–9* (pp. 49–50).
[8] *C 358* (p. 49). Cf. *Specimen Calculi Universalis*, *C 240* (p. 37): a primitive term is 'that of which no composite term is the equivalent'.
[9] Cf. *Specimen*, loc. cit.

the following table. (The numbers correspond to those in the text; Nos. 7 and 10 are omitted, as these are certain types of derivative terms and particles about which Leibniz cannot decide whether they are simple or composite.)

Terms	*Particles*
(1) Integral primitive simple	(2) Primitive simple
(3) Integral primitive composite	(4) Primitive composite[1]
(5) Integral derivative simple	(8) Derivative simple
(6) Integral derivative composite	(9) Derivative composite

On paper, this seems to be a tidy scheme; there is, however, a problem which concerns primitive terms. From what Leibniz has said, one might suppose that a primitive term must be simple, for any composite term is clearly analysable into the simple terms of which it is composed.[2] It is therefore surprising to find in this table integral primitive composite terms—or, as they are described in the text, 'Primitive integral terms composed of simple terms alone, and composed directly—i.e. without the mediation of particles or syncategorematic terms'.[3] This seems to indicate that a term can be primitive without being simple. It may be that all that Leibniz meant to do here was to distinguish between terms like A and AB—that is, between terms which are simple and those which are composed of simple terms. But if so, it is hard to see why he should have used the word 'primitive' in this context. Perhaps he means, then, that although a composite term is analysable, it is sometimes convenient to treat it as primitive. Whatever his views on this, the list which we have regarded as a specimen of the alphabet of human thoughts is declared to be a list of

---

[1] Not termed 'primitive' in the text, but consistency seems to demand this.

[2] It is not suggested that what Leibniz says here implies that the converse must be the case, i.e. that a simple term must be primitive. It seems clear that a simple term may be equivalent to a composite or derivative term which is not primitive, in which case it would not itself be primitive. (The point of the clause 'which is not primitive' is that, as will be seen later, Leibniz may think that there are some composite terms which are in a sense primitive.) It might be replied that Leibniz could understand by a 'simple' term here one which is not equivalent to any composite or derivative term; cf. the phrase 'a simple, i.e. a primitive concept' in the *Introductio ad Encyclopaediam Arcanam* (C *512*). This would mean, however, that the words 'simple' and 'primitive' would be equivalent, and it would be hard to see why Leibniz should use both of them in his classification.

[3] C *358* (p. 49).

primitive *simple* terms—or 'of those to be assumed for them in the mean time'.[1]

From the discussion of terms there is a gradual transition to what we have called the second part of the *Generales Inquisitiones*. The transition is made as Leibniz, after talking about integral terms, proceeds to the topic of 'partial' terms—i.e. those terms which cannot by themselves be the subject or predicate of a proposition. He begins with the term 'the same' or 'coincident', which he symbolizes in this paper by the sign for mathematical equality,[2] and which he defines by saying that 'A is the same as B' or 'A coincides with B' means that one term can be substituted for the other in any proposition without loss of truth.[3] On the basis of this definition he fulfils the task, which he set himself previously,[4] of showing that if A = B, then B = A. The next concepts introduced are those of subject and predicate. It is implied that these are partial terms,[5] perhaps because to speak of a subject or a predicate is to speak of the subject or predicate *of a proposition*. Leibniz explains these notions in terms of coincidence, and it emerges from what he says that his definition is of the subject and predicate of a universal proposition, so that in this context 'A is B' must be read as 'Every A is B'.[6] Leibniz has now used the notion of coincidence to prove a proposition and to define two concepts; it is not therefore surprising that he should go on to prove in terms of coincidence the conversion *simpliciter* of the particular affirmative proposition[7] and (after the introduction of negative propositions) subalternation.[8] At this stage he checks himself and says that a more rigorous (or, as he says, a 'more accurate') account of propositions is necessary if particles and partial terms are to be discussed adequately.[9] What Leibniz has seen is that such terms and particles are to be explained in the context of the propositions of which they form a part. As he proceeds, however, he seems to lose sight of terms and particles as such, and to concentrate on the development of a calculus, primarily in terms of coincidence.

---

[1] *C 360* (p. 51).
[2] This symbolization is first used in this paper in par. 3 (p. 54).
[3] *C 362* (p. 53). Cf. *G vii. 219* (p. 34).
[4] *C 362* (p. 52 n. 1).
[5] The notion of 'the same', Leibniz says, is the first partial term which occurs to him; 'subject' and 'predicate' are introduced as 'the next concept'; *C 362* (pp. 52–53).
[6] This is shown by the assertion (*C 362* (p.)) 53 that A is B if *every* A and *some* B coincide. For this symbolization, cf. *G vii. 218* (p. 33), *223* (p. 42).
[7] *C 362* (p. 53).
[8] *C 363* (p. 53).
[9] Ibid.

This 'more accurate' account is by no means easy to follow. Leibniz does not present us with an orderly, thought-out calculus; rather, we seem to be following the actual processes of his thinking. He begins by defining again the term 'coincides'. This definition precedes the series of numbered paragraphs which we have mentioned as constituting the second part of the *Generales Inquisitiones*, but it is clearly to be taken with them. The first four numbered paragraphs display, in the form of coincidences between terms, certain uses of the words 'not', 'true', and 'false'. It is noteworthy that Leibniz remarks that these propositions are *definitions* of the signs for truth and falsity, affirmation and negation.[1] Normally he regards a definition as an analysis, that is, as the breaking-up into other concepts of the concept to be defined. Here, on the other hand, he has provided what are now called 'implicit definitions', in which a term is defined by an axiom or axioms in which it occurs.[2] Another point of interest is the proof in par. 4 of the principle of bivalence—namely, that every proposition is either true or false—in which Leibniz uses the proposition that 'If not-p, then q' is equivalent to 'Either p or q', moving from 'If L is not true it is false' to 'L [or, as he says, 'Every proposition'] is either true or false'.[3]

Pars. 6 to 9 are said by Leibniz to contain axioms, which he declares to be corollaries of the definition of 'coincides'; the first of these is the proposition that if A = B, then B = A, which has been proved earlier. Pars. 10 and 11 contain respectively the proposition that A = A, which Leibniz declares to be true in itself, and that A = not-A, which he declares to be false in itself. In par. 16 Leibniz reintroduces the subject-predicate proposition 'A is B'. As mentioned earlier,[4] and as Leibniz himself declares in par. 28, he means by this 'Every A is B'. He takes this to be the same as 'A contains B',[5] or 'The concept of B is contained in the concept of A',[6] which indicates that here he is regarding the proposition intensionally. As before, he defines 'A is B' as '(Every) A is the same as some B';[7] he expresses this symbolically in par. 16

---

[1] *C 365* (p. 55).
[2] See also par. 38 (p. 58) and *LR*, pp. 74–75.
[3] Cf. *C 238*, in which Leibniz says that a disjunctive proposition can be regarded as a hypothetical. This comes from *De Varietatibus Enuntiationum*, a work which is related to the *Specimen* and *Addenda* (ibid.). See also *LR*, pp. 34–35.
[4] Cf. p. xxxi.
[5] Par. 16; cf. par. 4 (p. 55).
[6] Par. 28.
[7] Par. 16; cf. p. xxxi n. 6.

as 'A = BY', although he says that he suspects the symbol 'Y' to be superfluous.[1]

So far, Leibniz's calculus has been presented in a fairly systematic way. He has begun with definitions—namely, of 'coincides', 'not', 'false', and 'true'; he has stated corollaries of the first definition, and he has introduced the notion of a subject-predicate proposition. But when Leibniz goes on to prove subject-predicate propositions by expressing them as propositions which state coincidences between terms, he becomes aware of a lack of rigour in his presentation, and has to state points which, he says, should have been stated earlier. The first (par. 20) is that one letter can be put for any number of letters; the second (par. 26) says that 'What is generally asserted or concluded, not as an hypothesis, about any letters which have not yet been used, is to be understood of any number of other letters'. The second of these has already been stated in the *Addenda* as one of the 'principles of the calculus';[2] par. 18 also states the third of these principles—namely that A, AA, AAA etc. coincide—without, however, distinguishing it in any way. Also introduced in passing is the proposition that AB is B, which is regarded (as in the *Specimen* and *Addenda*) as indemonstrable.[3] Among the propositions proved are two of which Leibniz had given a less precise proof earlier:[4] these are subalternation (par. 29) and the conversion *simpliciter* of a particular affirmative (par. 52). Also of interest are par. 42, which contains another version of the principle of bivalence,[5] and pars. 43–46, which contain various versions of the principle of contradiction, understanding by this the assertion that what contains or implies a contradiction is false.[6]

Although Leibniz has already presented implicit definitions of the terms 'true' and 'false' he seems to think that explicit definitions also are required. Such definitions are given in par. 40, which states that a true proposition is one which either coincides with, or can be reduced to, the indemonstrable proposition 'AB is B', and in par. 35, which states that a false proposition is one which contains a contradiction. These definitions are introduced only in passing; in par. 56, however, Leibniz begins a detailed

[1] Par. 16 n. 1; cf. par. 83.
[2] *G vii. 221, 224* (pp. 40, 42).
[3] Par. 38; cf. p. xxiv above.
[4] *C 362* (p. 53); cf. p. xxxi above.
[5] Cf. p. xxxii. In the form of the assertion that of two contradictory propositions, the one is true and the other false, this is sometimes called by Leibniz the 'principle of contradiction'. Cf. *G ii. 62*; *G vi. 127, 413*; *Monadology*, par. 31; *LR*, p. 60.
[6] Cf. *G vii. 199*; *Monadology*, par. 31; Grua, p. 287.

discussion of the nature of truth and falsity, and of the problems to which his definitions give rise, which may be regarded as constituting a new section of the second part of the paper. He begins by defining truth and falsity again, saying that a proposition is true if it contains no contradiction (par. 56), and that 'false' means what is not true (par. 57). These definitions involve Leibniz in two difficulties. First, not only does he define a true proposition as one which either is or is reducible to an identical proposition,[1] but this is also his definition of a necessary truth.[2] It is hard to see, therefore, how there can be any truths which are not necessary; that is, how there can be any place for the concept of a contingent truth. Second, Leibniz has said that a proposition is true if it contains no contradiction; but he also says (par. 61) that a possible proposition is one of which it can be proved that no contradiction will arise when it is analysed, which seems to imply that every proposition which is possible is also true.[3]

The first difficulty is met by the notion that a contingent truth is a proposition such that the inclusion of the concept of the predicate in that of the subject can be shown only by an analysis of infinite complexity, whereas a necessary truth needs only a finite analysis. A necessary truth can therefore be proved by human beings, whereas a proof of a contingent truth would require an intellect which can grasp the infinite—namely, the intellect of God.[4] Leibniz's solution of the second difficulty is not altogether clear. He says in par. 61 that he describes as 'true' an incomplex term (i.e. what would now be called simply a term, or a concept)[5] which is possible, but that he has doubts about complex terms, i.e. propositions.[6] His assertion about incomplex terms may seem strange, for propositions, and not concepts, are normally said to be true or false. Leibniz probably means, however, that a possible term is a true term in the sense of a *genuine* term, as one speaks of a 'true friend'. With regard to propositions, Leibniz says in par. 61 that every analysis ends in axioms (or, 'propositions

---

[1] Cf. pp. xiv and xxv above.

   G vii. 300; C 17; FC, p. 181; Grua, p. 303.

   Expressed syllogistically, the inference would be: every proposition which contains no contradiction is true; every proposition which is possible is a proposition which contains no contradiction; therefore every proposition which is possible is true.

[4] Pars. 60–61; cf. pars. 134–6. Par. 137 suggests that this view is put forward for the first time in the *Generales Inquisitiones*; cf. Grua, p. 302 n. 128.

[5] Cf. par. 75, and C 346, 512.

[6] Ibid.

which are known through themselves') terms which are 'conceived through themselves' (i.e. primitive terms), and the data of experience. He may imply here that it is experience which enables us to distinguish between the actual and the merely possible.

It is certainly Leibniz's view in the *Generales Inquisitiones*[1] that experience is required for the proof of the possiblity of a term or concept; that is[2], for proving that it does not contain a contradiction. The problem of a proof of possibility had often exercised him, and at various times he offered three solutions, in the form of three methods of establishing possibility, two being *a priori* and one empirical. The first *a priori* method consists of giving what Leibniz calls a 'causal definition', that is, a definition which states a way in which the thing defined might be produced.[3] An example of this is Euclid's definition of a circle as a figure described by the motion of a straight line about one fixed end; this, according to Leibniz, makes it clear that such a figure is possible.[4] The other *a priori* method is the analysis into primitive concepts of the concepts whose possibility is in question.[5] Leibniz seems to have in mind here his view that the primitive concepts are concepts of God.[6] He believed that he had been able to give an *a priori* proof of the possibility of God,[7] from which it follows that any concept which can be analysed into primitive concepts must be possible. It is obvious that Leibniz could no longer think that this method of proof is usable, once he had decided that human beings cannot reduce derivative concepts to those that are absolutely primary, and it is surprising that as late as the early months of 1686, in which the *Discourse on Metaphysics* was written,[8] he should think that such an analysis was possible, 'though very rare'.[9] In the *Generales Inquisitiones*, however, not only is neither of these *a priori* methods mentioned, but Leibniz declares that the

[1] Pars. 61, 68.

[2] e.g. *C 261, 513*. Leibniz also states the problem in terms of establishing the possibility of things: *G ii. 55*; *G iv. 425*; *G vii. 310*; G.M., iii. 574.

[3] *G iv. 425*; *G vii. 310*; *DM*, par. 24.

[4] *G vii. 294*.

[5] *G iv. 425*; *DM*, par. 24. Cf. *G vii. 295, 319*.

[6] See p. xxvii, which quotes *C 513*; also *G iv. 425*, in which Leibniz says that the unanalysable concepts are (he should perhaps have said, are *of*) the absolute attributes of God.

[7] *A ii. 1, 271–2, 437–8*; cf. *Monadology*, par. 45.

[8] *DM*, Lestienne ed., pp. 9–10; *G ii. 11*.

[9] *DM*, par. 24. In the *Meditationes de Cognitione, Veritate et Ideis* of 1684 (*G iv. 423, 425*) Leibniz was more cautious, saying that he is not sure that a perfect example of this kind of analysis can be found, or that it will ever be found. He remarks in the former passage that our concept of numbers is close to a case of perfect analysis, but what he has in mind here is not clear. He may be referring to the reduction of non-prime to

only way of proving possibility is by experience[1]—a method which he had mentioned previously, but in company with the two *a priori* methods.[2] This method of proof is simple, being based on the Scholastic maxim *ab esse ad posse valet consequentia*. Suppose that we know by experience that X exists; now, what exists, or has existed, is possible, therefore X is possible.[3]

The meaning of the term 'exists' or 'existent' is discussed by Leibniz in pars. 71–73, after his account of truth and falsity. This is a topic on which he has already touched in the first part of the *Generales Inquisitiones*;[4] the questions at issue here verge on the metaphysical, and may be put briefly as follows. Take a proposition such as 'Peter exists', and assume this proposition to be true. Leibniz has said that a true proposition is one which either coincides with, or can be reduced to, the indemonstrable identical proposition 'AB is B';[5] or, what for him is the same, it is a proposition the concept of whose predicate is contained in that of the subject.[6] But if we say that the concept of existence is contained in that of Peter this will mean that Peter's non-existence is unthinkable, and will make of him a 'necessary being', like God. To avoid this conclusion Leibniz has to analyse the concept of existence, as applied to contingent things. The analysis in the *Generales Inquisitiones* is tentative and obscure, but the upshot seems to be that to say of a thing other than God that it exists is to say that its concept is such that, if there were a God, God would actualize it; and there is a God.[7] Leibniz adds (par. 73) that what makes a concept one that God will actualize is that it forms a part of the richest conceptual scheme, the 'most possible entity'. In this way, he escapes from the conclusion that everything that exists is a necessary being; turning to existential truths (par. 74), he says that these[8] are not necessary, since they involve an infinite analysis.

In par. 76 (*bis*) Leibniz resumes the development of a logical calculus. It soon emerges, however, that what is being presented

prime numbers (cf. *C 358* (p. 49), in which a primitive term is compared to a prime number), or he may be thinking of the possibility of expressing any number by means of 1 and 0, which he declares to be analogous to the fact that everything flows from God and from nothing (*C 430–1*; Grua, pp. 126, 364, 371).

[1] Par. 61 (p. 62), par. 68.
[2] *DM*, par. 24; *G iv. 425* (1684).
[3] *G iv. 425*; *G vii. 319*; *DM*, par. 24.
[4] *C 360* (p. 51).
[5] Cf. p. xxxiii above.
[6] *C 68, 401, 518*. Cf. *LR*, pp. 56 ff.
[7] Cf. *LR*, pp. 118 ff.
[8] He should have said, 'Other than the proposition that God exists', which for him is a necessary truth.

is not so much a development of what has gone before as a modification of it. Before his excursus into truth and falsity, Leibniz had proposed a way of symbolizing the four 'propositional forms'—the universal affirmative, the particular affirmative, the universal negative, and the particular negative. His proposal, which will for convenience be called 'Scheme I', was to render the universal affirmative, 'Every A is B', as 'A is (contains) B' (par. 47); the particular affirmative, 'Some A is B' as 'AY [sc. 'some A'] is (contains) B' (par. 48); and the universal negative, 'No A is B', as 'AY is not (does not contain) B' (par. 50).[1] The particular negative, 'Some A is not B', is not represented explicitly, but it may be assumed that it would be the negation of its contradictory, the universal affirmative, i.e. 'A is not (does not contain)B'. Between pars. 83 and 87 Leibniz offers, without distinguishing them clearly, what are in effect two further methods of symbolizing the propositional forms; these will be called 'Scheme II' and 'Scheme III' respectively. Scheme II is simply another version of Leibniz's previous symbolism, expressed in the form of equations. The universal affirmative is now 'A = AB' (par. 83), the particular affirmative is 'AY = ABY'[2] (par. 89), the universal negative is 'AY ≠ ABY' (par. 87), and the particular negative is 'A ≠ AB' (par. 84). The flaw in this version, as in the one which precedes, is in the representation of the universal negative; for such a proposition is true only when the inequality in question holds for *every* A,[3] or when *every* A is not B. However, Scheme III offers a better symbolization. In this, the universal affirmative and particular negative remain as 'A = AB' and 'A ≠ AB' respectively, but the universal negative is represented as 'A = A not-B' (par. 87) and the particular affirmative as 'A ≠ A not-B' (par. 85). It will be noticed that Leibniz here makes use of the indefinite or 'infinite' term 'not-B', about whose possible elimination he had speculated earlier (par. 80).

In par. 75 Leibniz expresses the hope that he will be able to conceive all propositions as terms, since this will simplify his symbolism. In pars. 108–9 he shows how this can be done, and how, conversely, any term can be regarded as a proposition. This occurs in the context of a method of representing the combinations of propositions, using as brackets lines drawn above the symbols for terms. The propositions combined state an identity

[1] For the equivalence here of 'is' and 'contains', cf. par. 4 (p. 55) and par. 16.
[2] The text has 'BY = ABY'; this has been altered for the sake of consistency.
[3] Cf. Kauppi, p. 177.

(or non-identity) between terms, each of which is quantified (par. 107). For example, $\overline{AB}$ might represent 'Every man is the same as some animal',[1] in which case $\overline{\overline{ABC}}$ might represent 'Every man-animal is the same as some mortal'. Leibniz next considers (par. 112) a difficulty which relates to his use of the indefinite symbol 'Y'. To assert the universal negative proposition 'No A is B' is to deny that some A is B; yet in Leibniz's symbolism 'Some A is B' is represented by 'AY is B', which states that *this* indeterminate A is B. The denial of this seems only to be the assertion of a particular negative; nevertheless, Leibniz insists that the denial of a particular affirmative must be a universal negative. This leads him to suggest two fresh ways of symbolizing the propositional forms, both of which involve the drawing of parallel lines; in the first, the proposition is regarded intensionally (pars. 113–21), whereas in the second it is regarded extensionally (pars. 122–3). The extensional form of the symbolism is only sketched, but is interesting in that it anticipates a symbolism suggested later by Johann Heinrich Lambert, the mathematician and friend of Kant, and one of the few symbolic logicians of the eighteenth century.[2] A somewhat similar symbolism to that presented in the *Generales Inquisitiones* is also to be found in Leibniz's paper *On the proof of logical form by the drawing of lines* (*De Formae Logicae Comprobatione per Linearum Ductus*),[3] written probably at about the same time. In this paper the proposition is first treated extensionally and then intensionally.[4]

Leibniz's use in the *Generales Inquisitiones* of a parallel line symbolism to represent the proposition from the intensional point of view is more complex than it appears, and since this symbolism also throws some light on his intensional treatment of the proposition in general, it will be worth while to comment on it. The four propositional forms are represented as follows:

Universal affirmative	A	![line]
	B	![line]
Particular affirmative	A	![line]
	B	![line]
Universal negative	A	![line]
	B	![line]
Particular negative	A	![line]
	B	![line]

[1] *C 362* (p. 53); cf. *C 233*.
[2] Cf. J. N. Keynes, *Formal Logic*, 3rd ed. (London, 1894), pp. 133 ff.
[3] *C 292* ff. For the date, cf. Kauppi, p. 184.
[4] See *C 292* ff. and *C 300* ff. respectively. This paper is also interesting in that it contains (*C 292–8*) the figures known generally as 'Euler's

The perpendicular lines represent 'the limits beyond which terms cannot, and within which they can, be extended without affecting the proposition', whilst the double, or thickened horizontal lines represent 'a minimum, or, that which cannot be taken away' without affecting the proposition (note to pars. 114–21).

The diagram for the universal affirmative shows, by means of the length and position of the unbroken horizontal lines, that the concept of A contains the concept of B; the dotted line probably shows that A and B may be identical terms, that is, that the concepts of A and B may consist of exactly the same component concepts. In such a case, Leibniz would still say that the concept of A 'contains' that of B;[1] in his usage, the concept of A contains that of B if every component of the concept of B (that is, each of the concepts which, taken together, constitute that of B) is also a component of the concept of A. The thickened lines in the diagram seem to indicate[2] that for every A to be B, it must at least be the case that all the components of the concept of B are the same as some of the components of the concept of A. The diagram which represents the particular affirmative needs more comment, and is perhaps best explained in the light of the essays of April 1679. In the *Elementa Calculi*[3] Leibniz says that in the particular affirmative proposition the concept of the predicate is contained in the concept of the subject 'with some addition or specification'. For example, in the case of the proposition that some metal is gold, the concept of gold is not contained in the concept of metal as such; but if one adds to the concept of metal the concept of, say, being soluble in *aqua regia*, then the concept of gold is contained in this complex concept. In the second diagram of the *Generales Inquisitiones* Leibniz expresses this by the use of overlapping unbroken lines, one end of each extending past one end of the other. The purpose of the dotted lines is not so clear, but Leibniz perhaps means that the unbroken line for A may be extended so that its right-hand end is level with the right-hand end

circles', published by Euler in 1768 in his *Lettres à une Princesse d'Allemagne*.

[1] *NE*, 4.17.8 (*A vi. 6, 486*).

[2] The interpretation of the thickened horizontal lines is complicated by the fact that, in the marginal note to pars. 114–21 in which Leibniz explains his symbolism, he says that a double, i.e. a thickened line 'does not seem necessary in the subject . . . . . . for I assume the subject arbitrarily'. It is not clear what this means; however, as Leibniz does not say that it is wrong, but only that it is superfluous, to thicken the line for the subject, it should not lead to any error if the diagrams are explained as they stand.

[3] *C 51* (p. 19). Cf. *C 55* (p. 23) and *C 85*.

of the unbroken line for B, in which case it would represent 'Every A is B'. That is, he seems to be taking 'some A' in the sense of 'at least one, and perhaps every A'.[1] The thickened lines in the diagram may be taken to express the proposition that, if some A is to be B, it must at least be the case that some components of the concept of A are the same as some components of the concept of B.

Although the diagram for the universal negative may appear to be of the same type as the last two, what it symbolizes is quite different. The diagrams discussed so far may be said to represent the fact that the concepts of A and B have, or do not have, concepts in common. The diagram for the universal negative, however, is not to be construed in this way. If it were, it would represent a proposition in which the concepts of subject and predicate have nothing in common; now, there may be universal negative propositions of this type, but there are undoubtedly very many which are not. It is obvious, for example, that the assertion that no ape is a man cannot be taken as saying that the concepts of ape and man have nothing in common, for they clearly have something in common—e.g. the concept of animality. What Leibniz must mean by his diagram is that the concepts of ape and man are *inconsistent*. This may be why he sometimes says[2] that in the proposition 'No A is B' the concept of A *excludes* that of B, where 'excludes' may be taken to mean, not that the concept of A does not contain any of the components of B, but rather that the concept of A as it were thrusts out that of B.[3] The diagram for the particular negative resembles that for the universal negative in one respect, and the other two diagrams in another. In the *Calculi Universalis Elementa* of April 1679, Leibniz argues that to say that some A is not B is to say that something is lacking in the concept of A which is required in that of B;[4] for example, to say

[1] As he also seems to do in *C 300–1, 328*, and *G vii. 208*. Considered in themselves, however, the definitions cited above from *C 55* and *C 85* suggest that 'some' is taken there to mean 'some only'; for to call B a species of A implies that some A is B and some is not (cf. *LR*, pp. 24–26).

It may be asked how, if every A is B, the concept of B can be said to be contained in that of A 'with some addition'. Perhaps the answer is that in such a case, the added concept may be regarded as being the same as one of the components of the concept of A. For to add a concept to itself does not alter that concept (cf. *Generales Inquisitiones*, par. 18), so that it is the same as if it had been said that every component of the concept of B is a component of the concept of A.

[2] e.g. *G vii. 208* (p. 112).

[3] It may be noted here that it is hard to see why the concepts of A and B are represented in the diagram by thickened lines; there would be little point in saying that, if no A is to be B, the concepts of A and B must at least be inconsistent, for they could hardly be more than inconsistent.

[4] *C 63–64*.

that some stone is not a man is to say that something can be a
stone without its concept containing all the components of the
concept of man. Leibniz symbolizes this in the *Generales Inquisitiones* by means of unbroken lines which do not overlap, showing
in this way that the concept of A lacks concepts which belong to
that of B. The diagram is differentiated from that for the universal
negative by the fact that the line for the concept of B is prolonged,
as a broken line, under the unbroken line for the concept of A,
indicating that the concepts of A and B may have some components
in common. So far, the symbolism is of the same type as in the
first two diagrams—common concepts are represented by the
overlap of lines, and the absence of common concepts by the lack
of overlap. But Leibniz also seems to want to allow for the possibility that no A is B, as is suggested by the fact that the line
under the line for the concept of A is dotted. If this dotted line is
not supposed to represent any concepts (i.e. is assumed not to be
there), then the diagram is in effect[1] the same as the diagram for
the universal negative, in which what is symbolized is, not a lack
of common concepts, but inconsistency. There is a similar
ambiguity in the use of thickened lines in this diagram. They are
probably meant to show that, if some A is not to be B, then the
concept of B must at least contain some components which the
concept of A does not. But the extreme case—that in which no A
is B—is not one in which all the components of the concept of B
are not components of the concept of A (i.e. in which the concepts
of A and B have no component in common), but one in which the
concepts of A and B are inconsistent.

Leibniz does not attempt to use these diagrams as a means of
testing inferences. It is easy to see from them the validity of the
conversion *simpliciter* of the particular affirmative and universal
negative, but it is not so clear how they are to be used to validate
some other inferences—for example, subalternation. A point
which it will be worth while to consider here relates to the symbolization of the syllogism. Couturat has argued[2] that the parallel-
line symbolism of the *De Formae Logicae Comprobatione* and the
Generales Inquisitiones is successful only if given an extensional
interpretation; for example, the mood *Celarent* cannot be shown

---

[1] 'In effect' because, if the dotted line under A is removed, there will be
no vertical line at the left-hand end of the continuous line for B, as there
is in the representation of the universal negative. This is because to assert
that some A is not B is not to say that no A is B, though what is said is
consistent with no A's being B.
[2] *C.L.*, pp. 30 ff.

to be valid if the symbolism is interpreted intensionally.[1] However, he makes this assertion on the basis of a diagram constructed in accordance with the rules stated in the *De Formae Logicae Comprobatione*. The symbolism of the *Generales Inquisitiones*, though it too involves the use of parallel lines, is not the same, and a diagram constructed in accordance with this symbolism gives a different result:

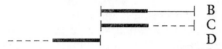

Here the second and third lines represent the premiss that no C is D, the first and second represent the premiss that every B is C, and the first and third the conclusion. It will be seen that, although the first and third lines are not exactly the same as Leibniz's diagram for the universal negative, yet they do not overlap, and so may be said to represent the proposition that no B is D, which is the conclusion of the syllogism in the mood *Celarent*.

In pars. 124–9 Leibniz returns to the problem, which had exercised him in June 1679, of finding a way of representing propositions numerically. This time he is satisfied that he has found a solution, and with it a solution of the problem of eliminating the indefinite 'Y', with which he had been concerned earlier in the *Generales Inquisitiones*.[2] His method of symbolizing the propositional forms, which will be called 'Scheme IV', is as follows. He takes the universal affirmative to mean that A can be divided by B, and the particular affirmative to mean that AB can be divided by B. Representing 'not-B' by $\frac{1}{B}$, he takes the universal negative to mean that A contains not-B; the particular negative he takes to mean that it is false that A can be divided by B. Here it is obvious that the universal affirmative and particular negative are contradictories, i.e. that if the one is true, the other is false; Leibniz adds[3] that it is also follows from his symbolism that the universal negative is the contradictory of[4] the particular affirmative, 'for if A is divided by B it cannot be the case that A is multiplied by B'. Leibniz offers two ways of expressing by equations this representation of the propositional forms. The first, which will be

[1] Cf. M. Dummett, *Journal of Symbolic Logic*, 1956, p. 199: 'Couturat is perfectly correct in saying that, as Leibniz explains the intensional interpretation, it is incapable of rendering the syllogism *Celarent*.'
[2] Cf. p. xxxiii above, and pars. 89–90.
[3] Par. 127.
[4] Leibniz says, 'the opposite of . . . '.

called 'Scheme V', is as follows (par. 128 and par. 129 n.): universal affirmative, $A = AB$; particular affirmative, $AB = AB$; universal negative, $A = \dfrac{A}{B}$; particular negative, $\dfrac{A}{B} = \dfrac{A}{B}$. The second, which will be called 'Scheme VI', is (par. 129 n.): universal affirmative, $\dfrac{A}{B} \neq \dfrac{A}{B}$; particular affirmative, $A \neq \dfrac{A}{B}$; universal negative, $AB \neq AB$; particular negative, $A \neq AB$. There seems to be a cross-division here. One would expect Leibniz to regard a pair of contradictory propositions as differing only in that whereas one states that two expressions are identical the other states that the same two expressions are not identical; so, for example, when the universal affirmative is represented as $A = AB$, the particular negative will be represented as $A \neq AB$, and so on. This would lead to the following representations of the propositional forms.[1] The first would be: universal affirmative, $A = AB$; particular affirmative, $A \neq \dfrac{A}{B}$; universal negative, $A = \dfrac{A}{B}$; particular negative, $A \neq AB$. This is the same as Scheme III; the other representation, which is not the same as any of the previous schemes, would be: universal affirmative, $\dfrac{A}{B} \neq \dfrac{A}{B}$; particular affirmative, $AB = AB$; universal negative, $AB \neq AB$; particular negative, $\dfrac{A}{B} = \dfrac{A}{B}$. As this is put forward by Leibniz later (par. 152) it will be called Scheme VII.

When Leibniz represents the universal affirmative and universal negative as $\dfrac{A}{B} \neq \dfrac{A}{B}$ and $AB \neq AB$ respectively, he might be thought to mean that 'Every A is B' says that A not-B is impossible, and that 'No A is B' says that AB is impossible. This appears to be confirmed by the fact that Leibniz says (par. 128) that when the particular affirmative, $AB = AB$, is false (i.e. when the universal negative is true), then AB is an impossible term. This can also be stated, and is stated by Leibniz, in terms of the representation of the universal negative in Scheme V, by saying that when $A = \dfrac{A}{B}$ (i.e. A not-B), then AB is impossible because A contains not-B (par. 128). One might ask why A should not contain not-B and AB still be possible; the answer (par. 130; cf. note to par. 129) is that

---

[1] The propositional forms are represented in this way by Kauppi, pp. 179–80.

what are in question here are *concepts*, so that to say that A contains not-B is in effect to say that A is *defined* as not-B, from which it follows that AB is impossible by definition. All this would have the consequence that when a universal proposition is true, it is necessarily true. This, however, is not what Leibniz wishes to say; he wants to distinguish between necessary and contingent universal propositions,[1] and after a brief glance at the difficulty in par. 128 he discusses it in detail in pars. 130–6, with special reference to universal negative propositions. In essence, his account adds nothing to the discussion of necessary and contingent truths in pars. 60–61.[2] He says that a proposition of the form 'No A is B' can be true without being necessarily true, provided that the analysis required to show that the concept of not-B is contained in the concept of A is infinite (par. 130). In such a case, the concept of AB may be called 'false' rather than 'impossible' (par. 128). In the same way a distinction is to be drawn between necessary and contingent universal affirmative propositions, so that 'A = AB, if the proof has been made by a finite analysis, must be distinguished from A = AB, if the proof has been made by an analysis *ad infinitum*' (par. 130 *bis*). It follows from this that the formulae mentioned at the beginning of the present paragraph, $\frac{A}{B} \neq \frac{A}{B}$ and AB $\neq$ AB, are also ambiguous, and that they represent necessary propositions only when A's containing B or not-B respectively can be shown in a finite number of operations.

In par. 137 Leibniz sums up the progress that he has made. He mentions his proof of a way in which all truths can be represented numerically (pars. 124–9), and his account of the nature of contingent truths (pars. 60–61, 130–6). He also claims to have shown that categorical and hypothetical propositions have the same laws. Strictly, he has not done so; he has merely expressed the hope that he will be able to treat hypothetical propositions as categorical (par. 75). However, what he claims to have done he performs in the next paragraph, in which he transforms the proposition '"C is D" follows from "A is B"' into the categorical proposition 'The B-ness of A contains the D-ness of C'.[3] Finally (perhaps referring

---

[1] In a marginal note to par. 129 (p. 76 n. 1) Leibniz says that when a particular affirmative—say, 'Some A is B'—is false, then it is impossible that there should be a concept AB. This, however, does not contradict what has been said above; Leibniz remarks that 'we are here considering abstract concepts, not the data of experience', which seems to mean that he is here considering necessary propositions alone, and is not asking how any universal propositions can be other than necessary.

[2] Cf. p. xxxiv.

[3] Par. 138; cf. C *260, 262, 407.*

to par. 109) Leibniz claims that he has explained how abstract terms are formed.

Leibniz decides that there is more to be said about abstract terms, and in pars. 139–43 he discusses their use in the representation of universality, of quantity, and of negation, besides considering abstractions as predicates. A new method of symbolizing the propositional forms is introduced when Leibniz discusses (pars. 144–70) what he expresses in traditional terminology as the problem of transforming propositions *tertii adjecti* into propositions *secundi adjecti*,[1] by which he means the transformation of propositions of the form 'A est B' ('A is B') into propositions of the form 'AB est' ('AB exists') or 'AB est res' ('AB is a thing'). In pars. 146–51 Leibniz uses the latter mode of expression to represent the propositional forms in the following way, which will be called 'Scheme VIII': universal affirmative, A not-B does not exist, or, A not-B is not a thing;[2] particular affirmative, AB exists, or, AB is a thing; universal negative, AB does not exist, or, AB is not a thing;[3] particular negative, A, not-B, exists, or, A not-B is a thing. It should be noted that Leibniz is here thinking of the proposition in conceptual, i.e. intensional, terms, so that 'exists' means 'can be conceived' (par. 144), and to say, for example, that AB does not exist is to say that A and B are inconsistent (par. 200).

[1] The terminology is Scholastic, but is ultimately derived from Aristotle. The Aristotelian connexions can be seen in Abelard (1079–1142), who distinguishes between the use of the word 'est' 'tertium adiacens', as in 'Socrates est homo', and its use 'appositum subiecto', as in 'Socrates est' (*Dialectica*, ed. de Rijk (Assen, 1956), pp. 135, 161; *Logica Ingredientibus*, ed. Geyer (Münster, 1919–27), p. 361; cf. Kneale, p. 207). He makes it clear (*Dialectica*, p. 161) that 'tertium adiacens' is related to Aristotle's terminology by citing a sentence from the *De Interpretatione* (19b 19–20), which in the Latin version is 'Quando autem "est" tertium adiacens praedicatur, dupliciter fiunt oppositiones'. The use of the term 'secundi adjecti' to refer to 'est' as it occurs in 'Socrates est' seems to be later; something like it may be found in Albert of Saxony (?1316–1390), who would have called 'Socrates est' a proposition 'de secundo adiacente', as opposed to a proposition 'de tertio adiacente', such as 'Socrates est homo' (Albert of Saxony, *Perutilis Logica*, iii. 1, 17; quoted by I. M. Bochenski, *Formale Logik* (Freiburg, 1956), p. 208).

Couturat supposes (*C.L.*, p. 350 n. 3) that Leibniz's use of the terms 'secundi adjecti' and 'tertii adjecti' comes from the fact that the predicate (*l'adjectif*) is the second in the one case ('AB est') and third in the other ('A est B'). But whether or not Leibniz thought that this was the meaning of the terms (and he offers no explanation of them, either in the *Generales Inquisitiones*, or in the *De Formae Logicae Comprobatione*, C *301*), it is clear that this cannot apply to propositions such as 'Socrates est'.

[2] This formulation, given in par. 150, replaces the 'Every A containing B exists' or 'A containing B is a thing' of par. 147.

[3] Also rendered as 'Every A containing not-B exists' (par. 149).

Couturat represents this scheme[1] in terms of Boolean algebra as: universal affirmative, A not-B $= 0$; particular affirmative, AB $\neq 0$; universal negative, AB $= 0$; particular negative, A not-B $\neq 0$. Care must be taken, however, not to ascribe to Leibniz a greater degree of logical sophistication than he had reached. A Boolean algebra is capable of many interpretations, and the formulae just cited could indeed be interpreted as saying that the logical product of two concepts is or is not a self-consistent concept, i.e. as giving Scheme VIII. It must be stressed, however, that in the *Generales Inquisitiones* Leibniz does not speak as if this scheme were one of several possible interpretations of an abstract calculus; the idea of such a calculus seems to have occurred to him only later.[2]

The *Generales Inquisitiones* contains another method of representing the propositional forms, which will be called Scheme IX. This scheme, which is stated more clearly in other works,[3] is as follows: universal affirmative, A $=$ YB; particular affirmative, YA $=$ ZB; universal negative, A $=$ Y not-B; particular negative, XA $=$ Y not-B. Each of these items can be found somewhere in the *Generales Inquisitiones*, and the last two and the first occur in one paragraph, par. 190.[4] However, Leibniz does not seem to have

---

[1] *C.L.*, p. 358. To be exact, what he represents is the very similar scheme put forward in the *Primaria Calculi Logici Fundamenta* of August 1690; cf. *C 236* (pp. 90–91).

[2] See p. lviii below, on Leibniz's study in the calculus of real addition. It is true that in the *Primaria Calculi Logici Fundamenta* Leibniz does not say how such sentences as 'AB is an entity' are to be taken; this, however, need not indicate that he is developing an abstract calculus. The work in question is a short one, perhaps meant for its author's eyes alone, and Leibniz may have thought it unnecessary to explain on paper sentences whose meaning was clear to him.
Another possible interpretation of Scheme VIII, relating it to medieval views, may be mentioned here. It has been argued that the Scholastic account of the verb 'est' in its use *secundo adiacens*—for example, in 'Socrates est' ('Socrates exists')—amounts to saying that the verb functions here as an existential quantifier, indicating that the subject term is to be 'taken for something' (E. A. Moody, *Truth and Consequence in Mediaeval Logic* (Amsterdam, 1953), p. 33). It may in consequence be thought that in Scheme VIII, which is stated in terms of propositions *secundi adiecti*, Leibniz is using the words 'est' or 'est res' in a similar way. However, it seems unlikely that he is; it has already been seen that in this context these words do not assert existence, as this would normally be understood, but rather assert consistency.

[3] Cf. *De Formae Logicae Comprobatione* (*C 302*) and *Primaria Calculi Logici Fundamenta* (*C 236* (pp. 90–91)); also *C 233–4*.

[4] For the universal affirmative, see also pars. 16, 158; for the particular affirmative, pars. 89, 159, 165.

the scheme clearly in mind in this paper, for par. 190 represents the particular affirmative, 'Some A is L', as 'AL = AL', which belongs to Scheme V, and also represents the particular negative by the appropriate formula from this scheme. This failure to state Scheme IX clearly in the *Generales Inquisitiones* may perhaps be due to Leibniz's wish to dispense with the indefinite symbols X, Y, and Z,[1] which are used in the scheme.

It will be useful at this stage to bring together the various schemes for the representation of the propositional forms discussed in the last few pages. The universal affirmative will be referred to as 'UA', the particular negative as 'PN', etc.

Scheme I

UA A is (contains) B
PA AY is (contains) B
UN AY is not (does not contain) B
PN A is not (does not contain) B

Scheme II

UA $A = AB$
PA $AY = ABY$
UN $AY \neq ABY$
PN $A \neq AB$

Scheme III

UA $A = AB$
PA $A \neq A \text{ not-}B$
UN $A = A \text{ not-}B$
PN $A \neq AB$

Scheme IV

UA A can be divided by B
PA AB can be divided by B
UN A contains $\frac{1}{B}$ (not-B)
PN It is false that A can be divided by B

Scheme V

UA $A = AB$
PA $AB = AB$
UN $A = \frac{A}{B}$
PN $\frac{A}{B} = \frac{A}{B}$

Scheme VI

UA $\frac{A}{B} \neq \frac{A}{B}$
PA $A \neq \frac{A}{B}$
UN $AB \neq AB$
PN $A \neq AB$

---

[1] Cf. p. xlii.

Scheme VII

UA $\quad \dfrac{A}{B} \neq \dfrac{A}{B}$

PA $\quad AB = AB$

UN $\quad AB \neq AB$

PN $\quad \dfrac{A}{B} = \dfrac{A}{B}$

Scheme VIII

UA $\quad$ A not-B does not exist
$\quad$ (A not-B is not a thing)

PA $\quad$ AB exists
$\quad$ (AB is a thing)

UN $\quad$ AB does not exist
$\quad$ (AB is not a thing)

PN $\quad$ A, not-B, exists
$\quad$ (A not-B is a thing)

Scheme IX

UA $\quad$ A = YB
PA $\quad$ YA = ZB
UN $\quad$ A = Y not-B
PN $\quad$ XA = Y not-B

The other symbolizations of the propositional forms offered in the *Generales Inquisitiones* are, with one exception, the same as one or other of these schemes. Thus, par. 152, which has already been mentioned as containing Scheme VII,[1] also contains a symbolization which is the same as Scheme VIII. Pars. 164–7 are the same as Scheme V, and par. 169 is the same as Scheme VIII, as is par. 199. What is in effect Scheme VIII is also contained in the note to par. 129, where instead of 'AB exists' or 'AB does not exist' Leibniz writes 'AB is a true concept' or 'AB is a false concept'. The exception mentioned above is a scheme put forward in pars. 158–61. This shows some signs of haste, in that Leibniz does not have a consistent symbolism for subject and predicate, D, A, and E being used for the subject and C, E, and F for the predicate. The scheme can be systematized as follows: universal affirmative, A = YB; particular affirmative, YA = ZB; universal negative, A = not-B; particular negative, YA = not-B. The first two items in this scheme belong to Scheme IX, but the other two do not belong to any scheme, and in fact are incorrect.[2] They are most easily corrected by changing 'A = not-B' to 'A = Y not-B', and

[1] Cf. p. xliii.
[2] For example, on this interpretation the universal negative 'No man is a stone' would be represented as ' "Man" = "not-stone" '. Replacing 'man' by 'not-stone' in the true proposition 'Every man thinks', we derive the conclusion 'Every not-stone thinks'. With regard to the particular negative, 'Some men do not laugh' will on this interpretation be ' "Some men" = "not-laughers" '. Similarly, 'Some stones do not laugh' will be ' "Some stones" = "not-laughers" '. But if a = b and c = b, then a = c; therefore 'some men' = 'some stones'.

'YA = not-B' to 'XA = Y not-B', the remaining formulae of Scheme IX.

Towards the end of the *Generales Inquisitiones* Leibniz makes several attempts at pulling together some of the threads of the argument by stating the principles of a calculus. Par. 156 may contain an attempt of this kind, and it is certain that the attempt is made in no fewer than three later paragraphs—pars. 171, 189, and 198. The last two sets of principles are distinguished from the rest in that they include propositions expressed, not in terms of equations, but in terms of containment, 'A contains *l*' being defined as 'A = *xl*'.[1] All four sets contain the proposition that AA = A;[2] those stated in pars. 156 and 171 contain the proposition that A = A;[3] those stated in pars. 171, 189, and 198 contain the proposition that not-not-A = A;[4] finally, those stated in pars. 189 and 198 contain the assertion that the expression 'A not-A', or any expression containing it, is to be rejected.[5]

The *Generales Inquisitiones* ends with the assertion that the fundamentals of logical form are contained 'in these few propositions' (*his paucis*),[6] which seems from the context to refer to the last set of principles stated—that is, those of par. 198. Leibniz makes little attempt at substantiating his claim, merely remarking (par. 199) that the oppositions and conversions of the propositional forms are 'evident' from his symbolization, which is that of Scheme VIII. He does not discuss the syllogism, here or at any other point in the *Generales Inquisitiones*, though he could argue that the symbolizations of the propositional forms which he has suggested can be used to symbolize the premisses and conclusions of syllogistic arguments, which he would probably try to justify in terms of containment.[7] Again, he has said nothing about relational arguments. Perhaps the discussion of terms and particles in the first part of the paper was meant to be used in this connexion; if so, the intention was unfulfilled. Leibniz, then, can hardly be said to have substantiated his claim to have stated the 'fundamentals of logical form'; but the more modest claim that in this paper he has made 'excellent progress'[8] seems amply justified.

---

[1] Par. 189 (no. 4); par. 198 (no. 9). Cf. par. 16.

[2] Par. 156 (no. 3); par. 171 (no. 3); par. 189 (no. 1); par. 198 (no. 2). Cf. par. 18 (p. xxxiii above).

[3] Par. 156 (no. 1); par. 171 (no. 1). Cf. par. 10.

[4] Par. 171 (no. 4); par. 189 (no. 2); par. 198 (no. 3). Cf. par. 2.

[5] Par. 189 (no. 3); par. 198 (no. 4). Cf. pars. 43–46 (p. xxxiii above).

[6] Par. 200.

[7] Cf. his views on the representation of hypothetical propositions, par. 138 (p. xliv above).

[8] *C 356* (p. 47, n.1).

4

The next paper translated here (No. 8) was sent by Leibniz in January 1687 to Jungius' editor, Vagetius; in it, Leibniz returns to the problem of relational arguments. He is here concerned with a proof of what (following Jungius)[1] he calls an inference from the direct to the oblique. The argument cited earlier[2] about the heads of horses is an instance of this type of inference; Leibniz's example, translated literally, is 'Painting is an art, therefore he who learns painting, learns an art', but its likeness to the previous example is brought out more clearly if the conclusion is rendered as 'therefore the student of painting is the student of an art'. Leibniz had remarked in an earlier letter[3] that a proof of such an inference could be based 'on the mutual substitution of equivalents', and the proof which he sent to Vagetius has such a basis; it may be compared with Jevons' proof of a similar argument in *The Principles of Science*.[4]

In the autumn of 1687 Leibniz began a journey to Italy, where his intention was to trace the connexions between the houses of Brunswick and of Este, and to engage in diplomacy, both political and ecclesiastical.[5] His next dated logical papers were written after his return in June 1690. These are two short papers, translated here as numbers 9 and 10, which were written on the first and second of August respectively of that year. The first is *The Primary*[6] *Bases of a Logical Calculus* (*Primaria Calculi Logici Fundamenta*), and the second *The Bases of a Logical Calculus* (*Fundamenta Calculi Logici*). These papers use and to a certain extent develop some of the ideas put forward in the *Generales Inquisitiones*. Both are based on the assumptions that 'A = B' is the same as 'A = B is true' and that 'A ≠ B' is the same as 'A = B is false' (cf. *Generales Inquisitiones*, pars. 1 and 5), and that AA = A (cf. *Generales Inquisitiones*, par. 18). The first, *Primaria Calculi Logici Fundamenta*, offers a number of ways of representing the propositional forms; these (which are taken for granted in the second paper) are related to several of the schemes put forward in

---

[1] Cf. Jungius, p. 391.
[2] Cf. p. xix.
[3] To Placcius, 16 November 1686; *D vi. 1*, p. 32.
[4] 2nd ed. (London, 1877), p. 18. Speaking of de Morgan's argument, 'Because a horse is an animal, the head of a horse is the head of an animal', Jevons says, 'I conceive that this amounts merely to replacing in the complete notion *head of a horse*, the term "horse" by its equivalent *some animal* or *an animal*'.
[5] Fischer-Kabitz, pp. 186 ff.
[6] In classical Latin 'primarius' means 'of the first rank, remarkable', but Leibniz normally uses the word to mean 'primary': cf. *C 25, 230, 400, 582, 593*.

the *Generales Inquisitiones*. Leibniz finally decides[1] on what was called earlier Scheme III; besides this, he offers a scheme which is very close to Scheme VIII, rendering the particular affirmative as 'AB is an entity', the universal negative as 'AB is a non-entity', and the particular negative as 'A not-B is an entity'.[2] Other representations are offered: that of the universal affirmative as A = YB, the particular affirmative as YA = ZB, and the universal negative as A = Y not-B resembles Scheme IX, whilst Schemes II and V are touched on when Leibniz represents the particular affirmative as YA = YAB and AB = AB respectively.

With regard to the content of these papers, Leibniz is again chiefly concerned with immediate inference; in the first, he proves the subalternation of the universal affirmative and the universal negative proposition, together with the conversion *simpliciter* of the particular affirmative and the universal negative,[3] whilst the second proves the subalternation of the universal negative and the conversion by contraposition of the universal affirmative.[4] What is most interesting, perhaps, is the proof in the first paper[5] of the equivalence between some of the items contained in the representations of the propositional forms in the *Generales Inquisitiones* —namely, between 'AB is a non-entity' (cf. Scheme VIII) and 'A = A not-B' (Scheme III), and between 'AB is an entity' (cf. Scheme VIII) and 'A ≠ A not-B' (Scheme III).

The next four translations (Nos. 11–14) form a group, having in common the fact that each is concerned largely, if not wholly, with the syllogism. The four in question are *A Mathematics of Reason* (*Mathesis Rationis*); *Of the Mathematical Determination of Syllogistic Forms* (*De Formis Syllogismorum mathematice definiendis*); an untitled paper on immediate inference and the syllogism, commonly referred to as *Logical Definitions* (*Definitiones Logicae*);[6] and an untitled paper concerned largely with conversion *per accidens* and with the representation of some syllogistic moods, often called *Some Logical Difficulties* (*Difficultates quaedam Logicae*), after its opening phrase. None of these works can be dated

---

[1] *C 236* (p. 91).
[2] Analogically, the universal affirmative would be rendered as 'A not-B is a non-entity', a definition which is given (*C 233*) in some remarks written on the same day, and on the same sheet of paper, as *Primaria Calculi Logici Fundamenta*.
[3] *C 236* (p. 91).
[4] Pars. 16 and 19 (p. 94).
[5] *C 237* (pp. 91–92).
[6] This title was given to it by the nineteenth-century editor Erdmann.

with precision, though it can at any rate be said that *Difficultates quaedam Logicae* was written some years after 1690.[1] The works are presented here in an order which (whether or not it is that in which they were written) seems at any rate to be a logical order. *De Formis Syllogismorum mathematice definiendis* is placed after *Mathesis Rationis*, of which it is the logical completion, since it contains a detailed account of a method of proving the valid moods of the syllogism which is only sketched at the end of the *Mathesis Rationis*.[2] In both these works, the proposition is considered from the standpoint of extension; they are followed here by *Definitiones Logicae*, in which Leibniz adopts the intensional point of view.[3] *Difficultates quaedam Logicae* is placed last, since in this work

---

[1] Leibniz refers there (*G vii. 212* (p. 116)) to his 'old analysis' of propositions; this is a reference to *Primaria Calculi Logici Fundamenta*, of August 1690 (cf. *C 236* (pp. 90–91) and *C 233*; also C.L., p. 358). There is no hint of how old the analysis was; Leibniz was still concerned with syllogistic problems in 1715, the year before his death (cf. *Schedae de Novis Formis et Figuris Syllogisticis*, *C 206* ff.), so *Difficultates quaedam Logicae* could be as late as that. It will be suggested later (p. liv n. 2) that it was probably written after the *Nouveaux Essais*, i.e. (cf. p. xx n. 4) after 1705. With regard to the other papers in the group, it has been suggested that *Mathesis Rationis* was written in about 1710 (cf. K. Dürr, *Leibniz' Forschungen im Gebiet der Syllogistik* (Berlin, 1949), p. 4). The evidence for this is a letter from Leibniz to Cornelius Dietrich Koch, dated 31 August 1710, in which Leibniz says that he would like to know who first thought of the theory which derives the quantity of predicates from the quality of propositions (*G vii. 481*). Such a theory is discussed in the *Mathesis Rationis* (*C 196* (p. 98)). However, it does not follow that Leibniz was writing this work at about the time he wrote to Koch; the question might have remained at the back of his mind for a long time, to receive expression when he was writing to someone who proposed to write a history of logic. (On Dürr's argument, cf. Kauppi, pp. 195–6.) Another suggestion (Schmidt, p. 516) is that the work must be dated much earlier, in fact before 1686. The reason for this is that Leibniz begins by saying (*C 193* (p. 95)) that he will prove the laws of the categorical syllogism by a consideration of the same and the different. As it was in 1686 that Leibniz first developed a calculus in terms of identity, and as this is not used in *Mathesis Rationis*, that work was probably not yet written. But there seems to be no reason why, once Leibniz had developed a calculus, he should always use it.

[2] *C 202* (p. 104).

[3] Dürr (op. cit., p. 37) argues that the *Definitiones Logicae* is probably to be placed after the *De Formis Syllogismorum* on the grounds that, at the end of the *Definitiones Logicae* (*G vii. 210* (p. 141)), Leibniz refers to the fact that there are only twenty-four moods of the syllogism, 'as I have shown elsewhere'. This, according to Dürr, may be a reference to the *De Formis Syllogismorum*. But in this work (*C 410* (p. 105)) Leibniz asserts that there are, not twenty-four, but twenty-seven moods of the syllogism.

Leibniz considers the proposition in both intensional and extensional terms.[1]

For the most part, Leibniz presents his arguments clearly in
these papers, which therefore need little comment. No. 11,
Mathesis Rationis, is a thorough account of the rules of syllogistic
inference; it is chiefly noteworthy for the fact that Leibniz con-
ceives the idea of the quantification of the predicate, only to reject
it.[2] *De Formis Syllogismorum*, No. 12, gives several examples of
the method of proof which Leibniz calls 'regress' (*regressus*), and
which is mentioned briefly at the end of the *Mathesis Rationis*.[3]
This method consists of assuming that the conclusion of a syllogism is false, and that one of its premisses is true, from which it
follows that the other premiss must be false. The method is
traditionally called 'reduction *per impossibile*', or 'indirect reduction';[4] it was used by Aristotle to validate the moods *Baroco* and
Bocardo,[5] though he did not state expressly the rule which he
used. This was done by the Stoics, as the first of their *themata*, or
principles for the analysis of propositions, which states that if
from two propositions a third is deduced, then either of the two
together with the denial of the conclusion entails the denial of the
other.[6] One surprising remark in the *De Formis Syllogismorum* is
that the fourth figure of the syllogism has nine valid moods,[7] and
not the six which Leibniz usually ascribes to it.[8] It has been suggested[9] that he was misled by his proposed method of proof, by
which some moods can be derived twice over, and it may be that

[1] *G vii. 215* (p. 119). There is an independent argument (cf. Kauppi,
p. 196) for placing at any rate the *Mathesis Rationis* before *Difficultates
quaedam Logicae*. In the former work, Leibniz uses S to stand for a
universal and I to stand for a particular proposition (*C 196* (p. 98)).
Couturat (*C 196* n.) traces this symbolism to the *De Arte Combinatoria*,
in which S stands for a singular proposition, there regarded by Leibniz
as equivalent to a universal proposition, and I for an indefinite proposition, regarded by him as equivalent to a particular proposition. This
suggests that when Leibniz wrote the *Mathesis Rationis* he was still regarding a singular proposition as equivalent to a universal proposition, a
view which he abandoned in *Difficultates quaedam Logicae* (*G vii. 211*
(p. 115)).
[2] *C 193–4* (p. 95).
[3] *C 202* (p. 104); *C 412–15* (pp. 107 ff.). Cf. *G vii. 212* (p. 115); *NE*, 4.2.1
(*A vi. 6, 363*).
[4] See, e.g., Jungius, pp. 146–7.
[5] *An. Pr.* ii. 8, 59b 28. Cf. Łukasiewicz, op. cit., p. 57; Kneale, pp. 76–77.
[6] Benson Mates, *Stoic Logic* (Los Angeles, 1961), p. 77. Cf. Kneale,
p. 169.
[7] *C 410* (p. 105).
[8] e.g. *G vii. 210* (p. 114); *NE*, 4.17.4 (*A vi. 6, 479*).
[9] Kauppi, p. 197 n. 1.

the absence from this paper of a proof of the moods of the fourth figure is due to Leibniz's discovery of his mistake.

Definitiones Logicae (No. 13), in which Leibniz considers immediate inference and the syllogism intensionally, is short and clearly stated, and needs no comment here;[1] there are, however, two points which are worth noting about the last paper in this group, *Difficultates quaedam Logicae*. The first is that in this paper Leibniz criticizes the view, which he had held since writing the *De Arte Combinatoria*, that a singular proposition can be regarded as a universal proposition.[2] In that work, he had argued for this view as follows:[3]

'Socrates is the son of Sophroniscus', if analysed somewhat after the manner of Johannes Raue, will be 'Whoever is Socrates is the son of Sophroniscus'. And it will not be wrong to say, 'Every Socrates is the son of Sophroniscus', even if he is the only son; for we are not talking about the name, but about the man. In the same way, if I say 'I give and bequeath to Titius all the garments I have', who will doubt that, even if I have only one garment, this is owed to him? . . . . . . Further, if it is assumed that Socrates has no brother, on this understanding I am right in saying 'Every son of Sophroniscus is Socrates'.

Now, however, a consideration of the opposition of singular propositions, and of a syllogism in which the conclusion is a singular proposition, leads Leibniz to modify this view and to say that a singular proposition is equivalent both to a universal and to a particular proposition.[4]

The second and perhaps more important point arises from problems relating to the conversion of propositions.[5] Leibniz begins by saying that an assertion such as 'Every laugher is a man' may be true even if no man laughs, i.e. even if there are no

---

[1] For a criticism of this approach to the syllogism, see Couturat's account of the *Definitiones Logicae*, C.L., pp. 19 ff.; this is answered in Kauppi, pp. 206 ff.

[2] Leibniz still held this view when writing the *Nouveaux Essais* (1703–5). There he remarks (4.17.8) that for 'The Apostle Peter has denied his master' one can say 'Whoever has been the Apostle Peter has denied his master'. Consequently, the syllogism 'St. Peter has denied his master, St. Peter has been a disciple, therefore some disciple has denied his master' can be regarded as having universal affirmative premisses, and so is in the mood *Darapti* of the third figure. It has already been remarked (p. lii n. 1) that this may mean that the *Difficultates quaedam Logicae* is to be put after 1705.

[3] *A vi. 1, 182–3.*

[4] *G vii. 211 (p. 115).*

[5] Ibid. Similar problems relate to subalternation, and are mentioned briefly by Leibniz towards the end of the *Difficultates quaedam Logicae* (*G vii. 216 (p. 120)*).

laughers—just as he had argued in the *Elementa Calculi* of 1679 that a proposition such as 'Every perfectly good man is happy' may be true even if there are no perfectly good men.[1] Leibniz's point can be made in terms of modern logic by saying that he regards 'Every laugher is a man' as equivalent to 'For all x, if x is a laugher then x is a man'; that is, he is saying that a universal affirmative proposition does not have 'existential import'. Leibniz then asks how one can infer from this universal proposition the particular proposition that some man is a laugher, which is not true unless some man laughs. He is not prepared to say that the conversion *per accidens* of a universal affirmative proposition is invalid; as this is so, it might seem that the obvious solution is to say that the universal affirmative proposition does after all have existential import, so that the proposition 'Every laugher is a man' is about actually existing laughers. Despite some hesitation, however, Leibniz seems to reject this, and to say instead that, whether the proposition is regarded intensionally[2] or extensionally,[3] neither the universal affirmative nor the particular affirmative proposition need have existential import.[4]

The last two papers translated (Nos. 15–16) are the most developed specimens of a logical calculus which Leibniz produced. They are undated, but are clearly later than the logical essays of August 1690.[5] Leibniz did not settle on a title for either paper, but No. 15 is sometimes referred to by later writers as *Non Inelegans Specimen Demonstrandi in Abstractis*, a title which he originally gave to it but deleted later. A number of considerations make it likely that this work is the earlier of the two. A distinctive feature of the symbolism used in these papers is the representation of the combination of concepts, not by 'AB' as in earlier works, but by 'A + B' in No. 15 and 'A ⊕ B' in No. 16.[6] The purpose of

---

[1] *C 53* (p. 20); cf. p. xxi above.
[2] *G vii. 211–15* (pp. 115–19).
[3] *G vii. 215–17* (pp. 119–21).
[4] Cf. *LR*, pp. 19–21.
[5] *C.L.*, p. 364. Kauppi argues that they were written before the essay *Specimen Geometriae Luciferae* (*G.M.* vii. 260 ff.), which presupposes some of the results of No. 16 and for which a date of about 1695–7 has been suggested (Kauppi, pp. 223–4). For a further account of Nos. 15 and 16, see e.g. Lewis, pp. 16 ff., *C.L.*, pp. 364 ff., Kauppi, pp. 222 ff., and Kneale, pp. 340 ff.
[6] Leibniz notes this in another paper: 'For A ⊕ B one could simply put AB' (*C 256*). It may be added that towards the end of No. 16 (*G vii. 245* (p. 142)) Leibniz forgets himself and writes AA, AB, and BA where he should consistently have written A ⊕ A, A ⊕ B, and B ⊕ A (cf. Lewis, p. 304).

the circle round the plus sign is to bring out the fact that the operation for which it stands, which Leibniz calls 'real addition', differs from mathematical addition.[1] The sign '$\oplus$', then, represents a more sophisticated concept than the sign '$+$' does, and it therefore seems likely that the paper in which the former sign occurs is the later of the two. The same conclusion is suggested by the fact that in No. 15 Leibniz uses the notion of subtraction (*detractio*),[2] which seems to have caused him some difficulty and is not found in No. 16. No. 16, again, is more elaborate and is rich in examples, the need for which is mentioned in the other paper.[3] Since No. 15, the former *Non Inelegans Specimen*, is distinguished by the use of the symbol for subtraction, it is called here 'A Study in the Plus-Minus Calculus';[4] the other, and later, paper is called 'A Study in the Calculus of Real Addition'.[5]

Despite their differences, there are many similarities between the two papers. Broadly, both are concerned with the relations of identity and inclusion, which they define in similar ways,[6] and they also have a number of theorems in common.[7] Each is very limited in scope, and neither is concerned directly with the problems of traditional logic, except to the extent that each contains what may be called[8] the 'principle of the syllogism', in the form of the proposition that if A is in B and B is in C, then A is in C.[9] Because of these similarities, the two papers can conveniently be discussed together.

Leibniz symbolizes 'A is in L' as 'A $+$ B $=$ L', or (in the second paper) as 'A $\oplus$ B $=$ L'. He notes that the $+$ sign does not function in the same way as the sign for arithmetical addition;[10] for if there are two partly overlapping lines, RS and YX, then the two taken together may be said to coincide with RX, though the lengths RS and YX added together do not equal the length RX. The difference is perhaps brought out more clearly by the fact

---

[1] *G vii. 246* (p. 143).

[2] *G vii. 229* (p. 124).

[3] *G vii. 232 n.* (p. 126, n. 1).

[4] Cf. Schmidt, p. 304.

[5] It may be noted here that Couturat and Kauppi refer to these papers as XIX and XX respectively, the numbers which they have in *G vii*.

[6] Identity ('the same') is defined in *G vii. 228* (p. 122) and *G vii. 236* (p. 131); inclusion ('being in' or 'being contained in') is defined in *G vii. 228* (p. 122) and *G vii. 237* (p. 132).

[7] Theorems 1, 2, 3, 3 Corol., 4, 5, 6, 7, and 7 (converse) of the first paper appear respectively as propositions 3, 4, 9, 10, 15, 18, 20, 14, and 13 of the second.

[8] *C.L.*, p. 370.

[9] *G vii. 231* (p. 126); *G vii. 240* (p. 135).

[10] *G vii. 229* (p. 123); cf. *G vii. 246* (p. 143).

that $A + A = A$ (or $A \oplus A = A$) is an axiom in these two papers.[1] The notion of subtraction is symbolized by the minus sign. Leibniz's definition[2] is somewhat clumsy, but its sense may be expressed, in terms derived from another paper,[3] by saying that $C - B = A$ if, and only if, $C = A + B$, and A and B have nothing in common, i.e. are what Leibniz calls 'uncommunicating' terms.[4] Leibniz's reason for saying that A and B must have nothing in common is that $A + A = A$, from which one would get $A = A - A$. But, as will be seen later, $A - A = 0$ in Leibniz's calculus, from which it follows that $A = 0$, which is contrary to the hypothesis.[5] Leibniz also notes that where concepts are concerned, subtraction differs from negation.[6] Thus, a non-rational man (i.e. a non-rational rational animal) is impossible, but the concept of a man from which the concept of rationality has been subtracted is possible, for this is simply the concept of a non-rational animal or brute. If one continues to subtract, and takes away from the concept of a rational animal the concept of animality as well as that of rationality, one is left with nothing, or mere non-entity. Couturat argues[7] that Leibniz has forgotten that 'non-entity' (*non-Ens*) is for him the same as the impossible or the self-contradictory, so that in the end there is no difference between subtraction and negation. Now, it is true that Leibniz often takes 'entity' (*Ens*) to mean 'possible',[8] but he need not always do so, so that the statement in No. 15 that 'non-entity' means the same as 'nothing'[9] may be internally consistent, whether or not it is consistent with Leibniz's usage elsewhere. It may be added that another respect in which Leibniz's usage, though not inconsistent, might be confusing is that his minus sign behaves like the minus sign of

---

[1] *G vii. 230* (p. 124); *G vii. 237* (p. 132).
[2] *G vii. 229* (p. 124).
[3] *C 267.*
[4] *G vii. 229* (p. 123); *G vii. 234* (p. 128). Cf. Kneale, p. 340.
[5] *C 267.* Kneale (loc. cit.) notes that if A and B have something in common, the operation of subtraction will not give a unique result. For example, in the equation $C - B = A$, let $A = N + M$ and $B = L + M$; then we might have, not only $C - (L + M) = N + M$, but also $C - (L + M) = N$. This is because $A + A = A$ in Leibniz's system, so that $N + M + L + M = N + L + M$. It may be added that the restriction on the overlapping of terms removes a difficulty noted by Lewis, pp. 17–18.
[6] *G vii. 232 n.* (p. 127 n. 1).
[7] *C.L.*, pp. 378–9.
[8] e.g. *C 259, 261, 271*; *G vii. 319*; Grua, p. 325.
[9] *Nihilum*; in the context, this is perhaps better rendered as 'The absence of all determination' (Kneale, loc. cit.). On the passage as a whole, see also Lewis, p. 17; Kauppi, p. 238.

arithmetic, in that $A - A = 0$,[1] whereas his plus sign does not, since $A + A = A$.

The reference to concepts in the last paragraph raises the question of the way in which Leibniz is thinking of the proposition in these papers: whether he is regarding it intensionally (i.e. in terms of the inclusion of the concept of the predicate in that of the subject), or extensionally (i.e. in terms of the inclusion of the subject in the predicate), or in both ways. The passage just discussed shows that in the study in the plus-minus calculus Leibniz is thinking of subtraction in terms of concepts, and it is reasonable to infer that he thinks of inclusion as the inclusion of the concept of the predicate in that of the subject, rather than of the subject in the predicate. Similarly, the many examples which he gives in the study in the calculus of real addition are phrased in terms of concepts. However, in that paper Leibniz makes it clear that he is not thinking exclusively in intensional terms, when he remarks[2] that he is not concerned with the question of the way in which those terms which are in something are related to each other or to the container. 'So our proofs hold even of those terms which compose something distributively, as all species together compose the genus.' The reference to species as composing the genus shows clearly that Leibniz is thinking of the extensional approach to the proposition; to adopt the intensional approach is to regard the species as containing the genus, as, for example, the concept of man contains the concept of animality.[3] The answer to the question raised earlier, then, is that Leibniz stresses the abstract nature of his calculus, and thinks that it is capable of interpretation in terms either of extension or of intension. Leibniz fails to note, however, that the meaning of the symbol $+$, or $\oplus$, will differ in accordance with the interpretation given to the symbols A, B, etc.[4] For example, if A stands for 'warrior' and B for 'happy', then if A and B are taken intensionally, 'A + B' will stand for 'happy warrior'. But if A and B are taken extensionally, then 'A + B' will represent the class of those who are either happy, or warriors, or both. Correspondingly, the sense of 'is in' will alter; thus, to say that the concept of happiness is in that of piety is to say that the concept of piety entails that of happiness, whereas to say that the class of pious men is in that of happy men is simply to say that one is a sub-class of the other, without any mention of entailment.

[1] G vii. 230 (p. 124). Cf. C 267.
[2] G vii. 244 (p. 141).
[3] Cf. C 52–53 (p. 20); C 81 (p. 29).
[4] Cf. Lewis, p. 16; Kneale, p. 343.

It is now time to make some general comments about Leibniz's place in the history of logic. There is widespread agreement that Leibniz was the first symbolic logician. The use of symbols in the representation of the structure of a deductive argument was by no means new with Leibniz, but goes back to the very beginnings of formal logic—to Aristotle's representation of terms by letters, i.e. by variables. What Leibniz did was to add symbols for the logical constants 'all' and 'some', making it possible to symbolize completely the structure of a proposition occurring in a deductive argument. But although Leibniz was the first symbolic logician, he cannot be called the founder of symbolic logic. To call someone a founder implies that others use, and perhaps build on, his work; but most of the papers translated below, and indeed most of Leibniz's logical papers in general, remained unpublished until late in the nineteenth or early in the twentieth century, by which time symbolic logic was a well-established discipline. The question now arises, why Leibniz published so little about logic. The short answer is that he left very little that was publishable. Of the works translated here that Leibniz did not publish, the bulk are merely rough sketches, often abandoned before Leibniz reached the end of his subject, and sometimes (as in the case of the *Generales Inquisitiones*) containing a number of attempts at stating a calculus. Leibniz wrote 'Finis' at the end of his paper on 'Some logical difficulties', and so presumably regarded it as complete; the study in the calculus of real addition also seems a finished work. But this, with the exception of such short papers as the proof sent to Vagetius (No. 8 below), is all.[1] This of itself needs explanation; in other words, the question why Leibniz published so little about logic turns into the question why he was able to complete so little. His many-sided activities, the 'thousand distractions' of which he complained,[2] doubtless constitute a partial explanation; yet in spite of all this, Leibniz succeeded in writing a great deal about

[1] To recapitulate what has been said earlier: the grammatical studies of *c.* 1678 are no more than fragments, as are the logical essays of August 1690. The logical papers of April 1679 were all abandoned as failures; the *Addenda* was written to correct the defects of the *Specimen Calculi Universalis*, but itself consists of two drafts of a calculus. The tentative nature of the *Generales Inquisitiones* has been mentioned immediately above, and the *Non Inelegans Specimen* seems to be a first draft of the study in the calculus of real addition. As for the works on the syllogism, the *Mathesis Rationis* does not offer a proof of the number of syllogistic moods; the *De Formis Syllogismorum* offers such a proof, but does not attempt to derive the moods of the fourth figure; finally, the *Definitiones Logicae* comes to the conclusion that there are thirty valid moods of the syllogism, a conclusion whose falsity is recognized by Leibniz.
[2] *G iii. 194.*

logic, and the question still remains, why so little of what he wrote took the form of completed works. One must look, then, for obstacles of another sort; one must try to see whether Leibniz's own views about logic hindered his progress as a symbolic logician.

Couturat has suggested[1] that one thing which hampered Leibniz was his excessive respect for tradition—in particular, his wish to preserve the validity of subalternation and conversion *per accidens*, and consequently those moods of the syllogism which depend on them.[2] These inferences Couturat regarded as illegitimate, as did many symbolic logicians at the time at which he wrote; now, however, logicians are much less ready to dismiss them in this way,[3] so that it can no longer be regarded as obvious that Leibniz was struggling to prove the validity of what is invalid. Another traditional view accepted by Leibniz was the belief that every proposition has a subject and a predicate; this, too, has been held to have had harmful effects on his logic.[4] That it did so is very probable, for it was almost certainly because of this belief that Leibniz failed to develop a calculus of relations.[5] However, the question now being discussed is, not why Leibniz's logic is as restricted as it is, but why he completed so little even in the restricted field in which he worked, and this does not seem to be explained by his belief that every proposition is of the subject-predicate form.

Perhaps the answer is to be found, not so much in his belief that every proposition has a subject and a predicate, as in his belief that to assert a proposition is to say that the concept of the predicate is contained in, or excluded from, that of the subject—that is, in his intensional view of the proposition. It has already been seen[6] that this view does not allow uniform treatment of the propositional forms, in that although the universal affirmative proposition can be regarded in terms of the inclusion of one concept in another, the 'exclusion' spoken of in the case of the universal negative refers to inconsistency rather than to mere non-inclusion. It was also mentioned earlier that the intensional approach, which Leibniz adopted because he believed that universal propositions do not

---

[1] *C.L.*, pp. 350, 386, 438.
[2] *Darapti, Felapton, Bramantip, Fesapo*, and the 'weakened moods' *Barbari, Celaront, Cesaro, Camestrop*, and *Camenop*.
[3] See, e.g., Bochenski, op. cit., p. 425; Łukasiewicz, op. cit., p. 130.
[4] Cf. Kneale, p. 324.
[5] Cf. pp. xix–xx. It may be added that Leibniz paid some attention to the symbolization of relations, making, in his *Analysis Didactica* (C 424–6), some comments on a symbolism proposed by an unknown author.
[6] Cf. p. xl.

have existential import,[1] could not easily be applied to existential propositions.[2] More important, however, is the fact that when Leibniz thought of one concept as including another, he thought of the including concept as being a conjunction of concepts. For example, to say that the concept of man includes the concept of animal is, for Leibniz, to say that the concepts of rational and of animal, into which the concept of man is analysable, include the concept of animal. Leibniz had little, if any, use for a concept such as that of rational *or* animal; in other words, he concentrated on the notion of a logical product at the expense of the notion of a logical sum—that is, he tended to think in terms of entities which are both A and B rather than in terms of those which are either A or B (or both). This is not to say that he ignored entirely the notion of a logical sum; it has been seen that his study in the calculus of real addition is capable of interpretation in terms of this notion,[3] and in about 1683 he wrote a short paper[4] in which he discussed what he called a *calculus alternativus*, where the formula 'x is abc' is taken to mean that x is either a or b or c. Nevertheless, these are exceptions; it remains true on the whole that Leibniz neglected the notion of a logical sum. It might be thought that what has just been said, like what was said earlier about Leibniz's belief that every proposition has a subject and a predicate, merely explains why Leibniz's calculi are more restricted than they need have been. But this is not so; the point is that it may have been because of his comparative neglect of the notion of a logical sum that Leibniz failed to state such laws as de Morgan's, which would have made the construction of his logical calculi much easier.[5]

---

[1] Cf. pp. xxi, lv.
[2] Cf. p. xxxvi, on *Generales Inquisitiones*, pars. 71–73.
[3] Cf. p. lviii.
[4] *C 556–7*.
[5] This point is rightly stressed by Couturat, *C.L.*, pp. 386–7. Couturat later asserted (*C 425 n. 2*) that Leibniz did state one of de Morgan's laws, and this is repeated by Russell, op. cit., p. vi. This, however, seems incorrect; Leibniz came close to stating such a law, but did not quite succeed in doing so. The passage in question, which occurs in the *Analysis Didactica* (cf. p. lx n. 5), is: 'A or B, that is, not neither A nor B' (*C 425*). Now, the correct formulation of the relevant de Morgan law would be: 'A or B if, and only if, not (not-A and not-B)', and although Leibniz approaches this, he does not take the important step of rendering 'neither A nor B' as 'not-A and not-B', and so does not state explicitly the relations between 'not', 'and', and 'or'.
  The same can be said of another passage in which Leibniz comes close to a formulation of de Morgan's laws; this is *C 43*, from *Elementa Characteristicae Universalis* (April 1679). In this, Leibniz says that for the particular affirmative, 'Some S is P', to be true, either S must be divisible by

Against the defects in Leibniz's logical work one must set his achievements, which were considerable. It has just been mentioned that his preference for the intensional approach to the proposition, though involving serious difficulties, was at any rate based on a general view about the nature of universal propositions—a view, it may be added, shared by many other symbolic logicians—and was not held merely because of an excessive reverence for Aristotelian logic. Further, Leibniz saw that difficulties arise about subalternation and conversion *per accidens* if a universal proposition is supposed not to have existential import, and in the *Difficultates quaedam logicae* he made a determined effort to overcome them. He developed the symbolism known as 'Euler's circles' long before Euler,[1] and he also discovered ways of expressing the propositional forms which can be regarded as an interpretation of Boolean algebra;[2] besides this, he anticipated an important idea of Boole by saying that it is possible to treat hypothetical propositions in the same way as categoricals.[3] Again, although he failed to develop a calculus of relations, he gave in his paper for Vagetius a proof of a relational argument which is similar to a proof given in the nineteenth century.[4] He gave accounts of the concept of identity which are close to those given by modern logicians,[5] and he stated what would now be called the rule of definitional substitution and the rule of substitution for term-variables.[6] But perhaps his greatest achievement is contained in the last paper translated in that volume, the study in the calculus of real addition. To have conceived the idea, and given an example, of an abstract

---

P or P by S, and for the universal negative 'No S is P' to be true, neither S must be divisible by P nor P by S. In discussing this passage, it will be convenient to replace 'Either S must be divisible . . . &c.' by 'A or B', and 'Neither S must be divisible . . . &c.' by 'Neither A nor B'. Now, the particular affirmative and universal negative are contradictories, i.e. if the one is false the other is true, and if the one is true the other is false. Leibniz could therefore be regarded as saying here that if not (A or B), then neither A nor B, or conversely; or that if not (neither A nor B), then A or B, or conversely. This would approach a statement of de Morgan's laws, 'Not (A or B) if, and only if, not-A and not-B' and 'A or B if, and only if, not (not-A and not-B)'. Once again, however, Leibniz does not take the important step of transforming 'Neither A nor B' into 'Not-A and not-B'.

[1] Cf. p. xxxviii n. 4.
[2] Cf. p. xlvi.
[3] Cf. pp. xxxvii and xliv; C.L., p. 354; Kneale, p. 413.
[4] Cf. p. l.
[5] Cf. p. xxvi.
[6] Cf. p. xxv n. 2, and p. xxxiii.

calculus which can be given more than one interpretation is to have displayed logical talent of the highest order.

It remains to say a few words about the texts from which the translations have been made, and about the translations as such. The texts used have been indicated on each occasion, and as many of them are standard and often quoted in works on Leibniz, their pagination has been indicated in the translations. It has not been thought necessary to indicate where Leibniz has made additions or deletions; this is done most easily in an edition of the original texts, as in that by Couturat, which may be consulted by those interested. Any obvious slips of the pen have been put right in the text of the translation, and the original indicated in a footnote.[1] Some measure of consistency has been imposed on Leibniz's symbolism; for example, his various signs for identity are always rendered here by '$=$', and the sign for identity prefixed by 'non' is rendered by '$\neq$'. Another respect in which consistency has been imposed is in the use of a hyphen to express a negative term, such as 'not-A'. It is important always to include this in an English translation, to distinguish between '. . . . is not A' and '. . . . is not-A'.[2] Leibniz, however, is not consistent in his use of the hyphen in such contexts, doubtless because the distinction is made adequately in Latin by the placing of 'non'— 'non est A' in the first case, and 'est non A' in the second.

To bracket an expression, Leibniz often uses parentheses; sometimes, however, he draws a line over the expression to be bracketed.[3] This is represented in the translation by parentheses, except where the lines are essential to the symbolism.[4] Footnotes indicated as Leibniz's (by the presence of 'L.-' at the beginning of the note) are marginal notes in the manuscript. Not every marginal note is presented as a footnote, however, as Leibniz often added in the margin what he clearly meant to go in the text.[5] Where any passages are omitted from the translations, as in Nos. 1 and 2, this is indicated by the use of six dots; gaps in Leibniz's text are indicated by the use of three dots.

One difficulty which faces the translator of Leibniz concerns the use of quotation marks. These, now commonly employed to indicate that a word or group of words is being mentioned as

---

[1] The only exceptions are to be found in the study in the calculus of real addition, in which Leibniz sometimes forgets to draw a circle round the $+$ sign; such oversights have been corrected without comment.
[2] e.g. *Generales Inquisitiones*, pars. 93, 169.
[3] e.g. *C 364* (p. 54); *C 235* (p. 90); *C 422* (p. 94); *G vii. 230* (p. 124).
[4] Cf. *C 380* ff. (pp. 69 ff.).
[5] e.g. pars. 40–41 of *Mathesis Rationis* (*C 200–1* (pp. 102–3)).

opposed to being used, are not used at all by Leibniz, who has no standard way of indicating the mention as opposed to the use of a word or words. Sometimes he uses a capital letter, as in 'substantivum Ens seu Res', which is naturally rendered as 'the substantive "entity" or "thing"'.[1] Sometimes he underlines a word or phrase (represented in print by italics); for example, he writes 'quidnam commune habet cum adverbio *fortiter*', naturally rendered as 'what has this in common with the adverb "bravely"?'[2] Sometimes he uses parentheses, and writes what would be rendered literally as '(A = B) is a true proposition'.[3] Sometimes he uses the Greek definite article, followed by the Latin word or words mentioned, as in 'Sed quaeritur quid significet τὸ existens', rendered here as 'But it is asked what "existent" means'.[4] Sometimes, again, he uses no distinguishing marks, as in 'Itaque cum dicitur sapiens credit, terminus erit non credit, sed credens', which is rendered below as 'So when it is said "The wise man believes" the term will be, not "believes", but "believer"'.[5] In all these, and in similar cases, the translation employs quotation marks in accordance with modern usage.

After this discussion of textual matters, it is now time to say something about the translations. Leibniz is far from being one of the great stylists of philosophical literature, and his sentences are sometimes awkward, especially in papers such as the *Generales Inquisitiones*, in which he is working out his problems as he writes. In making the translations, an attempt has been made to produce an accurate version, which keeps close to the text and yet reads as English and not as translator's jargon. Words which are different in Leibniz's text are not always rendered by different English words, if doing so would lead to a stilted translation. For example, the words 'conceptus' and 'notio', used by Leibniz in the same sense,[6] have both been translated here as 'concept', except when the one word is mentioned as equivalent to the other.[7] Similarly, both 'probatio' and 'demonstratio' are usually rendered as 'proof', and 'probare' and 'demonstrare' as 'prove'.[8] However, 'demonstration' is preferred when, for example,

[1] C *289* (p. 16).
[2] C *287* (p. 14).
[3] C *421* (p. 93).
[4] C *375* (p. 65).
[5] C *49* (p. 17).
[6] See, e.g. C *53, 85, 243*.
[7] e.g. C *243* (p. 39).
[8] That 'probatio' is equivalent to 'demonstratio', and 'probare' to 'demonstrare' is shown, e.g., by the fact that in C *50* Leibniz speaks of propositions as being 'probatae' after referring to their 'demonstratio',

Leibniz wishes to contrast 'demonstratio' with induction.[1] 'Propositio' and 'enuntiatio' are both translated as 'proposition';[2] however, as the words 'includere', 'continere', and 'involvere', which Leibniz often uses when speaking of propositions, can without awkwardness be distinguished in English, they are rendered as 'include', 'contain', and 'involve' respectively.

Some of the papers which appear below have not, to my knowledge, been translated before. In several cases, however, I have been able to compare my translations with other versions. For part of No. 1 (namely, pars. 87–88) I have compared Couturat's French translation in C.L., pp. 554 ff. For Nos. 3, 6, and 16, and parts of Nos. 1 and 5, I have compared the translations by L. E. Loemker, in *Gottfried Wilhelm Leibniz: Philosophical Papers and Letters* (Chicago, 1956). For Nos. 15 and 16 I have compared the translations by C. I. Lewis, in the appendix to his *Survey of Symbolic Logic*, and for Nos. 2(c), 3–7, 10–12, and 15–16 I have compared the German translations by F. Schmidt, in *Gottfried Wilhelm Leibniz: Fragmente zur Logik*.

---

and in *C 518–19* he speaks in turn of 'probatio a priori' and 'demonstratio a priori'. Again, in *C 377* he speaks of a proposition which cannot be proved ('probari'), just as he had said earlier (*C 376*) that one cannot reach a perfect proof ('demonstratio') of a certain proposition.

[1] *A vi. 1, 199* (p. 6).
[2] For this equivalence, see e.g. *C 364* and *C 513*, where Leibniz uses the two words in what is clearly the same sense.

1. From *Of the Art of Combination* (1666).[1]

Definitions

(1) 'Variation' here is a change of relation. For some change is
of substance, some of quantity, some of quality; some makes no
change in a thing, but changes only its relation, its situation, or its
conjunction with something else.

(2) 'Variability' is the quantity of all variations. For the limits
of powers, taken in the abstract, denote their quantity; so it is
often said in mechanics that the power of one machine is double
that of another.

(3) 'Situation' [*situs*] is the locality of parts.

(4) Situation is either absolute or relative; the former is that of
parts to whole, the latter is that of parts to parts. In the former,
one considers the number of places and their distance from the
beginning and the end; in the latter, no attention is paid either to
beginning or end, but one considers only the distance of a part
from a given part. Hence the former is expressed by a line, or by
lines which do not enclose a figure or return upon themselves, and
best of all by a straight line; the latter is expressed by a line or
lines which do enclose a figure, and best of all by a circle. In the
former, the greatest attention is paid to priority and posteriority;
in the latter, no such attention is paid. The former, therefore,
would best be called 'order',

(5) the latter, 'vicinity'; the former, 'disposition', the latter,
'composition'. In respect of order, therefore, the following situa-
tions are different: *abcd, bcda, cdab, dabc*. In respect of vicinity,
however, there is understood to be no variation, but only one
situation—namely

$$b$$
$$a \qquad\qquad c$$
$$d$$

Hence the witty Taubmann, when he was dean of the philosophical faculty at Wittenberg, is said to have put the names of

---

[1] References are given to the Academy edition. As this is perhaps not so
widely accessible as Gerhardt's edition, a table of correspondence
between the two editions, as far as concerns the passages translated
below, may be found useful: *A vi. 1, 171–3 = G iv. 36–38; A vi. 1,
177 = G iv. 44; A vi. 1, 192 = G iv. 61; A vi. 1, 194–6 = G iv. 64–66;
A vi. 1, 199 = G iv. 69–70; A vi. 1, 199–202 = G iv. 70–73.*

candidates for the Master's degree in a circular arrangement on the public programme, so that eager readers should not know who had 'the swine's place'.

(6) When we posit variations *par excellence* we shall usually understand variability of order; for example, four things can be transposed in twenty-four ways.

(7) The variability of a complexion we call 'complexions'; for example, four things can be joined to one another in fifteen different ways.

(8) The number of things to be varied we shall call simply 'number'; for example, four in the case imagined.

(9) A 'complexion' is the union of a smaller whole in a larger, as we have said in the preface.[1]

(10) For a certain complexion to be determined, the greater whole must be divided into equal parts assumed as the smallest (that is, which now at any rate are not divided further), from which there is composed and by whose variation there varies the complexion— i.e. the lesser whole. Because the lesser whole is greater or less as more parts enter into it at one time, the number of parts or unities to be taken together at one and the same time we shall call the 'exponent', after the example of geometrical progression. For example, let the whole be ABCD. If the lesser wholes are to consist of two parts—e.g. AB, AC, AD, BC, BD, CD—the exponent will be two; if of three—e.g. ABC, ABD, ACD, BCD— the exponent will be three.

(11) Given an exponent, we shall write the complexions as follows. If the exponent is two, we shall write 'com2nation' (combination); if three, 'con3nation' (conternation); if four, 'con4nation', &c.

A vi. 1,
173 (12) 'Complexions *simpliciter*' are all the complexions computed for all the exponents; e.g. for the number four, fifteen. These are composed of four (by union), six (by com2nation), four (by con3nation) and one (by con4nation) . . . . ..

Leibniz next states and gives solutions to two problems: to find the complexions for a given number and exponent, and to find the complexions *simpliciter* for a given number. He then describes various uses of these problems.

---

[1] The reference is to *A vi. 1, 171* (No. 8): 'A whole, and therefore number or totality, can be broken into parts, as smaller wholes. This is the basis of "complexions", provided that you understand that in the different smaller wholes there are common parts. For example, let the whole be ABC; the smaller wholes, its parts, will be AB, BC, AC. It is also possible to vary the disposition of the smallest parts, or of those taken as the smallest (namely, unities) in relation to each other and to the whole; this is called "situation".'

Uses of Problems I and II

(10) Since all things which exist or can be thought of are in the *A vi. 1,* main composed of parts, either real or at any rate conceptual, it is *177* necessary that those things which differ in species differ either in that they have different parts—and here is the use of complexions —or in that they have a different situation—and here is the use of dispositions. The former are judged by difference of matter, the latter by difference of form. Further, by the help of complexions not only the species of things but also their attributes are discovered. So almost the whole of the inventive part of logic, with regard both to simple and complex terms—in a word, both the theory of divisions and the theory of propositions—is based on complexions. This is to say nothing of the extent to which we hope to illuminate the analytic part of logic, i.e. the logic of judgement, by a diligent scrutiny of the moods of the syllogism in example six . . . . . .

Problems which relate to division are now discussed, in particular (*Use VI*) the determination of the number of moods of the categorical syllogism. Leibniz then continues:

(55) *Use X.* It is now time for us to leave divisions and come to *A vi. 1,* propositions, the other part of the logic of discovery. A proposition *192* is composed of subject and predicate; all propositions, therefore, are com2nations. It is, then, the business of inventive logic (as far as it concerns propositions) to solve this problem: 1. given a subject, to find its predicates. 2. Given a predicate, to find its subjects. In each case, this is to cover both affirmative and negative propositions . . . . . .

Leibniz now describes Raymond Lull's attempt at solving this problem. After rejecting Lull's list of 'simple terms', by the combination of which all propositions can be formed, he continues:

(63) So now, at long last, let us draw the first lines of the art *A vi. 1* of complications (we prefer this term, since not every complex is *194* a com2nation) as it seems to us that is should be constructed. Thomas Hobbes, everywhere a profound examiner of principles, rightly stated that everything done by our mind is a *computation,* by which is to be understood either the addition of a sum or the subtraction of a difference (*De Corpore*, Part I, Chap. 1, art. 2). So just as there are two primary signs of algebra and analytics, $+$ and $-$, in the same way there are as it were two copulas, 'is' and 'is not'; in the former case the mind compounds, in the latter it divides. In that sense, then, 'is' is not properly a copula, but

part of the predicate; there are two copulas, one of which, 'not', is named, whilst the other is unnamed, but is included in 'is' as long as 'not' is not added to it. This has been the cause of the fact that 'is' has been regarded as a copula. We could use as an auxiliary the word 'really'; e.g. 'Man is *really* an animal', 'Man is *not* a stone'. But this is by the way.

(64) Next, in order to establish what everything is made of, we must provide an analysis to fix the categories and as it were the matter of this art. The analysis is this: (1) Let any given term be analysed into formal parts, i.e. let its definition be given, and let these parts again be analysed into parts, i.e. let there be a definition of the terms of the definition, down to simple parts, i.e. indefinable terms. For 'we must not seek a definition of everything',[1] and these final terms are understood, not by further definition, but by analogy.

(65) (2) Let all the first terms discovered be placed in one class and designated by certain signs; it will be most convenient for them to be numbered.

(66) (3) Let there be placed among the first terms not only things, but also modes or relations.

(67) (4) Since all derived terms are at varying distances from the first as they are composed of more first terms, i.e. according to the exponent of the complexion, as many classes must be formed as there are exponents. Those terms which are formed from the same number of first terms are to be placed in the same class.

(68) (5) Terms which are derived by com2nation can only be written by writing the first terms of which they are composed; and since the first terms are designated by numbers, let there be written two numbers, designating two terms.

(69) (6) But terms which are derived by con3nation, or have any larger exponent—i.e. terms which are in the third and following classes—can be written in as many different ways as their exponent (no longer regarded as an exponent but as a number of things) has complexions *simpliciter*. This has its basis in Use IX.[2] For example, let the first terms be designated by the numbers 3, 6, 7, 9, and let the derived term be in the third class, i.e. composed by con3nation of the three simple terms 3, 6, 9. Further, let there be in the second class the following combinations: (1) 3, 6 (2) 3, 7

A vi. 1,
195

---

[1] The reference is to Aristotle, *Metaphysics*, 1048a 36–37: 'We must not seek a definition of everything, but be content to grasp the analogy' (trans. W. D. Ross).

[2] *A vi. 1, 191*: 'Given the species of a division, to find its subdivisions, i.e. the genera and subaltern species'.

(3) 3, 9 (4) 6, 7 (5) 6, 9 (6) 7, 9. I assert that the given term of the third class can either be written as 3, 6, 9, expressing all the simple terms, or by expressing one simple term, and in place of the other two simple terms writing their com2nation—e.g. $\frac{1}{2}$. 9, $\frac{3}{2}$. 6, or $\frac{5}{2}$. 3. What these quasi-fractions mean will soon be stated. The more remote a class is from the first, the greater the variation; for the terms of the preceding class are always the subaltern genera, as it were, to some of the terms of the following variation.

(70) (7) As often as a derived term is cited outside its class, let it be written as a fraction, in such a way that the upper number or numerator is the number of its place in the class, and the lower number or denominator is the number of the class.

(8) In setting out derived terms it is more convenient not to write all the first terms, on account of their great number, but to write the intermediate ones; and of those, the ones which occur most of all to someone thinking about the matter. But it is more basic to write all the first terms.

(71) (9) Now that this has been settled, all subjects and predicates—both affirmative and negative, universal and particular—can be found. For the predicates of a given subject are all its first terms; so are all derived terms nearer to the first terms, of which all the first terms are in the given subject. If, therefore, a given term which is to be a subject is written in its first terms, it is easy *A vi.* to find those first terms which are predicated of it; it will also be *196* possible to find the derived terms, if the complexions are arranged systematically. But if the given term is written in derived terms, or partly in derived and partly in simple terms, whatever is predicated of the derived term will be predicated of the given term. All these are cases of something wider being predicated of something narrower; but there is also predication of one equal of another, when a definition is predicated of a term. This is when either all its first terms together, or the derived terms (or the derived and simple terms) in which all the first terms are contained, are predicated of the given term. These are as many as the ways in which, as we have just said, the one term can be written. . . . . .

After discussing the problems described in par. 55, Leibniz adds an important warning about the scope of his symbolism.

(83) Finally, warning must be given that the whole of this art of *A vi. 1,* complications is directed to theorems, or, to propositions which *199* are eternal truths, i.e. which exist, not by the will of God, but by their own nature. But as for all singular propositions which might be called *historical* (e.g. 'Augustus was emperor of Rome'), or as for *observations* (i.e. propositions such as 'All European adults

have a knowledge of God'—propositions which are universal, but whose truth has its basis in existence, not in essence, and which are true as if by chance, i.e. by the will of God)—of these propositions there is no demonstration, but only induction; except that sometimes an observation can be demonstrated through an observation by the mediation of a theorem.

(84) All particular propositions which are neither the converses nor the subalterns of universal propositions are observations of this kind. It is clear from this in what sense it is said that there is no demonstration of particulars, and why the profound Aristotle put the *loci*[1] of arguments in the *Topics*, where there are both contingent propositions and probable arguments, whereas of demonstration there is one *locus*, definition. However, when something is to be said of a thing which is not derived from its inmost nature—for example, that Christ was born at Bethlehem—no one will reach this by definition, but history will supply the material and *loci* the memory of it . . . . . .

There follows what Leibniz calls a 'taste' of the art of combinations which he has sketched.

(87) Mathematics has seemed most suitable for an extemporary essay. Here we have started, not from first terms *simpliciter*, but from those which are first in mathematics; nor have we stated them all, but only those which we thought sufficient to produce by their complication the terms whose derivation we set ourselves. We could have set out by the same method all the definitions from Euclid's *Elements*, if time had permitted. However, as we have not started from first terms *simpliciter*, it has therefore been necessary to use signs by which the cases of words and other things which are necessary for the completion of discourse may be understood. If we had begun from first terms *simpliciter* we could have put terms for the variation of the cases themselves, whose origin from relations and from metaphysics Julius Caesar Scaliger has explained in his book, *De causis linguae Latinae*. We, however, have used the Greek articles. Plural number we have designated by 15 written in ( ) if it is indefinite; 2, 3 etc. if it is determinate.

A vi. 1, 200

(88) Let there be, therefore, a class I in which the first terms are:

1. Point. 2. Space. 3. Between. 4. Adjacent, or, contiguous. 5. Disjoined, or, distant. 6. Extremity, or, what are distant. 7. Contained [*insitum*]. 8. Included [*inclusum*]. E.g. the centre is contained in the circle, included in the periphery. 9. Part. 10. Whole. 11.

[1] Cf. Introduction, p. xv n. 7.

Same. 12. Different. 13. One. 14. Number. 15. Several, e.g. 2, 3, 4, 5 &c. 16. Distance. 17. Possible. 18. Every. 19. Given. 20. Becomes. 21. Direction. 22. Dimension. 23. Long. 24. Extended. 25. Deep. 26. Common. 27. Progression, or, continued.

Class II. 1. 'Quantity' is 14. of the 9 (15).
'Quantity' is the number of the parts.[1]
2. 'Outline' is 6.10.
An 'outline' is the whole extremity.

III. 1. 'Interval' is 2.3.10.
An 'interval' is the whole space between.
2. 'Equal', A of the 11.$\frac{1}{2}$.
'Equal' is of the same quantity.
3. A is 'continuous' with B if the 9. of A is 4. and 7. in B.
A is 'continuous' with B if a part of A is contiguous to and contained in B.

IV. 1. A is 'greater' if it has the 9.$\frac{2}{3}$. to B.
A is 'greater' than B if it has a part equal to B.
2. B is 'less' if it is $\frac{2}{3}$. to the 9. of A.
B is 'less' than A if it is equal to a part of A.
3. A 'line' is $\frac{1}{3}$. of 1 (2).
A 'line' is the interval of two points.
4. 'Parallel' is $\frac{2}{3}$. in 16.
'Parallel' is equal in distance.
5. A 'figure' is 24.8. in 18.21.
A 'figure' is something extended which is included in every direction.

V.1. 'Increasing' is that which 20.$\frac{1}{4}$.
'Increasing' is that which becomes greater.
2. 'Decreasing' is that which 20.$\frac{2}{4}$.
'Decreasing' is that which becomes less.
3. 'Implex' [*implexum*] is $\frac{3}{3}$. in the 11.22.
'Implex' is contiguous in the same dimension.
4. A 'secant' is $\frac{3}{3}$. in the 12.22.
A 'secant' is contiguous in a different dimension.

VI. 1.'Convergent' is $\frac{2}{5}$. in 16.
'Convergent' is decreasing in distance.
2. 'Divergent' is $\frac{1}{5}$. in 16.
'Divergent' is increasing in distance.

[1] For the convenience of the reader, an expanded version of each of Leibniz's definitions follows its statement in symbolic terms.

VII. 1. A 'surface' is $\frac{1}{3}$. of $\frac{3}{4}$.
A 'surface' is an interval of lines.
2. 'Infinite' is $\frac{1}{4}$. than 18.19.17.
'Infinite' is greater than every given possible.
3. A 'periphery' is $\frac{3}{4}$. 13. $\frac{2}{2}$.
A 'periphery' is a line which is the one outline.
4. A is said to be a 'measure', or B is measured, if 10. formed from A (15) $\frac{2}{3}$. is $\frac{2}{3}$. to B.
A is said to be a 'measure', or B is measured, if a whole formed from several equal A's is equal to B.

VIII. 1. The 'greatest' is $\frac{1}{4}$. not $\frac{2}{4}$.
The 'greatest' is greater and not less.
2. The 'least' is $\frac{2}{4}$. not $\frac{1}{4}$.
The 'least' is less and not greater.
3. A 'straight line' is $\frac{3}{4}$. $\frac{2}{3}$. to the 16 of its 6 (2).
A 'straight line' is a line equal to the distance of its two extremities.
4. What is not this, is a 'curve'.
5. An 'arc' is 9 of the $\frac{3}{7}$.
An 'arc' is a part of the periphery.

IX. 1. An 'ambit' is $\frac{1}{7}$. $\frac{2}{2}$.
An 'ambit' is a surface which is an outline.

X. 1. 'Commensurables' are those whose $\frac{4}{7}$. 26. is both 1. and 2.
'Commensurables' are those whose common measure is both a point and a space.

XI. 1. An 'angle' is that which $\frac{3}{4}$ (2). 4. $\frac{2}{6}$. make.
An 'angle' is what is made by two contiguous divergent lines.

XII. 1. A 'plane' is $\frac{1}{7}$. $\frac{2}{3}$. to the 16. of its 6.
A 'plane' is a surface equal to the distance of its extremities.

XIII. 1. A 'curved surface' is $\frac{1}{7}$. $\frac{1}{4}$. than the 16. of its 6.
A 'curved surface' is a surface greater than the distance of its extremities.

XIV. 1. A $\frac{5}{4}$. is 'rectilinear' whose $\frac{2}{2}$. consists of $\frac{3}{8}$ (15).
A figure is 'rectilinear' whose outline consists of several straight lines.
2. These are called 'sides'.
3. If it consists of $\frac{3}{8}$ (3). it is a 'triangle'.
If it consists of three straight lines it is a 'triangle'.
4. If it consists of $\frac{3}{8}$ (4). it is a 'quadrilateral', &c.
If it consists of four straight lines it is a 'quadrilateral', &c.

XV. 1. A 'lunule' is $\frac{1}{3}$. of $\frac{5}{8}$ (2). not $\frac{2}{3}$. 4 (2).
A 'lunule' is the interval of two arcs which are not equal and which are contiguous.
(I understand both a gibbous lunule, in which the concavities of two arcs face each other, and a sickle-shaped lunule, in which the convexity of the interior arc faces the other's concavity.)

XVI. 1. A 'right angle' is $\frac{1}{11}$. $\frac{2}{3}$. in 18. 21.
A 'right angle' is an angle equal in every direction.
2. A 'segment' is 3. of the $\frac{2}{2}$. and $\frac{3}{8}$. 7. in the $\frac{5}{4}$.
A 'segment' is between the outline and a straight line contained in the figure.

XVII. 1. A $\frac{5}{4}$. is 'equilateral' whose $\frac{2}{2}$. consists of $\frac{3}{8}$ (15). $\frac{2}{3}$.[1]
A figure is 'equilateral' whose outline consists of several equal straight lines.
2. An 'isosceles triangle' is $\frac{5}{4}$. whose $\frac{2}{2}$. consists of $\frac{3}{8}$ (3). $\frac{2}{3}$ (2).
An 'isosceles triangle' is a figure whose outline consists of three straight lines of which two are equal.
3. A 'scalene triangle' is $\frac{5}{4}$. whose $\frac{2}{2}$. consists of $\frac{3}{8}$ (3). not $\frac{2}{3}$ (3).
A 'scalene triangle' is a figure whose outline consists of three straight lines which are not equal.

XVIII. 1. An 'angle of contact' is that which is made by $\frac{3}{4}$ (2). *A vi. 1,* 4. $\frac{2}{6}$. not $\frac{4}{5}$. 27. if 17. *201*
An 'angle of contact' is that which is made by two contiguous divergent lines which are not secants, and continued if possible.

XIX. 1. 'Inscribed' is $\frac{5}{4}$. 7. whose $\frac{1}{11}$ (15). are 4. to the $\frac{2}{2}$.
A figure is 'inscribed' which is contained (in another) and whose several angles are adjacent to the outline (of that other).
2. That figure is 'circumscribed' in which the other is inscribed.

XX. 1. An 'obtuse angle' is $\frac{1}{4}$. than $\frac{1}{16}$.
An 'obtuse angle' is greater than a right angle.
2. An 'acute angle' is $\frac{2}{4}$. than $\frac{1}{16}$.
An 'acute angle' is less than a right angle.

XXI. 1. A 'diameter' is $\frac{3}{8}$. $\frac{1}{8}$. 7. in the $\frac{5}{4}$.
A 'diameter' is the greatest straight line contained in a figure.

XXII. 1. A 'circle' is $\frac{1}{12}$.[2] with 18. 6. in 18. 21. having 16. $\frac{2}{3}$. from a certain 19.1.
A 'circle' is a plane with every extremity in every direction having an equal distance from a certain given point.

---

[1] Following Couturat's emendation (C.L., p. 558). The original text reads: *Aequilaterum* est $\frac{5}{4}$. cujus $\frac{2}{2}$. est 8. τῶν $\frac{3}{8}$ (15).
[2] Deleting, with Couturat, the 8 which follows $\frac{1}{12}$. in the text (C.L., p. 559).

This is called 2. the 'centre' of the circle.

3.[1] A 'right-angled triangle' is $\frac{5}{4}$. whose $\frac{1}{11}$ (3). are all its angles, but of which 13. is $\frac{2}{3}$. in 18. 21.

A 'right-angled triangle' is a figure whose three angles are all its angles, but of which one is equal in every direction.

XXIII. 1. The 'centre of a figure' is 1.26 to $\frac{1}{21}$ (15).

The 'centre of a figure' is a point common to several diameters.

XXIV. 1. A given 'semi-figure' (e.g. a semi-circle) is 3. of the $\frac{1}{21}$.[2] and half of the $\frac{2}{2}$.

A given 'semi-figure' (e.g. a semi-circle) is between the diameter and half of the outline.

From these it will be easy to construct definitions, if what we said in No. 70 is observed: that in those symbols which are in the form of fractions the denominator indicates the number of the class and the numerator the number of the term in the class. E.g. the 'centre' is 1. (a point) 26. (common) to 15. (several) $\frac{1}{21}$. (diameters). A 'diameter' is $\frac{1}{8}$. (the greatest) $\frac{3}{8}$. (straight line) 7. (contained) in a $\frac{5}{4}$. (figure).

(89) We have spoken of the art of complication of the sciences, i.e. of inventive logic, whose categories, as it were, would be formed by a table of terms of this sort. From what we have said there flows as a corollary, or

Use XI: a universal writing, i.e. one which is intelligible to anyone who reads it, whatever language he knows. Several learned men of our day have attempted this, and in Book Seven of his *Technica Curiosa* the diligent Caspar Schott enumerates the following. First he lists a certain Spaniard, whom Kenelm Digby mentioned in his treatise on the nature of bodies,[3] Chap. 28 n. 8, and who was at Rome in the year 1653. His method was sought, ingeniously enough, from the very nature of things. He divided things into various classes, and in any class there was a certain number of things. So he wrote by means of numbers alone, citing the number of the class and of the thing in the class; though he added certain marks for grammatical and orthographical inflexions. The same would be done by the classes which we have described above, but in a more fundamental way, since in them the arrangement is more fundamental. Then Schott lists Athanasius Kircher, who has promised for a long time his *Polygraphia nova et universalis.* Finally he mentions Joh. Joachim Becher, chief physician of

---

[1] The text has '2'.

[2] Corrected by Couturat from the $\frac{1}{12}$. of the text (*C.L.*, p. 559).

[3] A reference to *Demonstratio immortalitatis animae rationalis* (Paris, 1655; Frankfurt, 1664).

Mainz, in a short work first published at Frankfurt in Latin, and then in German in the year 1661. Becher requires the construction of a Latin dictionary as a basis; in it, words are to be arranged in a purely alphabetical order and numbered. Then dictionaries are to be made in which words in individual languages are arranged, not alphabetically, but in the order in which the Latin words corresponding to them were arranged. What will be written will be numbers, which should be understood by everyone; the man who wishes to read them will refer in the dictionary of his native tongue to the word designated by the given number, and in this way he will translate. So it will be sufficient for the reader to understand his native tongue and to refer to its dictionary; but the writer (unless he has another alphabetical dictionary of his own language, referring to numbers) must know both his native tongue and Latin, and refer to the dictionary of each. But the system of both Becher and the Spaniard is obvious and impracticable. This is because of synonyms, of the ambiguity of words, *A vi. 1,* of the constant tedium of reference to a dictionary (as no one will *202* ever commit numbers to memory), and because of the difference of phrases in different languages.

(90) But when the tables or categories of our art of complication have been formed, something greater will emerge. For let the first terms, of the combination of which all others consist, be designated by signs; these signs will be a kind of alphabet. It will be convenient for the signs to be as natural as possible—e.g. for one, a point; for numbers, points; for the relations of one entity to another, lines; for the variation of angles or of extremities in lines, kinds of relations. If these are correctly and ingeniously established, this universal writing will be as easy as it is common, and will be capable of being read without any dictionary; at the same time, a fundamental knowledge of all things will be obtained. The whole of such a writing will be made of geometrical figures, as it were, and of a kind of pictures—just as the ancient Egyptians did, and the Chinese do today. Their pictures, however, are not reduced to a fixed alphabet, i.e. to letters, with the result that a tremendous strain on the memory is necessary, which is the contrary of what we propose. This, therefore, is Use XI of complexions; namely, in the formation of a universal polygraphy . . . . . .

2. From papers on grammatical analysis (*c.* 1678)

(a) From an untitled paper[1]

C *243* . . . . . . Before we may proceed in our logical inquiries, and make something out of these, we need grammatical inquiries first. In particular, reference must be made to Vossius's *Aristarchus*.[2]

A noun substantive and an adjective are distinguished in that an adjective has its gender governed by another. But as one can do without genders in a rational language, the distinction between substantive and adjective can be neglected.

Abstract terms [*abstracta*] are substantives made either from other substantives or from adjectives, such as 'humanity' and 'beauty'; 'human being' [*homo*] is 'that which has humanity', 'beautiful' is 'having beauty'. But we must see whether we cannot do without abstract terms in a rational language, at any rate as far as possible.

'Masculine' is an adjective, 'man' [*vir*] is a substantive, since for 'man' one can substitute 'masculine human being'; that is, it can be analysed into a substantive together with an epithet.

C *244* An epithet is an adjective joined to a substantive to make one term, i.e. without a copula, and governed in the same way.

Adverbs. 'Peter writes beautifully'; i.e. Peter writes something beautiful, or, Peter writes, and what Peter writes is beautiful. 'Peter stands beautifully': i.e. Peter is beautiful in so far as he is a stander [*quatenus est stans*].

Plural. 'Men write': i.e. Titius is a writer, Caius is a writer; Titius is a man, Caius is a man. Or, 'Men write': i.e. one man writes, another man writes.

A 'pronoun' is a noun put in place of another noun, i.e. designating another noun, though not explaining any attribute of it, but only an extrinsic denomination relative[3] to the discourse itself. An example is 'this', i.e. 'shown', 'said', 'present'. 'That' and 'this' differ as the nearer and the farther. 'I': that is, the one now

---

[1] This paper, already abbreviated by Couturat, is here abbreviated further.

[2] The reference is to *Aristarchus, sive de Arte Grammatica*, by Gerard Jan Vossius.

[3] Following Couturat's suggestion (C *244* n. 1) of 'relativam' for the 'relationem' of the text.

speaking. 'You': that is, the one now listening to hear what is said.

All oblique inferences—e.g. 'Peter is similar to Paul, therefore Paul is similar to Peter'—are to be explained by explanations of words. Such may be seen from the logic of Jungius. It is reduced to the propositions 'Peter is A now' and 'Paul is A now'.

All inflexions and particles are to be explained, and all are to be reduced to the simplest explanations, which can always be put in their place without affecting the sense. From these, definitions of everything are to be formed . . . . . .

There follows a list of authors from whom Leibniz proposes to borrow the definitions of various sciences. The last completed part of the paper (it is followed by uncompleted definitions of 'equal to', 'like' and 'given to') is an analysis of the genitive case:

C 245

The hand, son, horse, heat, title — of a man, that is, the hand, son, horse, heat, title[1] which is a part, effect, possession, accident, predicate in so far as a man is a whole, cause, master, substance, subject

(b) From *Grammatical Thoughts*

. . . . . . Distinction of gender is not relevant to a rational grammar; neither do distinctions of declensions and conjugations have any use in a philosophical grammar. For we vary genders, declensions and conjugations without any benefit, without any gain in brevity—unless perhaps the variation pleases the ear; and this consideration does not concern philosophy, especially as we can give beauty to a rational language by another method, in such a way that it will not be necessary to think up useless rules.[2] Certainly it is clear that the most difficult part of grammar is learning the different genders, declensions and conjugations. Yet a man who speaks a language and neglects these differences, as I heard a Dominican from Persia do in Paris,[3] is understood none the less.

C 286

---

[1] This is omitted in the text.
[2] Cf. *Lingua generalis* and *Lingua universalis* (C 277–80), where Leibniz states rules which produce words such as *bodifalemu, mubodilefa, humida,* and *mihuda.* In the second paper he suggests that his universal language might make use of musical intervals.
[3] Cf. *NE*, 3.2.1 (*A vi. 6, 279*).

One needs a catalogue of derivations, i.e. of terminations which make derivations, such as

—ble	—tive	—titude
lovable	active	rectitude

. . . . . . To some, a noun is what expresses a thing without time. By this definition, pronouns will be nouns, and participles will not.

A noun expresses a certain idea, but no truth, i.e. no proposition. In this sense, a pronoun and a participle are nouns. . . . . . .

Every verb indicates time. A noun also can indicate time, like the participle 'about to act', 'about to love'.

It can be disputed whether there are verbs which are not active, such as 'I am', 'I live', 'I run', or whether an accusative must always be understood, as 'to live one's life', 'to run one's course'. Scioppius[1] says that it must, but it does not seem to me to be at all necessary. For by joining with some noun the verb 'I am' (which Scioppius himself admits not to have an accusative) a verb can at once be made, such as 'I am a sick man' ('I ail'), 'I am a healthy man' ('I flourish').[2]

C 287   Particles which are clearly of a different nature are badly confused under the name of 'adverb'. For example, what has 'whether' [an], the adverb of interrogation, in common with the adverb 'bravely', i.e. 'with bravery'? Consequently, what are called adverbs of interrogation I would rather count as conjunctions. This, however, must be considered more carefully . . . . . .

Every adjective has a similar substantive, either explicit or implicit.

The genitive is the addition of a substantive to a substantive, by which that to which it is added is distinguished from another. For example, 'the sword of Evander', that is, 'the sword which Evander has'; 'a part of a house', that is, 'a part which a house has'; 'a reading of the poets', that is, 'an action by which a poet is read'. This will be the best way of explaining 'Paris is the lover of Helen', that is, 'Paris loves, *and by that very fact* [et eo ipso] Helen is loved'. Here, therefore, two propositions have been brought together and abbreviated into one. Or, 'Paris is a lover, and by that very fact Helen is a loved one'. 'The sword is the sword of Evander', that is, 'The sword is an article of property in so far as Evander is an owner'. A poet is read in so far as this or that person is a reader. For unless you analyse the oblique cases into several propositions,

---

[1] Kaspar Schoppe, *Grammatica Philosophica*, 1628.
[2] Leibniz has added the phrase, 'sum bonus; bon . . . o'.

you will never escape without being compelled, with Jungius, to invent new ways of reasoning . . . . . .

In a rational grammar, oblique cases and other inflexions are not necessary. Similarly, one can dispense with abstract nouns. To avoid inflexions, one must take a roundabout way; but it is worth the price to reason in a concise way, even if you do not express yourself concisely.

(c) From an untitled paper[1]

Vocables [*vocabula*] are either words [*voces*] or particles. Words   *C 288* constitute the matter, particles the form of discourse . . . . . .

In a philosophical language, cases are unnecessary when prepositions are used, and when cases are used one can do without prepositions . . . . . .

Just as prepositions govern the cases of nouns [*nominum*], so conjunctions govern the moods of verbs . . . . . .

There is a difficulty as to whether there ought to be as many moods of verbs as there are purely formal conjunctions, just as we wanted there to be as many cases of nouns as there are purely formal prepositions. It seems that, in the same way, a governing conjunction is unnecessary when a mood is used, and conversely that a mood is unnecessary when a governing conjunction is used, just as we said about preposition and case. However, I think that men have used these for the sake of greater effectiveness, to teach   *C 289* by saying the same thing twice. Conjunctions which connect periods to periods are non-governing. Moods affect the copula of the verb, i.e. the mode of affirmation . . . . . .

Not only verbs, but also nouns can have tense and place—just as we have seen in the case of participles, which are simply nouns derived from verbs by removing the copula and keeping the tense. Indeed, adverbs also can have a tense—e.g. if I were to coin the adverb 'amusingly-to-be' [*ridiculurè*], that is, that which is not immediately amusing, but which will be amusing at some time. Such was the badge of the tailors; a facetious painter had produced a splendid and elegant one, but in water-colours, and when these vanished there appeared an oil-painting of a goat, which in Germany is regarded as an insult. You could say that this man had painted something which was going to be amusing, or would be amusing in future; that is, that he had painted amusingly-to-be, i.e. amusingly with respect to future time . . . . . .

---

[1] This paper, of which the manuscript consists of nineteen folio pages, is abbreviated considerably by Couturat. Here it is abbreviated a little further.

In a rational language, the distinction between adjective and substantive is not of great importance . . . . . .

'Man' is the same as 'human entity' . . . . . .

If a verb is made from a noun substantive, an adverb is made from an adjective . . . . . .

Everything in discourse can be analysed into the noun substantive 'entity' or 'thing', the copula, i.e. the substantive verb 'is', adjectives and formal particles . . . . . .

The tenses of nouns: just as one speaks of 'loving', the act of one who loves, so there might be the 'has-been-loving' or 'about-to-be-loving' [*amavitio vel amaturitio*] of one who has loved, or is about to love. Just as the infinite has a preterite in Latin, so it should also have an imperfect . . . . . .

In Hebrew the root is a verb, but I would prefer it to be a noun, such as 'life'[1] . . . . . .

C 290   The multitude of declensions and conjugations is superfluous. It is superfluous to have inflexions in adjectives, for it is enough to have them in the substantive to which the adjective is attached. In the same way, number is unnecessary in the verb, for this is sufficiently understood from the noun to which it is attached. In Hebrew, Syriac, Chaldaic, Arabic and Ethiopian, verbs also have genders, which is incongruous enough. Also, the person of verbs can be invariable, as it is sufficient for 'I', 'you', 'he' &c. to be varied . . . . .

---

[1] From 'life' (*vita*) Leibniz forms *vivus, vivo, vivens, vivificatio, vivificare, vivificari, vivificamentum, vivificativum, vivificatorius, vitosus, vitalis.*

3. *Elements of a Calculus* (April, 1679)

(1) A 'term' is the subject or predicate of a categorical proposition. C 49 Under the heading of 'term', therefore, I include neither the sign of quantity[1] nor the copula; so when it is said, 'The wise man believes' the term will be, not 'believes', but 'believer', for it is the same as if I had said, 'The wise man is a believer'.

(2) By 'propositions' I understand here categorical propositions, unless I make special mention to the contrary. However, the categorical proposition is the basis of the rest, and modal, hypo-thetical, disjunctive and all other propositions presuppose it. I call 'categorical' the proposition 'A is B' or 'A is not B', i.e. 'It is false that A is B', together with a variation in the sign of quantity, so that either it is a universal proposition and is understood of every subject, or it is a particular proposition and is understood of some subject.

(3) Let there be assigned to any term its symbolic number [*numerus characteristicus*], to be used in calculation as the term itself is used in reasoning. I choose numbers whilst writing; in due course I will adapt other signs both to numbers and to speech itself. For the moment, however, numbers are of the greatest use, because of their certainty and of the ease with which they can be handled, and because in this way it is evident to the eye that everything is certain and determinate in the case of concepts, as it is in the case of numbers.

(4) The one rule for discovering suitable symbolic numbers is this: that when the concept of a given term is composed directly of the concepts of two or more other terms, then the symbolic number of the given term should be produced by multiplying together the symbolic numbers of the terms which compose the C 50 concept of the given term. For example, since man is a rational animal, if the number of animal, a, is 2, and of rational, r, is 3, then the number of man, h, will be the same as ar: in this example, 2×3, or 6. Again, since gold is the heaviest metal, if the number of metal, m, is 3, and the number of heaviest, p, is 5, then the

---

[1] For this meaning of the word *signum*, compare the following passage (*C 85*) from *Calculus Consequentiarum*, probably written (cf. p. xxi n. 1) at about the same time as the *Elements of a Calculus:* '. . . . . . the sign, that is, 'every' or 'some'—i.e. the quantity'.

number of gold, s,[1] will be the same as mp, i.e. in this example
3×5, or 15.

(5) We shall use letters (such as a, r, h or m, p, s above) when
numbers are either not available, or they are at any rate being
treated generally and not considered specifically. This we must do
here, when we are establishing the elements of the subject. The
same thing is done in algebra, so that we are not compelled to
show in individual cases what we can show once and for all of an
indefinite number of instances. The method of using letters here
I shall explain below.

(6) The rule given in article 4 is sufficient for our calculus to cover
all things in the whole world, as far as we have distinct concepts of
them, i.e. as far as we know some of their requisites by which,
after we have examined them bit by bit, we can distinguish them
from all others; or, as far as we can assign their definition. For
these requisites are simply the terms whose concepts compose the
concept which we have of a thing. We can distinguish many
things from others by their requisites, and if there are any whose
requisites are difficult to assign, we will assign to them in the mean
time some prime number, and use it to designate other things. In
this way we shall be able to discover and prove by our calculus at any
rate all the propositions which can be proved without the analysis
of what has temporarily been assumed to be prime. (In the same
way, Euclid never uses the definition of a straight line in his proofs,
but instead used certain assumptions which he took to be axiomatic.
But when Archimedes wanted to go further, he was compelled to
analyse and define the straight line itself—namely, as the least
distance between two points.) In this way we shall discover, if
not all, at any rate innumerable things; both those which have
already been proved by others, and those which can ever be proved
by others from the definitions, axioms and experiments which are
already known. This is our prerogative: that by means of numbers
we can judge immediately whether propositions presented to us
are proved, and that what others could hardly do with the greatest
mental labour and good fortune, we can provide with the guidance
C 51   of symbols alone, by a sure and truly analytical method. As a
result of this, we shall be able to show within a century what many
thousands of years would hardly have granted to mortals otherwise.

(7) To make evident the use of symbolic numbers in propositions,
it is necessary to consider the fact that every true universal
affirmative categorical proposition simply shows [*significat*] some

---

[1] Leibniz here refers to gold by its alchemical name, *Sol*.

connexion between predicate and subject (a *direct* connexion, which is what is always meant here). This connexion is, that the predicate is said to be in the subject, or to be contained in the subject; either absolutely and regarded in itself, or at any rate in some instance, i.e. that the subject is said to contain the predicate in a stated fashion. This is to say that the concept of the subject, either in itself or with some addition, involves the concept of the predicate, and therefore that subject and predicate are related to each other either as whole and part, or as whole and coincident whole, or as part to whole. In the first two cases the proposition is a universal affirmative; so when I say 'All gold is metal' I simply mean that in the concept of gold the concept of metal is contained directly, since gold is the heaviest metal. Again, when I say, 'Every pious man is happy', I mean simply this: that the connexion between the concepts of the pious man and of the happy man is such that anyone who understands perfectly the nature of the pious man will realize that the nature of the happy man is involved in it directly. But in all cases, whether the subject or predicate is a part or a whole, a particular affirmative proposition always holds. For example, some metal is gold; for although metal does not by itself contain gold, nevertheless some metal, with some addition or specification (e.g. 'that which makes up the greater part of a Hungarian ducat') is of such a nature as to involve the nature of gold. There is, however, a difference in the method of containment between the subject of a universal and of a particular proposition. For the subject of a universal proposition, regarded in itself and taken absolutely, must contain the predicate; thus the concept of gold, regarded in itself and taken absolutely, involves the concept of metal, for the concept of gold is 'the heaviest metal'. But in a particular affirmative proposition, it is enough that the inclusion should hold with some addition. The concept of metal, regarded absolutely and taken in itself, does not involve the concept of gold; for it to do so, something must be added. This 'something' is the sign of particularity; for there is some certain metal which contains the concept of gold. However, when we say later that a   *C 52* term is contained in a term or a concept in a concept, we shall understand 'simply and in itself'.

(8) Negative propositions merely contradict affirmatives, and assert that they are false. So a particular negative proposition simply denies that an affirmative proposition is universal. For example, when I say 'Some silver is not soluble in common *aqua fortis*', I simply mean that the universal affirmative proposition 'All silver is soluble in common *aqua fortis*' is false. For, if we believe certain chemists, there is a contrary instance, which they call 'fixed silver'

[*Luna fixa*]. A universal negative proposition merely contradicts a particular affirmative. For example, if I say 'No wicked man is happy', I mean that it is false that some wicked man is happy. So it is evident that negatives can be understood from affirmatives, and conversely, affirmatives from negatives.

(9) Further, in every categorical proposition there are two terms. Any two terms, in so far as they are said to be in or not to be in, i.e. to be contained or not to be contained, differ in the following ways: that either one is contained in the other, or neither is. If the one is contained in the other, then either the one is equal to the other or they differ as whole and part. If neither is contained in the other, then either they contain something which is common, but not too remote, or they are totally different. However, we will explain this species by species.

(10) Two terms which contain each other and are nevertheless equal I call 'coincident'. For example, the concept of a triangle coincides in effect with the concept of a trilateral—i.e. as much is contained in the one as in the other. Sometimes this may not appear at first sight, but if one analyses each of the two one will at last come to the same.

(11) Two terms which contain each other but do not coincide are commonly called 'genus' and 'species'. These, in so far as they compose concepts or terms (which is how I regard them here) differ as part and whole, in such a way that the concept of the genus is a part and that of the species is a whole, since it is composed of genus and differentia. For example, the concept of gold and the concept of metal differ as part and whole; for in the concept of gold there is contained the concept of metal and something else— e.g. the concept of the heaviest among metals. Consequently, the concept of gold is greater than the concept of metal.

C 53

(12) The Scholastics speak differently; for they consider, not concepts, but instances which are brought under universal concepts. So they say that metal is wider than gold, since it contains more species than gold, and if we wish to enumerate the individuals made of gold on the one hand and those made of metal on the other, the latter will be more than the former, which will therefore be contained in the latter as a part in the whole. By the use of this observation, and with suitable symbols, we could prove all the rules of logic by a calculus somewhat different from the present one—that is, simply by a kind of inversion of it. However, I have preferred to consider universal concepts, i.e. ideas, and their combinations, as they do not depend on the existence of individuals. So I say that gold is greater than metal, since more is required for the concept of gold than for that of metal and it is a

greater task to produce gold than to produce simply a metal of some kind or other. Our language and that of the Scholastics, then, is not contradictory here, but it must be distinguished carefully. However, it will be evident to anyone who considers the matter that I have not made any linguistic innovation which does not have some reason and some utility.

(13) If neither term is contained in the other they are called 'disparate'; and then, as I have said, they either have something in common or they differ totally. Those terms have something in common which are under the same genus, and which you could call 'conspecies'; as 'man' and 'brute' have the concept of animal in common. 'Gold' and 'silver' have in common the concept of metal, 'gold' and 'vitriol', that of mineral. From this it is evident that two terms have more or less in common as their genus is less or more remote. For if the genus is very remote, there will be little that the species have in common. If the genus is most remote, we say that things are 'heterogeneous', i.e. that they differ totally, like body and spirit; not because they have nothing in common— for they are both substances, at any rate—but because this common genus is very remote. From this it is evident that what is to be called heterogeneous or not is a relative matter. However, in our calculus it is enough for two things to have no concepts in common out of certain fixed concepts which are designated by us, even though they may have others in common. *C 54*

(14) What we have just said about terms which, in various ways, contain or do not contain each other, let us now transfer to their symbolic numbers. This is easy, since we said in article 4 that when a term helps to constitute another, i.e. when the concept of the term is contained in the concept of another, then the symbolic number of the constituent term is a factor of the symbolic number to be assumed as standing for the term to be constituted; or, what is the same, the symbolic number of the term to be constituted (i.e. which contains another) is divisible by the symbolic number of the constituent term (i.e. which is in the other). For example, the concept of animal helps to constitute the concept of man, and so the symbolic number of animal, a (e.g. 2), together with another number r (such as 3), will be a factor of the number ar, or h (2×3, or 6)—namely, the symbolic number of man. It is therefore necessary that the number ar or h (i.e. 6) can be divided by a (i.e. by 2).

(15) When two terms are coincident, e.g. 'man' and 'rational animal', then their numbers, h and ar, are in effect coincident (as 2×3 and 6). Since, however, the one term contains the other in this way, although reciprocally (for 'man' contains 'rational

animal', and nothing besides; and 'rational animal' contains 'man', and nothing besides which is not already contained in 'man'), it is necessary that the numbers h and ar (2×3 and 6) should also contain each other. This is the case, since they are coincident, and the same number is contained in itself. Furthermore, it is necessary that the one can be divided by the other, which is also the case; for if any number is divided by itself, the result is unity. So what we said in the previous article—that when one term contains another the symbolic number of the former is divisible by the symbolic number of the latter—also holds in the case of coincident terms.

(16) Hence we can also know by symbolic numbers which term does not contain another; for we have only to test whether the number of the latter can divide exactly the number of the former. For example, if the symbolic number of man is assumed to be 6, and that of ape to be 10, it is evident that neither does the concept of ape contain the concept of man, nor does the converse hold, since 10 cannot be exactly divided by 6, nor 6 by 10. If, therefore, it is asked whether the concept of the wise man is contained in the concept of the just man, i.e. if nothing more is required for wisdom than what is already contained in justice, we have only to examine whether the symbolic number of the just man can be exactly divided by the symbolic number of the wise man. If the division cannot be made, it is evident that something else is required for wisdom which is not required in the just man. (This 'something else' is a knowledge of reasons; for someone can be just by custom or habit, even if he cannot give a reason for the things he does.) I will state later how this minimum which is still required, or, is to be supplied, can also be found by symbolic numbers.

(17) From this, therefore, we can know whether some universal affirmative proposition is true. For in this proposition the concept of the subject, taken absolutely and indefinitely, and in general regarded in itself, always contains the concept of the predicate. For example, all gold is metal; that is, the concept of metal is contained in the general concept of gold regarded in itself, so that whatever is assumed to be gold is by that very fact assumed to be metal. This is because all the requisites of metal (such as being homogeneous to the senses, liquid when fire is applied in a certain degree, and then not wetting things of another genus immersed in it) are contained in the requisites of gold, as we explained at length in article 7 above. So if we want to know whether all gold is metal (for it can be doubted whether, for example, fulminating gold is still a metal, since it is in the form of a powder and explodes rather than liquefies when fire is applied to it in a certain degree)

C 55

we shall only investigate whether the definition of metal is in it. That is, by a very simple procedure (once we have our symbolic numbers) we shall investigate whether the symbolic number of gold can be divided by the symbolic number of metal.

(18) But in the particular affirmative proposition it is not necessary that the predicate should be in the subject regarded in itself and absolutely; i.e. that the concept of the subject should in itself contain the concept of the predicate; it is enough that the predicate should be contained in some species of the subject, i.e. that *the concept of some instance or species of the subject should contain the concept of the predicate*, even though it is not stated expressly what the species is. Consequently, if you say, 'Some experienced man is prudent', it is not said that the concept of the prudent man is contained in the concept of the experienced man regarded in itself. Nor, again, is this denied; it is enough for our purpose that some species of experienced man has a concept which contains the concept of the prudent man, even though it is not stated expressly   *C 56* just what that species is. For even if it is not said expressly here that the experienced man is a prudent man who also has natural judgement, it is enough that it is understood that some species of experienced man involves prudence.

(19) If the concept of the subject, regarded in itself, contains the concept of the predicate, then the concept of the subject with some addition (i.e. the concept of a species of the subject) will contain the concept of the predicate. This is enough for us, since we do not deny that the predicate is in the subject itself when we say that it is in a species of it. So we can say that some metal is liquid in fire, properly applied, though we could have stated more generally and more usefully that every metal is liquid in fire, properly applied. However, a particular assertion has its uses, as when it is sometimes proved more easily than a general one, or when the hearer will accept it more readily than a general proposition, and a particular proposition is sufficient for our purposes.

(20) Since, therefore, all that is required for a particular affirmative proposition is that a species of the subject should contain the predicate, it follows that the subject is related to the predicate either as species to genus, or as a species to something which coincides with itself (i.e. a reciprocal attribute), or as genus to species. That is, the concept of the subject will be related to the concept of the predicate either as whole to part, or as a whole to a coincident whole, or as a part to the whole (see above, articles 7 and 11).

It will be related as whole to part when the concept of the predicate, as genus, is in the concept of the subject, as species: e.g. if 'bernicle' is the subject and 'bird' the predicate. It will be related as whole to coincident whole when two equivalents are stated of each other reciprocally, as when 'triangle' is the subject and 'trilateral' the predicate. Finally, it will be related as part to whole, as when 'metal' is the subject and 'gold' the predicate. So we can say 'Some bernicle is a bird', 'Some triangle is a trilateral' (even though I could also have stated these two propositions universally), and lastly 'Some metal is gold'. In other cases a particular affirmative proposition does not hold. I prove this as follows. If a species of the subject contains the predicate, it will contain it either as coincident with itself or as a part; if it contains it as equal to itself, i.e. as coincident, then the predicate is a species of the subject, since it coincides with a species of the subject. But if a species of the subject contains the predicate as a part, the predicate will be a genus of a species of the subject, by article 11; therefore predicate and subject will be two genera of the same species. Now, two genera of the same species either coincide or, if they do not,

C 57

they are necessarily related as genus and species. This is easily shown, since the concept of the genus is formed simply by casting-off [*abjectio*] from that of the species; since, therefore, from a common species of two genera, genera will appear on both sides by continued casting-off (that is, they will be left behind as superfluous concepts are cast off), one will appear before the other, and so one will seem to be a whole and the other a part.[1] So we have a paralogism, and with it there falls much that we have said hitherto; for I see that a particular affirmative proposition holds even when neither term is a genus or species, such as 'Some animal is rational', provided only that the terms are compatible. Hence it is also evident that it is not necessary that the subject can be divided by the predicate or the predicate by the subject, on which we have so far built a great deal. What we have said, therefore, is more restricted than it should be; so we shall begin again.

[1] Leibniz has written in the margin: diamond $\left\{ \begin{array}{l} \text{2, 3, 4, 5} \\ \text{sensible body} \\ \text{homogeneous} \\ \text{most durable} \end{array} \right.$

This is perhaps meant to illustrate how different genera can be obtained from the species 'diamond' (*adamas*) by 'casting-off' concepts successively.

4. Rules from which a decision can be made, by means of numbers, about the validity of inferences and about the forms and moods of categorical syllogisms (April, 1679).

I have derived these rules from a higher principle, and with certain changes I can adapt them to modal, hypothetical and any other syllogisms, variously multiplied, continued, transformed and rearranged, in such a way that when a numerical sum has been worked out it will appear, even in the longest reasonings, whether an inference is valid. So far, however, logicians can examine only the commoner and simpler arguments, arranged in a certain order, and are compelled to make tedious reductions of other arguments to these. This, not without reason, has dissuaded men from putting logicians' rules to use. I also have a way of inventing certain symbols which, on being applied to things, permit one to decide whether an argument is valid by virtue of its matter, if not by virtue of its form. Indeed, from the same principle other discoveries can be made which are of much greater importance and usefulness than those which I have touched on; for the moment, however, I think it sufficient to expound the easiest way of reducing to numbers the forms of the inferences which are well known in the Schools.

Every categorical proposition has a subject, a predicate, a copula, a quality and a quantity. Subject and predicate are called 'terms'. For example, in 'The pious man is happy', 'the pious man' and 'happy' are the terms, of which 'the pious man' is the subject, 'happy' the predicate, and 'is' the copula. The 'quality' of a proposition is affirmation or negation: thus, the proposition 'The pious man is happy' affirms, whilst the proposition 'The wicked man is not happy' denies. The 'quantity' of a proposition is its universality or particularity. So when I say 'Every pious man is happy', or 'No wicked man is happy', these are universal propositions, the former being a universal affirmative and the latter a universal negative.[1] But if I say, 'Some wicked man is wealthy', or 'Some pious man is not wealthy', these are particular propositions, the former being affirmative and the latter negative.

C 77

C 78

---

[1] Corrected by Couturat, from the 'particularis negativa' of the text.

I come now to the numbers by which terms are to be expressed, and to that end I shall give the following rules or definitions:

(I) Any term of any proposition, whether a subject or a predicate, is to be written as two numbers, the one being modified by a plus sign and the other by a minus sign. For example, let the proposition be 'Every wise man is pious', and the number corresponding to 'wise man' be $+20$ -21, and the number corresponding to 'pious', $+10$ -3. In what follows I shall call these the 'symbolic numbers' of each term (assumed in the interim). The one thing to be avoided is this: the two numbers of the same term must not have a common divisor. If, instead of $+20$ -21, we had taken for 'the wise man' the numbers $+9$ -6 (both of which can be divided by the same number, namely by 3), they would have been in no way suitable. We can also use letters in place of numbers, as in algebra. Any number satisfying these same conditions may be understood by letters; supposing, for example, the number of 'pious' to be $+a$ $-b$, satisfying the one condition that a and b should be prime in relation to each other, i.e. should have no common divisor.

(II) A true universal affirmative proposition, for example

Every wise man is pious

$+70$ -33 $+10$ -3

$+cdh$ $-ef$ $+cd$ $-e$

is one in which any symbolic number of the subject (e.g. $+70$ and -33) can be divided exactly (i.e. in such a way that no remainder is left) by the symbolic number of the same sign belonging to the predicate ($+70$ by $+10$, -33 by -3). So, if you divide $+70$ by $+10$ you get 7, with no remainder, and if you divide -33 by -3 you get 11, with no remainder.[1] Conversely, when this does not hold the proposition is false.

C 79 (III) A particular negative proposition is true when a universal affirmative is not, and conversely. For example,

Some pious man is not wise

$+10$ -3 $+70$ -33

$+cd$ $-e$ $+cdh$ $-ef$

It is evident that neither can $+10$ be divided by $+70$, nor -3 by -33.[2] Of these two defects even one would be enough to make a

---

[1] In the text Leibniz wrote 2 for 7, -21 for -33, and 7 for 11, since he had originally written $+20$ -21 instead of $+70$ -33.

[2] The text has -21 here.

particular negative true (or, what is the same, to make a universal affirmative false). Thus, if you say

Some wise man is not wealthy

$+70$ -33 $+8$ -11

$+cdh$ $-ef$ $+g$ $-f$

it is evident that $+70$ cannot be divided exactly by $+8$; which is enough, even though -33 can be divided by -11.

Theorem 1. Hence a universal affirmative and particular negative are opposed to each other as contradictories, and so are not true at the same time or false at the same time.

(IV) A true universal negative proposition, for example

No pious man is unhappy

$+10$ -3 $+5$ -14

$+cd$ $-e$ $+l$ $-cm$

is one in which two numbers of different signs and different terms have a common divisor. (For example, $+10$ and -14, since the former has the sign $+$ and the latter the sign $-$; the former is taken from the subject, the latter from the predicate, and $+10$ and -14 can both be exactly divided by 2.) Conversely, when this does not hold the proposition is false.

Theorem 2. Hence a universal negative proposition can be converted *simpliciter*; that is, from 'No pious man is unhappy' there follows 'No unhappy man is pious', or conversely. This is because it makes no difference which of the two you say, and which term you have for subject or which for predicate; for mention of the subject or the predicate does not enter differently into the condition of a true universal negative proposition, but it is enough that one term's number of one sign can be divided by the other term's number of the other sign, whichever of these two terms is the subject or the predicate.

(V) A particular affirmative proposition is true when a universal negative is not true, and conversely. For example,   C 80

Some wealthy man is unhappy

$+11$ -9 $+5$ -14

$+n$ $-p$ $+l$ $-cm$

This is because neither $+11$ and -14, nor -9^1 and $+5$ have a common divisor (either of which would be enough to make a universal negative proposition true). Similarly

Some wise man is pious

$+70 \quad -33 \quad +10 \quad -3$

$+cdh \quad -ef \quad +cd \quad -e$

since neither $+70$ and -3, nor -33 and $+10$ have a common divisor.

Theorem 3. A universal negative and a particular affirmative proposition are opposed to each other as contradictories (i.e. in such a way that they cannot be true at the same time or false at the same time). This is evident from what has been said.

Theorem 4. A particular affirmative proposition can be converted *simpliciter*: e.g. 'Some wealthy man is unhappy, therefore some unhappy man is wealthy', 'Some wise man is pious, therefore some pious man is wise'. This appears in the same way in which we showed that a universal negative proposition (which contradicts this) can be converted *simpliciter* (see theorem 2).

These are the definitions or conditions of true categorical propositions, in accordance with their different quality and quantity; in these definitions are contained the principles of a whole logical calculus. From these we will now prove, simply by the use of numbers which has already been explained, the better-known logical inferences. These are either simple or syllogistic. The better-known simple inferences are subalternation, opposition and conversion. 'Subalternation' is when a particular is inferred from a universal. Let this, then, be

Theorem 5. Subalternation is always valid, i.e. a particular can always be inferred from a universal.

Every wise man is pious

$+70 \quad -33 \quad +10 \quad -3$

$+cdh \quad -ef \quad +cd \quad -e$

Therefore some wise man is pious.

I prove this as follows. -33 can be divided by -3^2 (since this is a universal affirmative proposition, by rule 2). Therefore $+70$ and -3^2 do not have a common divisor (otherwise*[3] $+70$ and -33 would have the same common divisor, which is contrary to rule 1).

C 81

---

[1] -7 in the text. Cf. Schmidt, pp. 221, 489.

[2] 11 in the text. Cf. Schmidt, p. 222.

[3] The meaning of this and of the following asterisk is explained at the end of this paragraph.

Similarly, $+70$ can be divided by $+10$ (by rule 2), therefore -33 and $+10$ do not have a common divisor (for otherwise* -33 and $+70$ would also have a common divisor, which is contrary to rule 1). Since, therefore, both $+70$ and -3, and -33 and $+10$ do not have a common divisor, the particular affirmative proposition 'Some wise man is pious' will be true (by rule 4). (The reason for the inference indicated by * is obvious to anyone who knows the nature of numbers, since a divisor of a divisor is also a divisor of the dividend. For example, if -33, as the third number, and $+10$, as the divisor, have a common divisor, this divisor of the divisor $+10$, and of the number -33,[1] will also be the divisor of the dividend of $+10$, namely $+70$. It would therefore follow that -33 and $+70$ have a common divisor.)

This can be proved in the same way in the case of negative propositions. For example,

No pious man is unhappy

$+10$	-3	$+5$	-14
$+cd$	$-e$	$+l$	$-cm$

Therefore some pious man is not unhappy

For since $+10$ and -14 have a common divisor (as this is a universal negative, by rule 4), -3 and -14 do not have a common divisor; for otherwise -3 and $+10$ would also have a common divisor, contrary to rule 1. Therefore -3 cannot be divided by -14; for otherwise they would have a common divisor, since the divisor of a divisor is also a divisor of the dividend. Now, -3 cannot be divided by -14, therefore the particular negative proposition is true (by rule 5). Q.E.D.

These two proofs are of the greatest importance; not, indeed, to make more certain a thing which is clear of itself, but for laying the foundations of our calculus, and for the recognition of their harmony. Certainly, when I had discovered these proofs, on whose success everything else depended, it was then above all that I knew that I had found the true laws of the calculus. The reason for this is that as I was considering universal concepts, I was particularly looking for a transition from genus to species. For I do not consider a genus as something greater than the species, i.e. as a whole composed of species, as is commonly done (and not done wrongly, since the individuals of the genus are related to the individuals of the species as whole to part). I consider the genus as a part of the species, since the concept of the species is produced from the concept of the genus and of the   *C 82*

---

[1] Leibniz's text has $+33$. Cf. Schmidt, pp. 223, 489.

differentia. On this principle I constructed this method of calculation, since I considered ideas and not individuals. However, proceeding in this way it was very difficult to descend from the genus to the species, since it is a progress from the part to the whole. But I have made a road to this point by these very proofs, by which one goes from universals to particulars.

Opposition comes after subalternation. Opposition is either contradictory, contrary or subcontrary. It is contradictory when two opposite propositions cannot be true at the same time or false at the same time (this was said to hold between a universal affirmative and a particular negative, theorem 1,[1] and between a universal negative and a particular affirmative, theorem 3). It is contrary when they cannot be true at the same time but can be false, and it is subcontrary when they can be true at the same time, but not false.

Theorem 6. A universal affirmative and a universal negative are opposed to each other as contraries; for example

Every wise man is wealthy

$+70$ $\quad-33$ $+8$ $\quad\quad-11$

$+cdh$ $\quad-ef$ $+g$ $\quad\quad-f$

and $\qquad\qquad$ No wise man is wealthy

cannot be true at the same time. For if they are, it will follow from the latter that some wise man is not wealthy (by theorem 5), whereas the former was 'Every wise man is wealthy'. Therefore these two will be true at the same time, contrary to theorem 1. But they can be false at the same time; for it can happen that neither can $+70$ be divided by $+8$ (and therefore the first is false, by rule 2), nor do either $+70$ and -11 or -33 and $+8$ have a common divisor (and therefore the second is false, by rule 4). (Another example could also be assumed in which a number which replaces -33 cannot be divided by a number which replaces -11; but it comes to the same.)

Theorem 7. A particular affirmative and particular negative are opposed to each other as subcontraries, i.e. they can be true at the same time, but not false: e.g. 'Some wise man is wealthy', and 'Some wise man is not wealthy'. This follows from the preceding theorem; for since the contradictories of universals of contrary sign are particulars (by theorems 1 and 3), when the former are true the latter are false, and conversely. But the former can be false at the same time (by theorem 6), therefore the latter can be true at the same time. The former cannot be true at the same time

C 83

---

[1] Corrected by Couturat from the 'theor. 2' of the text.

(by the same theorem, 6), therefore the latter cannot be false at the same time.

Conversion is either *simpliciter* or *per accidens*. Conversion *simpliciter* is valid in the universal negative, by theorem 2 ('No pious man is unhappy, therefore no unhappy man is pious', or conversely). It is valid in the particular affirmative by theorem 4 ('Some wealthy man is unhappy, therefore some unhappy man is wealthy', and conversely). Conversion *per accidens* is valid in the universal affirmative, as I shall soon show; neither kind of conversion is formally valid in the particular negative. Of conversion by contraposition I do not speak here, as this assumes a new term. For example, 'Every wise man is pious, therefore the man who is not pious is not wise, i.e. no[1] not-pious man is wise'. For there we have three terms: 'wise', 'pious' and 'not-pious'. Here, however, I am concerned with simple inferences where the same terms are kept. Further, the use of this conversion is in no way necessary to prove the figures and moods of the syllogism. The properties of this sort of infinite terms, 'not-pious', 'not-happy' &c., should and can be proved by our calculus separately, just like the modal propositions. For they have many peculiarities: if you use them, a syllogism can have four terms and still be valid,[2] and there are many other things which are not relevant here, since what we have proposed is to show by our calculus the general moods and figures of three-termed categorical syllogisms.

Theorem 8. A universal affirmative can be converted *per accidens*. Every wise man is pious, therefore some pious man is wise. For since every wise man is pious, therefore (by theorem 5) some wise man is pious; therefore (by theorem 4) some pious man is wise.

From simple inferences in which there are only two terms I pass to three-termed inferences, i.e. categorical syllogisms. One now needs a little more care if one is to assume the numbers of terms suitably; for the same term (the middle term) is in each premiss, and therefore its symbolic numbers must be adapted to the rules of each premiss. To this end, the middle term should first be   *C 84*
adapted to one of the extreme terms (namely, either to the major or the minor term) and the other extreme term should later be adapted to it. Here it must be noted that it is better to adapt the

---

[1] Leibniz wrote 'Omnis non-pius est sapiens'. 'Nullus' is read above in place of 'omnis', on the basis of *C 91*: 'A universal affirmative proposition can be converted universally by what is called "contraposition". "Every wise man is pious, therefore no-one who is not pious is wise" . . . . . . This may be written otherwise as "No not-pious man is wise".'
[2] Examples of what Leibniz has in mind are: 'Every C is B, every not-D is C, therefore some B is not D' and 'No man is a stone, no man is an angel, therefore some not-angel is not a stone' (*C 320*).

subject to the predicate than conversely, as will be evident if one considers the above rules. So if there should be a premiss in which the middle term is the subject one should begin with it, and after assuming arbitrarily the numbers of its predicate one should adapt to it the numbers of its subject, the middle term. When the numbers of the middle term have been invented in this way, the numbers of the other term in the other premiss may also be adapted to these. Once the symbolic numbers of the major and minor term are in one's possession it will readily appear whether they observe between them that law which the form of the conclusion prescribes, that is, whether the conclusion is derived formally from the premisses.

So that this assumption of numbers may be made more easily I will lay down certain rules.

5. A Specimen of the Universal Calculus (1679-86?)

(1) A universal affirmative proposition will be expressed here as follows:

a is *b*, or, (every) man is an animal.

We shall, therefore, always understand the sign of universality to be prefixed. Negative, particular and hypothetical propositions we shall not touch at present.

(2) A proposition true in itself:

ab is *a*, or, (every) rational animal is an animal.

ab is *b*, or, (every) rational animal is rational.

Or, omitting *b*,

a is *a*, or, (every) animal is an animal.

(3) An inference true in itself:

If *a* is *b* and *b* is *c*, then *a* is *c*. Or, if (every) man is an animal and (every) animal is a substance, then (every) man is a substance.

(4) From this there follows:

If *a* is *bd* and *b* is *c*, then *a* is *c*. (Every) man is a rational animal. (Every) animal is a substance. Therefore (every) man is a substance.

This is proved as follows:

If *a* is *bd* (by hypothesis) and *bd* is *b* (by no. 2), then *a* is *b* (by no. 3). Again, if *a* is *b* (as we have proved) and *b* is *c* (by hypothesis), then *a* is *c* (by no. 3).

(5) A true proposition is one which arises by means of inferences from what is assumed and what is true in itself.

Note: even if certain propositions are arbitrarily assumed, as the definitions of terms, yet there arises from these a truth which is far from arbitrary. For it is at any rate absolutely true that the conclusions arise from the definitions which have been assumed, or (what is the same) that the connexion between conclusions or theorems, and definitions or arbitrary hypotheses, is absolutely true. This appears in the case of numbers. The signs for these, and the decimal system also, have been established arbitrarily; but the calculations derived from these signify absolute truths, namely the connexion between the symbols assumed and the formulae deduced from them, by which there are also signified the connexions of things (which remain the same, whatever the symbols assumed). It is useful for the sciences that symbols are so assumed that from a few assumptions many deductions can easily be made;

and this is the case if symbols are assigned to the simplest elements of thought.

(6) If some term can be substituted everywhere in place of another without loss of truth, then the other in turn can be substituted everywhere in place of it. For example, since 'trilateral' can be substituted everywhere in place of 'plane triangular figure', 'triangle' can also be substituted everywhere in place of 'trilateral'. For let there be two terms, a and b, and let b be capable of being substituted everywhere in place of a; I state that a, in turn, can be substituted everywhere in place of b. I show this as follows. Let there be a proposition 'b is c', or 'd is b'; I state that a can be substituted in these. For let us suppose that it cannot be substituted, i.e. that it cannot be said that a is c, and d is a; then these propositions will be false. So the following two propositions, at any rate, will be true: 'It is false that a is c' and 'It is false that d is a'. Now, b can be substituted for a (by hypothesis), and therefore the two propositions 'It is false that b is c' and 'It is false that d is b' will also be true. But this is contrary to the hypothesis, for we assumed these as true; therefore the proposition is proved. The same can be proved in another way.

(7) Those terms are 'the same' of which one can be substituted in place of the other without loss of truth, such as 'triangle' and 'trilateral', 'quadrangle' and 'quadrilateral'.

(8) All universal affirmative propositions (which are the only subject of discussion here) in which there occurs a given letter, a, can be reduced to these forms:

G vii.
220

a is d

ab is e

c is a

—though it might seem that more can be enumerated.

a is d

a is fg is reduced to a is d, on the assumption that fg is d.

a is $fh\beta$ is reduced to a is d, on the assumption that $fh\beta$ is d, i.e. that $h\beta$ is g and fg is d. &c.

ab is e

ab is ik is reduced to ab is e, on the assumption that ik is e. &c.

alm is e is reduced to ab is e, on the assumption that b is lm. For if b is lm, ab will be alm.

alm is ik is reduced to ab is e; for ik is e, and ab is alm. &c.

c is a

np is a is reduced to c is a, on the assumption that c is np. &c.

q is ab (abc, &c.) is reduced to q is a, for ab is a.

rs is *ab* (*abc*, etc.) is reduced to *q* is *a*, on the assumption that
rs is *q*. &c.

a is *a* is reduced to *d* is *a*, on the assumption that *d* is *a*; or to
a is *c*, on the assumption that *a* is *c*.

a is *at* (*aθλ*, &c.) is reduced to *a* is *d*, on the assumption that
at is *d*; or to *a* is *a*, since *at* is *a*.

$$ab \text{ is } \begin{cases} a \\ av \\ awx \text{ (\&c.)} \end{cases}$$
$$abc \text{ is } \begin{cases} a \\ az \\ a\mu w \text{ (\&c.)} \end{cases}$$

All these can be reduced in two ways
from what precedes, by retaining *a* either
in the subject or in the predicate.

&c.

All, however, can be reduced to the three mentioned above, provided that we note that for *df* or *dfg* or *bc* or *cn*, *ab*, *abc*, &c., one letter can be put which is equal to this conjunction of several (just as for the term 'rational animal' we put, for the sake of brevity, the one term 'man'); and for the composite term *ab* or *abc*, found in the predicate, there can be substituted the simple term *a*. For if you say '*c* is *ab*', or, 'Man is a rational animal', you can also say, '*c* is *a*', or, 'Man is an animal'. It is different, however, in the case of a subject; for though I may say, 'Every rational animal is a man', I cannot say, 'Every animal is a man'. So I cannot reduce the proposition '*ab* is *c*' to a simpler one in which *a* also appears. The rest I can, as is evident from what has been said.

G vii.
221

(9) If *a* is *f* and *f* is *a*, *a* and *f* will be the same, i.e. the one can be substituted in place of the other. I prove this as follows. First I shall show that *f* can always be substituted in place of *a*. By what precedes, all propositions in which *a* occurs can be reduced to three, namely, *a* is *d*, *ab* is *e*, and *c* is *a*. From this I shall show that there can be substituted these three: *f* is *d*, *fb* is *e*, and *c* is *f*. For since *f* is *a* and *a* is *d*, *f* will also be *d*. Again, because *f* is *a*, *fb* will also be *ab* (by what has been proved in the additions to this paper);[1] now, *ab* is *e*, therefore *fb* will be *e*. Finally, because *c* is *a* and *a* is *f*, *c* will also be *f*. In the same way in which we have shown that *f* can be substituted in place of *a*, it will also be shown that *a* can be substituted in place of *f*; both because it was a matter of choice whether we picked on *a* or *f*, and because we showed above in no. 6 that substitution is reciprocal.

---

[1] 'per demonstrata in additionibus'. This seems to be a reference to the proof of 'If *b* is *c*, then *ab* is *ac*' in the *Addenda to the Specimen of the Universal Calculus*, G vii. *222–3* (p. 41 below).

An 'entity' is what is signified by any term, such as a, or b, or ab.[1]

C 239   To investigate what 'one' and 'several' are, we must consider examples. We say, 'Peter is one apostle', or, 'Some one apostle is Peter'; 'Paul is one apostle', or, 'Some one apostle is Paul'; 'Peter and Paul are several apostles'. But if I say, 'Peter, the disciple of Christ, is one apostle' and 'The disciple who denied Christ is one apostle', this does not, on that account, make several apostles; for Peter the disciple of Christ, and the disciple who denied Christ, are the same. So if a is m and b is m, and a is b and b is a (i.e. if a and b are the same), then m is one.

So if you say, 'a is m', it follows from this that there is one m, for it is as if you were to say, 'a is m and b is m', supposing a and b to be the same.

If a is m and b is m, and neither a is b nor b is a (i.e. if a and b are 'disparate'), there are several m.

C 240   If a is m and b is m, and a is b but b is not a, it is uncertain whether there are several m or only one. Take, for example, 'Adam is a rational animal and a man is a rational animal'. This leaves it uncertain whether there are several rational animals, for there might be no other man than Adam.

If a is m	one
b is m	... } two
c is m	.... } three
d is m	.... } four
and a, b, c, d	in a word,
are disparate,	several m.
there will be	

If a is b, then *only* b will be a; i.e. if every man is an animal, only an animal will be a man. This, then, is the definition of 'only'.

If only b is a, then a will be b.

If only a is b and only b is a, then a and b will be the same. For if only a is b, then b is a; if only b is a, then a is b (by the definition of 'only'). Now if b is a and a is b, a and b will be the same, by what has been proved above.

'Equivalent terms' are those by which the same things are signified, such as 'triangle' and 'trilateral'.

A 'simple term' is that in which there is only one term, such as a. A 'composite term' is that which consists of several, such as ab.

---

[1] At this point, Gerhardt's transcription of the manuscript ceases, with the remark that the remainder assumes more of the character of a study.

A 'primitive term' is that of which no composite term is the equivalent; a 'derivative term' is that of which some composite term is the equivalent. So if we assume that bc is equivalent to a, and de to b, but that to c no composite term is equivalent, a will be a derivative [1] term, and so will b, but c will be primitive.

This can be illustrated by the example of primitive numbers. Let a be a multiple of 30, b of 15, c of 2, d of 3 and e of 5;[2] then it is evident that a is the same as bc, i.e. that a multiple of 15 and 2 is equivalent to a multiple of 30, and that b is the same as de, i.e. that a multiple of 3 and 5 is equivalent to a multiple of 15. It is also evident that no other known numbers are equivalent to a multiple of 2 (taken generally and absolutely), just as they are not equivalent to multiples of 3 or 5. So 'multiple of 2', 'multiple of 3' and 'multiple of 5' are primitive terms.   *C 241*

A term which is 'prior by nature' is one which appears in place of a composite term, by substituting simple terms; a term which is 'posterior by nature' is one which appears in place of simple terms, by substituting a composite term. Or, what is the same, a term which is prior by nature appears through analysis, and one which is posterior by nature through synthesis; the one from the other. So, in the previous example, 'multiple of 15' is prior by nature to 'multiple of 30', and 'multiple of 2' is also prior by nature to 'multiple of 30'. Again, the term 'multiple of 15 and 2' is prior by nature to 'multiple of 30'. 'Multiple of 3' is prior by nature both to 'multiple of 15' and to 'multiple of 30'; so also is 'multiple of 5'. So is 'multiple of 3 and 5' also; for although a number which is a multiple of 3 and 5 is the same as that which is a multiple of 15,[3] yet it is another *term*, although an equivalent one. It can be asked whether 'multiple of 2' is not a term prior by nature to 'multiple of 15'. According to the definition which I have given it will be neither prior nor posterior by nature; for one does not constitute the other, nor does it arise from the other through synthesis or analysis. But if you give a definition of this kind: a term 'prior by nature' is one which consists of terms which are less derivative, and a 'less derivative' term is one which is equivalent to fewer

---

[1] Leibniz erased 'compositus' in front of 'terminus', probably intending to substitute 'derivativus'. Similarly, the last word of the sentence in the text is 'simplex', very probably an error for 'primitivus'.

[2] Literally, a, b, c, d, and e are called respectively a 'tricenary', 'quindenary', 'binary', 'ternary', and 'quinary' (*tricenarius, quindenarius, binarius*, &c.). That these are multiples is shown by *C 241*: 'binarius numerus (seu per 2 divisibilis)'—literally, 'a binary number (i.e. one which is divisible by 2)'.

[3] Corrected by Couturat, from 'tricenarius'.

simple primitive terms . . .[1] From this it is evident that if a simple
and a composite term can be predicated of each other, then the
composite term is prior by nature.

A 'name' is a term, assumed arbitrarily, which signifies a thing.
So 'circle' is the name of a figure of such and such a kind; but
that it is a figure, is uniform, and has the most area of those
figures which have an equal perimeter, are its attributes.

An 'attribute' is the predicate in a universal affirmative proposition of which the name of a thing is the subject. For example,
every multiple of 30 is a multiple of 2; every multiple of 30 is a
multiple of 2 and 15; God is just, merciful, &c. Consequently,
being a multiple of 2 is an attribute of being a multiple of 30;
being just is an attribute of God.

A 'property' is the subject in a universal affirmative proposition,
of which the predicate is the name of the thing whose property it
is said to be. Thus, in 'a is b' I call a the property. For if every a
is b, then only b will be a (as above), i.e no not-b will be a; and a
is the property of b.[2] So being a multiple of 30 is a property only of
a multiple of 2, for only a multiple of 2 can be a multiple of 30.
Again, being God is a property of a just being alone; for even if
this does not belong to every just being, it does belong to a just
being alone. So also reason is a property of living things, for it
belongs to living things alone.

C 242

A 'proper attribute' is that which is the subject of a term in
one affirmative proposition, and the predicate of the same term in
another—for example, 'multiple of 30' and 'multiple of 2 and 15';
'God' and 'omnipotent'. From this it is evident that a proper
attribute is the same as what is commonly called a 'reciprocal
property'; consequently 'name of a thing' and 'proper attribute of
a thing' are equivalent terms.

A 'definition' is an equivalent term prior by nature; a 'defined
term' is an equivalent term posterior by nature. In this way, some
composite term can be a defined term; e.g. a 'conic section' is
a line common to the surface of a cone and a certain plane. But if
we prefer definition to be of single names alone, then we must say:

[1] There seems to be a confusion in the manuscript here; this sentence is
clearly unfinished, and the sentence which follows (a later addition)
refers to a fact already noted, namely that a term such as 'multiple of 15
and 2' is prior to 'multiple of 30'. This does not answer the question
whether 'multiple of 2' is prior to 'multiple of 15'. However, it is probable
that Leibniz would say that the former is prior, in that it is 'less derivative'.
[2] Corrected by Couturat from the 'b ipsius a' of the text.

A 'definition' is a composite term equivalent to a simple term; a 'defined term' is a simple term equivalent to a composite term. Or finally, assuming that the simple term is a name,

A 'definition' is a proper attribute of a name; a 'defined term' is a name of a proper attribute.

But if one considers the matter rightly it seems that another explanation must be given, namely

A 'definition' is the term which is more composite, and a 'defined term' or 'name' is the term which is more simple, in a reciprocal proposition which is assumed arbitrarily and consists of a simple and a composite term. So a definition is a proposition of which no reason is given, but which we use only for the sake of abbreviation. A definition, then, is some hypothesis about whose truth one may not dispute, but only about whether it is apt, clear and intelligently assumed.

It is evident that a defined term can be a composite term, if a definition is composed of the definitions of its parts (or from the definition of one part and from the other part); namely, when a thing does not have some single name, such as a conic section. From this it is evident that a name can be a composite term. But if the defined term is a composite term, the definition is not an assumed proposition, but must be proved; it being assumed that the parts of the defined term have their separate definitions which, taken together, must be equivalent to a definition of the defined term. Unless, perhaps, we consider the defined term as one name, though not as one vocable: e.g. 'intervallum', where one does not explain both 'inter' and 'vallum', just as in the case of 'Fort-royal'[1]—that is, one which is regular and has a certain exact magnitude—one does not explain the word 'royal'.

However, as we shall give a single name to each concept there is no need for these precautions. For us, every simple term is a name, and every definition is the composite reciprocal predicate of the name, from which everything else is proved. I prefer this to an arbitrary predicate, for, as I shall state later, I shall transfer everything from the arbitrary to certain laws.

C 243

By 'term' I understand, not a name, but a concept, i.e. that which is signified by a name; you could also call it a notion, an idea.

---

[1] 'Munimentum Regium'. A 'Fort-royal' is defined as 'A fort that has 26 fathoms for the line of defence' in the 1706 edition of Edward Phillips' *The new world of English words: or, a general dictionary* (quoted in the *Oxford English Dictionary*).

6. *Addenda to the Specimen of the Universal Calculus* (1679–86 ?)

For the nature of this calculus to be understood, it must be noted that whatever is stated by us in certain letters which have been arbitrarily assumed can be stated in the same way in any other assumed letters. So when I say that the proposition 'ab is a' is always true, I understand to be true not only the example 'A rational animal is an animal' (taking 'animal' to be signified by a, and 'rational' by b), but also the example 'A rational animal is rational' (taking 'rational' to be signified by a, and 'animal' by b). I understand the same to hold with any other example; e.g. 'An organic body is organic'. Therefore instead of 'ab is a' it could also be said that bd is d.

It must also be noted that it makes no difference whether you say ab or ba, for it makes no difference whether you say 'rational animal' or 'animal rational'.

The repetition of some letter in the same term is superfluous, and it is enough for it to be retained once; e.g. aa or 'man man'.

So if a is bc, b is d, and c also is d, it is superfluous to say that a is dd, for it is enough to say that a is d. For example, 'Man is a rational animal; every animal is sentient; again, everything rational is sentient'. But it is superfluous to say, 'Man is a sentient sentient', for this is merely to say 'Man is sentient'. But if anyone wishes to say that man is sentient in a double sense, this must be expressed in another way, in accordance with the rules of our symbolism.

Different predicates can be joined into one; thus, if it is agreed that a is b, and (for some other reason) that a is c, then it can be said that a is bc. For example, if man is an animal, and if man is rational, man will be a rational animal.

Conversely, one compound predicate can be divided into several. For example, a is bc, therefore a is b and a is c; put into words, 'Man is a rational animal, therefore man is an animal and man is rational'.

As this division is self-evident, composition can be proved from it. For assume that man is an animal and that man is rational, but that man is not a rational animal; therefore the proposition, 'Man is a rational animal' will be false. But its falsity can be proved in three ways only; first, by showing that man is not an animal, which is contrary to the hypothesis; second, by showing that man is not rational, which is again contrary to the hypothesis; third, that he is not both at once, i.e. that these two terms are incompatible, which is also contrary to the hypothesis, since we have assumed that he is at once both an animal and rational.

In the subject, composition is valid, but not division. For if *b* is *a* and *c* is *a*, *bc* also will be *a*. If every animal lives, and everything rational lives, then every rational animal lives. This is proved as follows:

bc is *b*, *b* is *a*, therefore *bc* is *a*.
bc is *c*, *c* is *a*, therefore *bc* is *a*.

Also, by mixing in various ways the compositions and divisions of terms there will arise many inferences not yet touched by logicians, especially if we employ negative and particular propositions also.

If *b* is *c*, then *ab* will be *ac*; i.e. if man is an animal, it follows that a wise man is a wise animal. This is proved as follows:

ab is *b*, *b* is *c*, therefore *ab* is *c*, by the first rule of inferences.
ab is *c*, *ab* is *a*, therefore *ab* is *ac*, by what has been proved above.

However, one cannot infer conversely, '*ab* is *ac*, therefore *b* is *c*'. For it can happen that *a* is *ad* and *bd* is *c*. But if *a* and *c* have nothing in common, the inference '*ab* is *ac*, therefore *b* is *c*'[1] is valid. Here, however, we are concerned with the discussion of general inferences alone. Afterwards we shall proceed to more particular inferences; these, however, are of greater importance than the general ones, and have not yet received the attention they deserve. For the whole of analysis rests on certain inferences which seem to be formal errors but in fact are not, because a certain general relation of the terms is always observed.

G vii.
223

If *a* is *b*, *a* is *d* and *d* is *b*, then *ab* will be equivalent to *bd*. This is proved from what has gone before: *a* is *b*, *a* is *c*, *d* is *b*, *d* is *c*, therefore *ad* is *bc*, assuming *c* to be *d*. But it is evident from what has been said above that there is no need of so many suppositions to draw this conclusion, and '*a* is *b*' is sufficient. For from this it follows that *ad* is *bd*.

If *a* is *b* and *d* is *c*, then *ad* will be *bc*. This is a fine theorem, which is proved in this way:

a is *b*, therefore *ad* is *bd* (by what precedes),
d is *c*, therefore *bd* is *bc* (again by what precedes),
ad is *bd*, and *bd* is *bc*, therefore *ad* is *bc*. Q.E.D.

In general, if there are as many propositions as you please—*a* is *b*, *c* is *d*, *e* is *f*—it is possible to make from these the one

---

[1] '*ergo b est c*' is added by Schmidt (p. 489) to Gerhardt's text.

proposition *ace* is *bdf*, by adding the subjects on the one side and the predicates on the other.

In general, if there is a proposition *m* is *bdf*, three propositions can be made from this: *m* is *b*, *m* is *d*, *m* is *f*.

All this is easily proved from the one assumption that the subject is as it were a container, and the predicate a simultaneous or conjunctive content; or conversely, that the subject is as it were a content, and the predicate an alternative or disjunctive container.[1]

A 'term' is *a*, *b*, *ab*, *bcd*; such as 'man', 'animal', 'rational animal', 'rational visible mortal'.

A 'universal affirmative proposition' I represent as *a* is *b*, or, '(every) man is an animal'. For I want the sign of universality always to be understood, where *a* is the 'subject', *b* the 'predicate' and 'is' the 'copula'.

G vii.
224 *Postulate:* Let it be a permissible supposition that a letter is equivalent to one letter or to several at once; e.g. that *d* is equivalent to *a* and the one can be substituted in place of the other, or that *c* is equivalent to the term *ab*—for example, 'man' is the same as 'rational animal'. I understand this to hold, provided that nothing has already been assumed which is contrary to these suppositions.

Propositions true in themselves:

(1) *a* is *a*. An animal is an animal.

(2) *ab* is *a*. A rational animal is an animal.

(3) *a* is not not-*a*. An animal is not a not-animal.

(4) Not-*a* is not *a*. A not-animal is not an animal.

(5) That which is not *a*, is not-*a*. That which is not an animal, is a not-animal.

(6) That which is not not-*a*, is *a*. That which is not a not-animal is an animal.

From these, several propositions can be deduced.

An inference true in itself: a is *b* and *b* is *c*, therefore *a* is *c*. God is wise, he who is wise is just, therefore God is just. This chain can be continued further: e.g. God is wise, he who is wise is just, he who is just is severe, therefore God is severe.

Principles of the calculus

(1) Whatever is concluded in terms of certain indefinite letters must be understood to be concluded in terms of any other letters which have the same conditions. For example, because it is true

---

[1] What follows is written in the margin of the manuscript.

that *ab* is *a*, it will also be true that *bc* is *b*, and also that *bcd* is *bc*. For, substituting *e* for *bc* (by the postulate) it is the same as if we had said, '*ed* is *e*'.

(2) The transposition of letters in the same term changes nothing: e.g. *ab* coincides with *ba*, or, 'rational animal' and 'animal rational'.

(3) Repetition of the same letter in the same term is superfluous, such as *b* is *aa*, or *bb* is *a*: man is an animal animal, or man man [*homo homo*] is an animal. For it is enough to say, *a* is *b*, or, man is an animal.

(4) From any number of propositions it is possible to make one proposition, by adding together all the subjects into one subject and all the predicates into one predicate. From *a* is *b*, *c* is *d* and *e* is *f* we get *ace* is *bdf*. For example, God is omnipotent, man is endowed with a body, a person crucified suffers; therefore a God-man crucified is an omnipotent being, endowed with a body, and suffering. Nor does it matter that what are joined in this way are sometimes incompatible, as, for example, 'A circle is non-angled, a square is a quadrangle, therefore a square circle is a non-angled quadrangle'. For this proposition is true from an impossible hypothesis. This observation is especially useful in long-drawn-out chains of reasoning, for example in this way: 'God is wise; God is omnipotent; a just omnipotent being punishes evil men; God does not punish some evil men in this life; he who punishes, and does not punish in this life, punishes in another life; therefore God punishes in another life'.

G vii.
225

(5) From any proposition whose predicate is composed of several terms several propositions can be made, any one of which has the same subject as before, but in place of the predicate has some part of the former predicate. *a* is *bcd*, therefore *a* is *b*, *a* is *c* and *a* is *d*. For example, man is rational, mortal and visible, therefore man is rational, man is mortal and man is visible.

If *a* is *b* and *b* is *a*, then *a* and *b* are said to be 'the same'. For example, every pious man is happy, and every happy man is pious, therefore 'happy man' and 'pious man' are the same.

From this it is easily proved that the one can everywhere be substituted in place of the other without loss of truth; or, if *a* is *b* and *b* is *a*, and *b* is *c* or *d* is *a*, then *a* is *c* or *d* is *b*. For example, every pious man is happy, and every happy man is pious. Every happy man is chosen; every martyr is pious. Therefore every pious man is chosen, and every martyr is happy. (Note that by 'pious' I understand here 'persevering', or, 'dying in grace'.)

Those terms are 'different' which are not the same, such as 'man' and 'animal'; for although every man is an animal, not every animal is a man.

a and *b* are 'disparate' if *a* is not *b* and *b* is not *a*, such as 'man' and 'stone'. For a man is not a stone, and a stone is not a man. So all disparates are different, but not conversely.

If *a* is *m* and *b* is *m*, and *a* and *b* are the same, then *m* is said to be 'one'. For example, Octavian is Caesar and Augustus is Caesar, but because Octavian and Augustus are the same, only one Caesar is enumerated.

If *a* is *m*.................⎞
     there are said to be⎬   two⎞
and *b* is *m*................⎠   ⎬ three⎞
     several *m*   ⎠   ⎬ four
and *c* is *m*....................⎞ ⎠
and *d* is *m*............................⎠

        provided that *a*, *b*, *c*, *d* are disparate.

G vii.
226

If we have assumed some simple term as equivalent to some composite term, i.e. as expressing the same thing, then the simple term will be the 'defined term' and the composite term will be the 'definition'. This defined term, expressed by a symbol, we shall call henceforth the 'name' of the thing. For example, if for *ab* we say 'rational animal', and wish for the sake of brevity to say later *c* or 'man', then *c* (or, the word 'man') will be the name of that thing whose definition is 'rational animal'; i.e. the word 'man' will be the name of man.

If in a universal affirmative proposition the subject is a thing but the predicate is neither a thing nor a definition, but is some other term, then that term will be said to be an 'attribute'. So the definition of God, whose name is 'God', is 'the most perfect being', and the attributes are: merciful, omnipotent, a creator, an entity, an entity in itself [*Ens a se*]. So if *c* is a thing and *ab* a definition, and if *c* is *d*, and *d* is not the term *ab*, then *d* will be called an attribute of *c*.

If in a universal affirmative proposition the predicate is a thing, but the subject is not a thing nor the definition of a thing, but is another term, that term will be called a 'property'. For example, every man is an animal, and so 'man' is a property of 'animal'. For only an animal can be a man, although not every animal is a man; for we are defining here, not a property 'in the fourth kind', but a property in general, i.e. that which belongs to one thing alone. So if *c* is a thing, and *ab* the definition of the thing, and the (universal affirmative) proposition '*d* is *c*' is given, then *d* will be a property of *c*, provided that the term *c* or *ab* is not understood by the term *d*.

A 'genus' is a common attribute; thus the genus of the terms *d* and *e* is *a*, assuming that *d* is *ab* and *e* is *ac*—i.e. if *d* is *a*, but *a* is not *d*.

A 'proper genus' is an attribute common to several, but to them alone; e.g. 'animal' is the proper genus of 'man' and 'brute'. That is, if d is a and e is a, and if anything which is not-d and not-e is not-a, then a will be the proper genus of the species d and e.

An 'accident' is the predicate[1] both in a particular affirmative and in a particular negative proposition which have the same subject. For example, some man is learned, and some man is not learned; therefore 'learned' is an accident of 'man'. If some a is b and some a is not b, then b is an accident of a.

A 'proper attribute' is that which is at the same time both an attribute and a property. Thus, suppose that the definition of a thing c (e.g. man) is ab ('a rational animal'). Suppose also that there are given two propositions: one is that c is d ('man is a rational mortal'), on account of which d is an attribute, and the other is that d is c ('a rational mortal is a man'), on account of which d is a property. Then it is evident that d is a proper attribute. It is also evident that 'name', 'definition' and 'proper attribute' are equivalent terms, i.e. that they express the same thing. This is what is commonly called a 'property in the fourth kind', or, a 'reciprocal property'.

A 'substantive'[2] is (a name) which includes (the name) 'entity' or 'thing'; an 'adjective' is that which does not include these. Thus 'animal' is a substantive, i.e. is the same as 'animal entity'. 'Rational' is an adjective, for it becomes a substantive if you add 'entity', by saying 'a rational entity' or (to abbreviate this into one word, if a joke is allowed) 'a rational'—just as from the term 'animal entity' there comes 'animal'.

G vii.
227

A 'genus' is a substantive which is the common attribute of several, which are called 'species'.

Attribute { Every difference can be specific with another genus.

A 'specific difference' is an adjective which, with the genus, constitutes a term equivalent to a species (or rather, the definition of a species?)

A 'generic difference' is that which is the specific difference of a genus.

---

[1] The text has 'subjectum'.

[2] L.– These definitions are adapted to Scholastic usage; but in symbols it is not necessary that the difference between a noun substantive and an adjective should appear, nor has that difference any use.

A 'definition' is a composite substantival term, equivalent to a species.

A 'property' is the adjectival subject of a universal proposition, whose predicate is a substantive.

An 'accident' is the adjectival predicate of a substantival subject in a particular affirmative proposition only.

7. *General Inquiries about the Analysis of Concepts and of Truths*[1] (1686)

Let us, for the present at any rate, omit all abstract terms, so that all terms are understood to refer to concrete things alone— whether these are substances, like the Ego, or phenomena, like the rainbow. So we shall not at present be concerned with the distinction between abstract and concrete terms; or at any rate, we shall not at present use any abstract terms other than those which are logical or conceptual, as, for example, 'The B-ness of A' merely stands for 'The fact that A is B'.

'The privative' is not-A. Not-not-A is the same as A.

'The positive' is A—that is to say, if it is not a not-Y of any kind, it being assumed at the same time that Y is not not-Z, and so on. Every term is understood to be positive, unless notice is given that it is privative. A positive term is the same as an 'entity'.

'Non-entity' is that which is purely privative, i.e. is the privative of everything, or, not-Y; that is, not-A, not-B, not-C, &c. This is what is meant when it is commonly said that nothingness has no properties.

We shall also accept every term here as complete, i.e. as a substantive, so that 'big' is the same as 'big entity', or, so to speak, as 'a big one'—just as a man with a big nose is called 'Nosey'. So we do not require the distinction between an adjective and a substantive, except perhaps to emphasize what is meant.

An entity is either in itself [*per se*] or accidental [*per accidens*]; or, a term is either necessary or mutable. Thus, 'man' is an entity in itself, but 'learned man' or 'king' are accidental entities. For that thing which is called 'a man' cannot cease to be a man except by annihilation; but someone can begin or cease to be a king, or learned, though he himself remains the same.

A term is either 'integral', i.e. complete, or it is 'partial', i.e. incomplete. It is integral or complete if, without any addition, it can be the subject or predicate of a proposition—e.g. 'entity', 'learned', 'the same as A', or 'similar to A'. It is partial or incomplete—e.g. 'the same' or 'similar'—when something (namely, 'to A') must be added for an integral term to arise. Further, what has to be added is added obliquely; a direct term which is added to an

---

[1] L.– Here I have made excellent progress.

integral can always be added and omitted without affecting the
integrity of the term. Two integral terms are joined 'directly' when
they constitute a new integral term. However, not every term to
which another is added 'obliquely' is partial; thus, 'sword' is
integral, even if by oblique addition it becomes 'the sword of
Evander'. So something non-direct can be omitted without
affecting the integrity of a term, as in this case the oblique 'of
Evander'. On the other hand an oblique term, if the direct term
is omitted, does not make an integral term. Therefore, if a term
which is integral in itself is added to another by means of some
inflexion or mark of connexion, in such a way that if the other is
omitted it does not make an integral term, then it is added obliquely.
But it is possible for an integral term to be made from an oblique
one which has been separated from an integral term; e.g. from the
oblique 'of Evander' there can be made 'that which is the property
of Evander', or, 'Evandrian'. But it will be useful to see that
terms are made integral. Some general signs of things or terms will
therefore be needed; so if we wish always to use in our symbolism
integral terms alone, we must say, not 'Caesar is like Alexander',
but 'Caesar is like the A which is Alexander', or 'like the thing
which is Alexander'. So our term will be, not 'like', but 'like the
A'. In the same way we shall not use the verbal expression 'the
sword of Evander', but shall speak of 'the sword which is the
property of Evander', in such a way that 'which is the property of
Evander' is one integral term. In this way we shall be able to
divide any composite term into integral terms. How far and in
what way this may be carried out, our progress will show. If we
always succeed in this, we shall have no other nouns but integrals.
We shall also see whether it will similarly be possible to form
integrals from particles themselves—e.g. 'A inexistent[1] in another,
which is B' in place of 'A in B'.

From this it is also evident that there are integral terms which
are analysed into partial terms, and direct terms into which (if
you analyse them, i.e. substitute a definition for what is defined)
C 358 it is manifest that oblique terms enter. Therefore, before one
explains the integral terms which are analysed into partial terms
and particles, partial terms must be explained, and also the particles
which, when added to oblique terms, make direct terms out of
them, and which make integral terms when added to partial terms.

---

[1] The word 'inexistent' (cf. pp. 122 ff. and 133 ff. below) renders the Latin
'inexistens'—literally 'existing in'. It must be stressed that in the word
'inexistent' the prefix 'in' does not have a negative sense; it resembles
the 'in' of 'inhere' rather than the 'in' of 'inactive'.

However, before partial terms and particles there must be explained those integral terms which either are not analysed, or are analysed only into integral terms. Such integral terms at any rate must be independent of partial terms; at least this is true of general integral terms, such as 'term' and 'entity'. For the partial terms themselves need these if they are to be transformed into integrals. For since the ultimate complement of a partial or an oblique term, which makes it into an integral one, is itself integral, it cannot again be analysed into an integral and a partial term. Such integral terms, which we cannot analyse into oblique and partial terms, must be enumerated; this will be done by analysis of the remainder. At first it will be sufficient to enumerate as purely integral those whose analysis into non-integral terms seems less necessary. Also, the analysis is to be carried out to such an extent that, by the use of a few integral terms, composed of partial and oblique terms, all the rest can be compounded from these directly, i.e. similarly, or, without oblique terms. So it will be possible to establish a few integral terms—or at any rate certain definite terms, or terms progressing in a definite series—which can be considered as primitive in a direct analysis and from which the other more composite terms arise, like derivative numbers from prime numbers. In this way each concept, in so far as it is analysed without obliquity, can have its own symbolic number assigned to it.

We have, therefore: first, *integral primitive simple terms*, which are unanalysable, or assumed in place of unanalysable terms, such as A. (I understand an integral term, for partial terms are made from an integral term and a particle; e.g. a 'part' is 'an entity in another', &c.) Second, *simple particles*, i.e. primitive syncategorematic terms, such as 'in'. Third, *primitive integral terms* composed of simple terms alone, and composed directly—i.e. without the mediation of particles or syncategorematic terms—such as AB. Fourth, *composite particles*, composed of simple particles alone, without the mediation of a (categorematic) term, such as 'with-in' [*cum-in*]. If this particle is later added to categorematic terms we can use it to designate a thing which *with* something is *in* something. Fifth, we have *integral derivative simple terms*. I call 'derivative' those which arise, not through composition alone—namely, similar composition, i.e. of a direct term with a direct term, such as AB—but through the mediation of some inflexion, or of a particle or syncategorematic term; for example, 'A in B', where A and B enter dissimilarly a term which is composed of them, namely 'A in B'. This difference between composition and derivation is in some degree observed by grammarians also. There are, therefore, simple derivative terms which cannot be analysed into

C 359

other derivative terms, but only into simple primitive terms with particles. Sixth, we have *integral derivative composite terms*, namely those which are compounded directly, i.e. similarly, from other derivative terms, and the latter are also obliquely compounded from primitive composite terms together with particles. Seventh, of those *derivative terms which consist of simple primitive terms and composite particles*, one may doubt whether they are simple rather than composite. Certainly, they cannot be analysed into other categorematic terms except by the duplication of one primitive term, in so far as, by compounding this now with one and now with another of the simple particles which make up the composite particle, two new simple derivative terms can be made, from which there can be made the proposed derivative term, as if it were composite. Eighth, just as we have primitive and derivative categorematic terms, so also there can be *derivative particles*. These again are *simple*[1] if composed of a simple particle and a primitive term, but (ninth) are *composite* if composed of a composite particle and a primitive term; these can be analysed into several derivative simple particles. Tenth, one may similarly doubt here what is to be said of a *derivative particle*,[1] *composed of a primitive composite term and a simple particle*.[2]

Now, however, we must consider the fact that not even the primitive simple particles are united so similarly as the primitive simple terms. And so many varieties can occur in the composition of particles. For example, if I say 'Paul's Peter's John'—i.e. John, the son of Peter, who was the son of Paul—there is a certain similarity of composition. But if I say 'Socrates, the son of Sophroniscus, from Athens', the composition of the particles or inflexions is dissimilar. From this there will doubtless arise various relations and various obliquities and mixtures of obliquities, in the accurate arrangement of which the chief part of the art of symbolism is contained. But it is not possible to judge adequately of these before the primitive simples, both in terms and in particles, are quite accurately determined; or, at any rate, before there are assumed in their place meanwhile certain terms which are derivative and composite, but which are fairly close to the primitive

---

[1] These words are not underlined in the text, but this should in consistency have been done.

[2] L.– Perhaps, however, it is better to arrange things so that all particles are left aside, just as all the oblique terms are, as has been said on the previous page. Unless perhaps there is the obstacle that in this way it will not appear easily what is to be referred to what.

(The reference to 'the previous page' is to the first page of the MS., which extends from the beginning of the paper to the end of the previous paragraph.)

simples, until gradually the way to a further analysis opens of its
own accord. Under 'particles' I also understand here some
primitive partial ones, if there are any which cannot be analysed
into other primitive partials. But I think that in fact they arise
from 'entity', or another integral term, with a particle.

Let the *primitive simple terms*, or those to be assumed for them
in the meantime, be the following:

'Term' (by which I understand both entity and non-entity).
'Entity', or, the possible. (I always understand something concrete, for I have excluded abstract terms as unnecessary.) 'Existent'. (Though in fact it is possible to assign a cause to existence,
and 'existent' can be defined as 'that which is compatible with more
things than anything else which is incompatible with it.' But at
present we keep away from these matters, as being too profound.)
'Individual'. (For even if every entity is really an individual, we
are defining terms which designate either any individual of a
certain given nature, or some certain determinate individual. For
example, 'man' or 'any man' means any individual who partici-
pates in human nature; but a certain individual is *this* one, whom I
designate either by pointing or by adding distinguishing marks.
For although there cannot be marks which distinguish it perfectly
from every other possible individual, there are however marks
which distinguish it from other individuals which we meet.) 'I'.
(There is something special and difficult to explain in this concept,
but since it is integral I thought it should be put here.)

Also primitive simple terms are all those confused phenomena
of the senses, which we perceive clearly but cannot explain distinctly, or define by other concepts, or designate by words. Thus,
we can say much to a blind man about extension, intensity, shape
and the other varieties which accompany colours; but besides
these accompanying distinct concepts there is something confused
in colour which a blind man cannot conceive by the assistance of
any words of ours, unless it is granted to him to open his eyes at
some time. In this sense, 'white', 'red', 'yellow' and 'blue', in so
far as they consist of this inexplicable expression of our imagina-
tion, are a kind of primitive terms. But since they are confused and
are of no assistance to our reasoning, it will be useful to avoid them
as far as possible by using instead of definitions their accompanying
distinct concepts, as far as these suffice to distinguish between
confused concepts. Sometimes it will even be useful to mix both
methods as convenience dictates, and so we can give their own
marks to primary terms of such a kind, after explaining the rest
through them. Thus, 'coloured' is a term explicable through its
relation to our eyes; but since that relation cannot be expressed

accurately without many words, and the eye itself, as a kind of machine, again needs a lengthy explanation, it will be possible for 'coloured' to be taken as a primitive simple term, by the addition to which of certain differentiating marks the various colours can be designated. Perhaps, however, 'coloured' can be defined through the perception of a surface without sensible contact. But which of these is the best will appear as we proceed.

It seems that there can be counted among primitive simple terms all concepts which contain matter of a certain quantity, i.e. in which homogeneous things agree—for example, 'having magnitude', 'extended', 'enduring', 'intensive'. But these concepts, unless I am mistaken, can be analysed further. In particular, it can be doubted whether the concepts of 'extended' and 'thinking' are simple. Many think that these are concepts which are conceived in themselves, and need no further analysis; but 'extended' seems to be 'continuous, with co-existing parts', and the term 'thinking' seems not to be integral, since it is related to some object which is thought. However, there is in thought itself some absolute reality which it is difficult to explain in words, and in extension we seem to conceive something else besides continuity and existence. Nevertheless, it seems a complete enough concept of extension if we conceive continued co-existence, such that all co-existents make one, and whatever is existent in the extended thing is continuable, i.e. continuously repeatable. Meanwhile, if it seems advantageous to assume as primitive simples 'extended', or even 'situation' (i.e. 'existing in a space'), and also 'thinking' (i.e. 'one thing expressing several with immanent action, or, conscious'), this will do no harm—especially if we then add certain axioms from which all other propositions may be deduced by the addition of definitions. But all this, as I have often said, will appear better as we actually proceed. And it is better to proceed, than to stick at the very beginning through being too fastidious.

Let us now try to explain 'partial terms', i.e. relative terms, from which there also arise the particles which denote the relation of terms. The first which occurs to me on inquiry is 'the same'. That A is the same as B means that one can be substituted for the other in any proposition without loss of truth.[1] For those relations are explained through propositions or truths. For example,

C 362

---

[1] L.– We must see whether, it being assumed that A can everywhere be substituted for B, it also follows that conversely B can be substituted everywhere for A. If these terms are similar in their inter-relations, the substitution is mutual. But if they are not related similarly, neither are they related in the same way to any third term, nor in consequence can the one be substituted for the other.

'Alexander the Great' and 'the king of Macedonia who conquered Darius', and again 'triangle' and 'trilateral', can be substituted for each other. That these coincide can always be shown by an analysis: namely, if they are analysed until it appears *a priori* that they are possible, and if the same terms appear formally, then different terms are the same. Let there be a term A and a term B: if for each of the two a definition is substituted, and for any constituent term another definition, until one arrives at primitive simple terms; if, moreover, there appears in the one what appears in the other, i.e. what is formally the same, A and B will therefore be 'coincident', or virtually the same. In this way, therefore, there can be defined:

'A coincides with B' if the one can be substituted in place of the other without loss of truth, or if, on analysing each of the two by substitution of their values (i.e. of their definitions) in place of the terms, the same terms appear on both sides: the same, I mean, formally—for example, if L, M and N appear on both sides. For those changes are made without loss of truth which are made by substituting a definition in place of a defined term, or conversely. Hence it follows that if A coincides with B, B also coincides with A.

The next concept is that A is the 'subject' and B the 'predicate' if B can be substituted in place of A without loss of truth; i.e. if, on analysing A and B, the same terms which appear in B also appear in A. The same can be explained in another way: that A is B if *every* A and *some* B coincide.

We have therefore the marks: 'coincident with B', 'subject' and 'predicate', 'is', 'every' and 'some'.

If it is said, 'Some A is B', the sense is, 'Some A and some B coincide'. From this there also follows, 'Some B is A'.

If every A and some B coincide, some A and some B also co-incide. But it appears that this can be proved from negatives; let us therefore proceed to these. $\quad$ *C 363*

Just as A and A are the first coincidentals, so A and not-A are the first disparates. A term is 'disparate' if it is false that some A is B. So if B = not-A, it is false that some A is B.

In general, if A is B, it is false that A is not-B.

If it is false that some A is not-B, it will be said that no A is not-B, i.e. that *every* A is B.

Hence this inference can be proved: Every A is B, therefore some A is B. The proof is this: every A and some B coincide, therefore some A and some B coincide. For if every A and some B coincide, it is therefore false that some A and some not-B coincide (by the definition of 'every'). Therefore it is true that some A and some B coincide.

But it is worth while to discuss more accurately the whole subject of propositions, and the relations of terms which arise from various propositions. For the origin of many partial terms and particles is to be derived from this.[1]

I say that propositions 'coincide' if one can be substituted for the other without loss of truth, or, if they imply each other reciprocally.

(1) The (direct) proposition L and the (reflexive) proposition 'L is true' coincide. Hence there coincide 'It is true that L is true' and 'Therefore L is true', and 'It is false that L is true' and 'Therefore L is false'. (These are rather to be distinguished in accordance with the propositions explained.) (In general, even if A is a term, it can always be said that 'A is true' coincides with something.)

    * 'L is true' and 'That L is false is false' coincide.

'That L is false is true' and 'L is false' coincide. I can prove this as a theorem, in this way. That L is false is a proposition which may be called M. Now, 'M is true' and M coincide (by 1). Therefore, substituting for M its value, 'That L is false is true' and 'L is false' coincide.

(The same is proved in another, though more prolix way by the use of * also. That L is false is true coincides with the proposition that it is false that L is false is false (by *), and that again with the proposition that it is false that L is true (also by *), and that, finally, with the proposition that L is false (by 1).)

(2) If A and B coincide, so also do not-A and not-B.

A not-A is a 'contradictory term' [*contradictorium*].

That which does not contain a contradictory term, i.e. A not-A, is 'possible'. That which is not Y not-Y is possible.

Not-not-A and A coincide; so if not-A and B coincide, not-B and A will also coincide.

(3) 'Not true' and 'false' coincide.

So 'not-false' and 'true' will coincide also.

If A = B, not-A = not-B.

If A = some truth, then not-A = not-(some truth), i.e. no truth, i.e. falsity, for not-A contains not-AY.[2]

C 364

---

[1] L.– (Any letter, such as A, B, L, &c., means for me either some integral term, or another integral proposition.)

(When one term is put for several, the latter are the definition or the assumed value, the former is the defined term: e.g. if for AB I put C, or when A = BC is a primitive proposition.)

(A and B coincide if, by the substitution of assumed values in place of terms, and conversely, the same true (or false) formula appears on both sides.)

[2] L.– Understand in all this that the terms are possible; for otherwise

(4) 'It is true that L is true' and 'It is not true that L is not true' coincide; so L and 'It is false that L is false' coincide. For L is the same as 'L is true', and this is the same as 'It is true that L is true' (by 1), which is the same as 'It is not true that L is not true'; and this is the same as 'It is false that L is false' (by 3).

L and 'It is not false that L is not false' coincide. For L is the same as 'It is true that L is true' (by 1), and this is the same as 'It is not false that L is not false' (by 3).

That L is false and that it is not false that L is not true coincide.

That L is false and that it is not true that L is not false coincide. These are easily proved from what precedes.

In general, if a proposition is called true or not true, false or not false, then true multiplied by true, and false by false, makes true. 'Not' multiplied by 'not' is equivalent to the omission of each 'not'.

C 365

From these it is also proved that every proposition is either true or false: i.e. if L is not true it is false. If it is true it is not false; if it is not false it is true; if it is false it is not true. (All this by 3.)

Propositions 1, 2, 3 and 4 serve as definitions, and so have been assumed without proof; for they indicate the use of certain signs, namely of truth and falsity, affirmation and negation.[1]

A is B (i.e. B is in A, or, B can be substituted for A).

A 'proposition' is 'A coincides with B', 'A does not coincide with B'.

(A and B can signify terms, or other propositions.)

(5) 'A does not coincide with B' is the same as 'It is false that A coincides with B'.

(6) If A coincides with B, B coincides with A.

(7) If A does not coincide with B, B does not coincide with A.

(8) If A coincides with B and B coincides with C, then A also coincides with C.

(9) If A coincides with B, not-A coincides with not-B.

These four axioms are corollaries of the definition that those terms coincide of which the one can be substituted for the other.

(10) A 'proposition true in itself' is 'A coincides with A'.

neither truth nor falsity has any place in the propositions into which these terms enter.

[1] L.– I say that something is impossible or contains a contradiction, whether it is an incomplex term which contains A not-A, or is a proposition which either says that there coincide those terms of which the one contains the contradictory of the other, or contains an impossible incomplex term. For as often as those terms of which one contains the contradictory of the other are said to coincide, this term contains a contradictory term; and as often as something contains that whose contradictory it contains, it contains a contradictory term. So when an impossible proposition is used, a contradictory incomplex term appears.

(11) A 'proposition false in itself' is 'A coincides with not-A'.

(12) From this it is inferred that it is false that not-A coincides with A (by 6).

(13) It is also inferred that it is true that A does not coincide with not-A (by 5).

These propositions could be regarded as true by inference.

C 366 　As I have remarked, A here means either a term or a proposition; so not-A means either a term which is the contradictory of a term or a proposition which is the contradictory of a proposition.

(14) If a proposition is assumed and nothing is added, it is understood to be true. This coincides with 1.

(15) Not-B coincides with not-B. This is a corollary of 10, assuming that not-B coincides with A.

(16) An 'affirmative proposition' is 'A is B', or, 'A contains B', or, as Aristotle says, 'B is in A' (that is, directly). That is, if we substitute a value for A, 'A coincides with BY' will appear. For example, man is an animal, i.e. man is the same as a —— animal (namely, man is the same as a rational animal). For by the sign Y I mean something undetermined, so that BY is the same as some B, or a —— animal (where 'rational' is understood, provided that we know what is to be understood), or, some animal. So 'A is B' is the same as 'A is coincident with some B', or, A = BY.[1]

(17) So there coincide the propositions that A is B and that some B coincides with A; or, BY = A.

(18) From the nature of this symbolism A, AA, AAA &c. coincide —or 'man', 'man man' and 'man man man'. So if anyone should be called both a man and an animal, by analysing 'man' into 'rational animal' he will be called equally a rational animal and an animal, i.e. a rational animal.[2]

(19) If A is B, B can be put for A, where only containing is in question: e.g. if A is B and B is C, A will be C. This is proved from the nature of coincidence, for coincidentals can be substituted for one another. (Except in the case of propositions which you could call formal, where one of the coincidentals is assumed

C 367 　formally in such a way that it is distinguished from the others; but these are reflexive, and do not so much speak about a thing, as

---

[1] L.– It is noteworthy that for 'A = BY' it is also possible to say 'A = AB', and so there is no need for the assumption of a new letter. But this notation presupposes that AA is the same as A, for a redundancy arises.

[2] L.– From this it is also evident that from AC = ABD we may not infer C = BD; for it is evident that in A = AB we may not omit A on both sides. For it to be inferred from AC = ABD that C = BD, it must be presupposed that nothing which is contained in A is contained in C unless it is also contained in BD, and conversely.

about our way of conceiving it—where there is a distinction between these.) So when (by 16) A = BY and B = CZ, A = CYZ; or, A contains C.[1]

(20) It must be noted—and this should have been stated earlier in this calculus—that one letter can be put for any number of letters together: e.g. YZ = X. However, this has not yet been used in this calculus of reason, so that confusion does not arise.

(21) Definite letters I indicate by the earlier letters of the alphabet, indefinite letters by the later ones, unless otherwise indicated.

(22) For any number of definite letters there can be substituted one definite letter, whose value, or definition, is those letters for which it has been substituted.

(23) For any definite letter there can be substituted an indefinite letter not yet used. One can in the same way substitute for any number of definite letters, and for definite and indefinite letters: i.e. one can put A = Y.

(24) To any letter a new indefinite one can be added; e.g. for A we can put AY. For A = AA (by 18) and A is Y (or, for A one can put Y, by 23); therefore A = AY.

(25) That A is B (A contains B) implies (contains) that some B is (contains) A.

For (that A is B) = (BY = A) (by 17) = (BY = AY) (by 24) = Some B is A (by 17).

(26) We must note something else about this calculus which we should have stated earlier: namely, that what is generally asserted or concluded, not as an hypothesis, about any letters which have not yet been used, is to be understood of any number of other letters. So if A = AA, it will also be possible to say B = BB.

(27) Some B = YB, and therefore similarly some A = ZA. The latter may be said in imitation of the former (by 26), but a new indefinite letter—namely, Z—is to be assumed for the latter equation, just as Y had been assumed a little earlier.

(28) I usually take as universal a term which is posited simply: e.g. 'A is B', i.e. 'Every A is B', or, 'The concept of B is contained in the concept of A'.

(29) A is B, therefore some A is B; or, that A contains B implies or contains that some A contains B. For A is B = AY is B (by 24).

(30) That A is B and B is A is the same as that A and B coincide;   C 368

---

[1] L.–We may also have some general indefinite term, such as 'some entity' or 'something', as in common speech, and then no coincidence arises.

i.e. A coincides with B, which coincides with A. For A = BY and B = AZ; therefore (by 31) A = AYZ. Therefore YZ are superfluous letters; or, Z is contained in A. Therefore for 'B = AZ' one can say 'B = A'.

(31) One must also note this: if A = AY, then either Y is superfluous (or rather is a general term, such as 'entity') and can be omitted with impunity, like unity in the case of arithmetical multiplication, or Y is in A. Indeed, Y is always in A, if it is said that A = YA.

(32) A 'negative proposition' is 'A does not contain B', or 'It is false that A is (contains) B'.[1]

(32)[2] B not-B is impossible; or, if B not-B = C, C will be impossible.[3]

(33) So if A = not-B, AB will be impossible.

(34) 'That which contains B not-B' is the same as 'impossible'; or, 'EB not-B' is the same as 'impossible'.

(35) A 'false proposition' is one which contends that AB contains not-B (assuming that B and A are possible). I understand B and Y both of terms and of propositions.[4]

(36) A = B, therefore A is B; or, A = B contains that A is B. For if there is a superfluous Y we shall have A = BY, i.e. A is B.[5] The same is proved in another way: A = B is the same as that A = BY and B = AY, therefore A = B contains A = BY. Also, A = B, therefore AA = BA; therefore A = BA; therefore A is B.

(37) B is B. For B = B (by 10), therefore B is B (by 36).

C 369 (38) AB is B. This is indemonstrable, and is either an identical proposition or a definition, either of 'is', or of 'contains', or of 'a true proposition'. For what is meant is that AB (or, that which contains B) is B, i.e. contains B.

(39) If B contains C, then AB contains C. For AB is B (by 38), B is C (by hypothesis), therefore AB is C (by 19).

---

[1] L.– N.B. If B is a proposition, not-B is the same as that B is false, or, B's being false ['τὸ B esse falsum']. Not-B, understanding B of a proposition which is materially necessary, is either necessary or impossible. However, this does not hold in the case of incomplex terms.

I take a concept to be both incomplex and complex, and a term to be an incomplex categorematic concept.

[2] *Sic.* In this paragraph Leibniz puts a dot between 'B' and 'non-B'; as this is omitted in par. 34 it is omitted in the translation.

[3] L.– In the case of complex terms 'impossible' is 'non-entity'; in the case of complex terms it is 'false'.

[4] L.– That A contains B and A contains C is the same as that A contains BC. So if A contains B, it also contains AB. So if AB contains not-B, AB will also contain AB not-B.

[5] The text has 'A = B', but 'A est B' must be meant.

(40) A 'true proposition' is one which coincides with 'AB is B', or, which can be reduced to this primary truth. (I think that this can also be applied to non-categorical propositions.)

(41) Therefore, since a false proposition is one which is not true (by 3), it follows (by 40) that a false proposition is the same as a proposition which does not coincide with 'AB is B'; or, a false proposition is the same as one which cannot be proved.

Propositions of fact cannot always be proved by us, and so they are assumed as hypotheses.

(42) Of the propositions 'A contains B' and 'A does not contain B', the one is true and the other is false, i.e. they are 'opposites'. For if one can be proved, the other cannot, provided that the terms are possible; therefore (by 41) they are not at the same time true or false.

(43) It is false that B contains not-B; or, B[1] does not contain not-B. Each of these is evident from what precedes. For however you analyse them, this pattern [*forma*] always remains, and will never become 'AB is B'. This is also evident in another way. B contains B (by 37): therefore it does not contain not-B, otherwise it would be impossible (by 32).

(44) In the same way it is evident that it is false that not-B contains B.

(45) It is false that B and not-B coincide. This is evident from 43 and 44.

(But these assume that the term B is possible.)

(46) It is false that AB contains not-B; or, AB does not contain not-B. (I suppose AB to be possible.) This is proved in the same way as 43; for AB contains B, therefore it does not contain not-B, since it is not impossible (by 32).[2]

(47) 'A contains B' is a 'universal affirmative in respect of A', the subject.

(48) 'AY contains B' is a 'particular affirmative in respect of A'.

(49) If AB is C, it follows that AY is C; or, it follows that some A is C. For it can be assumed, by 23, that B = Y.

(50) 'AY is not B' is a 'universal negative'.

(51) Hence it follows that a universal negative and a particular affirmative are opposites; or, if the one is true, the other is false (by 48 and 50).

(52) A particular affirmative can be converted *simpliciter*; i.e., if some A is B it follows that some B is A. I prove this as follows. AY is B, by hypothesis; that is (by 16) AY coincides with BY.

C 370

---

[1] Corrected by Couturat from the 'A' of the text.
[2] L.– We must take care not to use syllogisms which we have not yet proved to be legitimate.

Therefore (by 6) BY coincides with AY; therefore (by 16) BY is A. Q.E.D.[1]

(53) A universal negative is converted *simpliciter*; i.e. if no A is B, it follows that no B is A. For AY is not B (by hypothesis); therefore AY does not coincide with BY (by 16); therefore BY does not coincide with AY (by 6); therefore (by 16) BY is not A. Q.E.D.

(54) A universal affirmative is converted *per accidens*; i.e. if every A is B, it follows that some B is A. For A is B (by hypothesis); therefore some A is B (by 29); therefore (by 52)[2] some B is A. This can be shown more briefly. A coincides with BY (by 16); therefore BY coincides with A (by 6); therefore (by 36) BY is A. It will be worth while to compare these two proofs, so that it may be seen whether they come to the same, or whether they reveal the truth of some proposition assumed hitherto without proof.[3]

(55) If A contains B and A is true, B also is true. By 'a false letter'[4] I understand either a false term (i.e. one which is impossible, or, is a non-entity) or a false proposition. In the same way 'true' can be understood as either a possible term or a true proposition. As is explained later, I count the whole syllogism as a proposition also. What I assert here can also be stated in this way: any part of the true is true, or, what is contained in the true is true.

This can be proved from what follows.

(56) 'True' in general I define in this way: A is 'true' if, when we substitute a value for A, and treat in the same way as A (if possible) anything which enters into the value of A, there never arises B and not-B, i.e. a contradiction. From this it follows that for us to be certain of a truth, either the analysis must be continued to primary truths—at least, either to that which has already been treated by such a method, or to that which is agreed to be true—or it must be proved that from the very progression of the

C *371*

---

[1] L.– Fundamental, i.e. undemonstrated propositions should be denoted by capitals, such as LI (or, at the same time, by common [?] and different numbers).
    (The word rendered as 'common' is obscure in the MS.)
[2] Corrected by Couturat from the '53' of the text.
[3] L.– We must speak of the comparison between 'No A is B' and 'Every A is not-B'; also of the conversion by contraposition of the universal affirmative. Will it be correct to say 'Every A is not B' for 'No A is B'?
[4] After first writing 'Per falsam literam . . . . . .' Leibniz later inserted the phrase 'veram vel' between 'per' and 'falsam', giving 'By "a true letter" or "a false letter" . . . . . .'. However, in this sentence he is defining a false letter only (cf. Schmidt, p. 489).

analysis, i.e. from a certain general relation between preceding analyses and the one which follows, nothing of this kind will ever appear, however long the analysis is continued. This is particularly worth noting, for in this way we can often be freed from a long continuation of an analysis. It can also happen that the analysis of letters itself contains something about the analyses of those which follow, such as the analysis of 'true' here. It can also be doubted whether every analysis must necessarily end with primary truths, i.e. with what is unanalysable—especially in the case of contingent truths, as there is no time for these to be reduced to identical propositions.

(57) I define 'false in general' as that which is not true. For it to be established that something is false, therefore, it is necessary either that it should be the opposite of a truth, or that it should contain the opposite of a truth, or that it should contain a contradiction (i.e. B and not-B), or that it should be proved that, however long an analysis is continued, it cannot be proved that it is true.

(58) Therefore what contains the false is false.

(59) But something can contain a truth and yet be false—namely, if (by 58) it also contains something false.

(60) We also seem able to learn from this the distinction between necessary truths and others—namely, that necessary truths are those which can be reduced to identical propositions, or whose opposites can be reduced to contradictory propositions, and that impossible propositions are those which can be reduced to contradictory propositions, or whose opposites can be reduced to identical propositions.

(61) Possible propositions are those of which it can be proved that a contradiction will never arise in their analysis. True contingent propositions are those which need an analysis continued to infinity. False contingent propositions are those whose falsity can be proved only by the fact that it cannot be proved that they are true. It seems doubtful whether it is sufficient to prove a truth that, on continued analysis, it should be certain that no contradiction will arise; for it will follow from this that everything possible is true. For my part, I call an incomplex term which is possible 'true', and one which is impossible I call 'false'. But doubt is possible about a complex term, such as 'that A contains B', or 'that A is B'. (I understand the analysis of a complex term into other complex terms.) Thus, let (that A is B) = L, let B = CD, let (that A is C) = M, and let (that A is D) = N; then we shall have L = MN. If the subject A is analysed, part of its value cannot be substituted for A, but its whole value must be

C 372

substituted. (I give this reminder in passing.) And if C = EG, D = FG, and A = EFG, M can be analysed into the two equations (A = EFG) = P and (EFG = EG) = Q; i.e. we shall have M = PQ. Similarly, N can be analysed into the two equations (A = EFG) = P and (EFG = FG) = R; therefore L = PQR. These are primary truths, for P is an hypothesis—namely, a definition or a datum of experience [*experimentum*]—whilst R and Q are primary axioms. However, if we proceed further, it is required of a definition that there should be agreement that it is possible. That is, it is necessary that it should be proved that A is possible, or, that it should be proved that EFG does not involve a contradiction; i.e. that X not-X is not involved. But this can be known only by experience, if it is agreed that A exists, or has existed, and so is possible. (Or at least, if it is agreed that something like A has existed. However, perhaps this case cannot really arise, for two complete things are never similar, and where incomplete things are concerned it is sufficient that one of two similar things should exist for the incomplete thing, i.e. the common denomination, to be called possible. (However, this seems to be useful; thus, if one sphere has existed, it can rightly be said that any sphere is possible.))[1] So it is evident that the argument proceeds in the same way in the case of complex and of incomplex terms. For to prove that a complex term is true is to reduce it to other true complex terms, and these finally into complex terms which are primary truths—that is, into axioms (i.e. propositions which are known through themselves), definitions of incomplex terms which have been proved to be true, and the data of experience. Similarly, incomplex terms are proved to be true by reducing them to other true incomplex terms, and these finally into other incomplex terms which are primary truths; that is, into terms conceived through themselves, or else into terms which we have experienced. (Or whose like we have experienced. Though there is no need to add this, for it can be

C 373

proved that if one possible thing exists out of a number of similar things, the others are possible[2] also.) The result is that every analysis, both of complex and of incomplex terms, ends in axioms, terms conceived through themselves, and the data of experience. This analysis is made by substituting a value for any term; for even when a content is substituted for a container, an indefinite value is substituted, as we have shown above in no. 16.

(62) But every true proposition can be proved. Therefore (since the data of experience are again true propositions) it follows that,

---

[1] L.– If something like a thing is possible, that thing itself is also possible.
[2] Corrected by Couturat from the 'similia' of the text.

if there is no other means of proof than that described a little before, the data of experience can again be analysed into axioms, terms conceived through themselves, and data of experience. But there can be no primary data of experience unless they are known through themselves, i.e. are axioms.

(63) It is a question whether the data of experience can be analysed into others *ad infinitum*, and (without reference to data of experience) whether it is possible for some proof to be such that it is found that the proof of the proposition always presupposes the proof of another, which is neither an axiom nor a definition, and so needs proof again. Hence it is also necessary that some incomplex terms can be analysed continually in such a way that one never arrives at terms which are conceived through themselves. Otherwise, when the analysis has been completed, it will appear whether the virtual coincidence becomes formal or express, i.e. whether a reduction has been made to an identical proposition.

(64) The question is, therefore, whether it is possible for the analysis of incomplex terms to be sometimes capable of being continued *ad infinitum*, so that one never arrives at terms which are conceived through themselves. Certainly, if there are in us no concepts conceived through themselves which can be grasped distinctly, or only one (e.g. the concept of entity), then it follows that no proposition can be proved perfectly by the reason. For even if it can be proved perfectly, without the data of experience, from the definitions and axioms assumed, yet the definitions presuppose the possibility of the terms, and so their analysis either into terms which are conceived through themselves, or into those discovered in experience; so we return to the data of experience, or, to other propositions.

(65) But if we say that the continuation of an analysis *ad infinitum* is possible, then it can at any rate be noticed whether one's progress in analysis can be reduced to some rule; from this a similar rule of progression will appear in the proof of complex terms, which have as ingredients incomplex terms which can be analysed *ad infinitum*.

C 374

(66) But if, when the analysis of the predicate and of the subject has been continued, a coincidence can never be proved, but it does at least appear from the continued analysis (and the progression and its rule which arise from it) that a contradiction will never arise, then the proposition is possible. But if, in analysing it, it appears from the rule of progression that the reduction has reached a point at which the difference between what should coincide is less than any given difference, then it will have been proved that the proposition is true. If, on the other hand, it appears

from the progression that nothing of this sort will ever arise, then it has been proved to be false—that is to say, in the case of necessary propositions.[1]

(67) A necessary proposition is one whose opposite is not possible, or, such that if one assumes its opposite one reaches a contradiction on analysing it. Therefore that proposition is necessary which can be proved by means of identical propositions and definitions, with no use of experience other than for it to be agreed that a term is possible.

(68) But something still has to be examined, if I am to know that I am proceeding correctly as I define something. If I say that A = EFG, then I must know not only that E, F and G are severally possible, but also that they are compatible with each other. But it is evident that this cannot be done except by experience, either of the thing itself or of another thing which is like it, at any rate in the respect under consideration. Someone may say that I can, at all

C 375

events, know this from the ideas which are contained in my mind whilst I know by experience [*experior*] that I am conceiving EFG, which I call A. I reply that when I say that I conceive E, I can either conceive something which I know by experience to involve nothing else, or conceive something which is again composite and is confusedly apprehended by me. If I know by experience that E involves nothing else, i.e. is conceived through itself, then it can be admitted that it is possible. Only identical propositions, however, can be asserted about such a thing; otherwise I have stated falsely that I know by experience something which involves nothing else. If I know by experience that E involves several things, these are again to be treated similarly; but as often as I combine several things which are not conceived through themselves, experience is needed—not only of the fact that they are conceived by me at the same time in the same subject (for such a

---

[1] L.– A doubtful point: is everything true which cannot be proved false, or everything false which cannot be proved true? What, then, of the cases of which neither of these holds? It must be said that both truth and falsity can always be proved, at any rate by an analysis which is carried to infinity. But then it is contingent, i.e. it is possible that it is true, or that it is false. The same is the case with concepts: namely, that in an analysis which is carried to infinity they are manifestly true or false, that is, to be admitted to existence, or not. N.B. In this way, will a true concept be existent, a false one non-existent? Every impossible concept is false, but not every possible concept is true; so that concept will be false which neither exists nor will exist, as a proposition of such a kind is false; &c. Unless, perhaps, we prefer to take no account of existence in these cases, and a true concept here is the same as a possible one, and a false concept the same as an impossible one—except when, for example, 'Pegasus existing' is said.

concept is confused), but also of the fact that they really exist in the same subject.

(69) So it is one of the first principles that terms which we discover to exist in the same subject do not involve a contradiction. Or, if A is B and A is C, then BC is possible, i.e. does not involve a contradiction.

(70) God, from the data of his intellectual experience alone [*ex solis . . . . . . intellectus sui experimentis*] and without any perception of anything else, judges about the possibility of things.

(71) What is to be said about the propositions 'A is an existent', or, 'A exists'? Thus, if I say of an existing thing, 'A is B', it is the same as if I were to say 'AB is an existent'; e.g. 'Peter is a denier', i.e. 'Peter denying is an existent'. The question here is how one is to proceed in analysing this; i.e. whether the term 'Peter denying' involves existence, or whether 'Peter existent' involves denial—or whether 'Peter' involves both existence and denial, as if you were to say, 'Peter is an actual denier', i.e. is an existent denier; which is certainly true. Undoubtedly, one must speak in this way; and this is the difference between an individual or complete term and another. For if I say, 'Some man is a denier', 'man' does not contain 'denial', as it is an incomplete term, nor does 'man' contain all that can be said of that of which it can itself be said.

(72) So if we have BY, and the indefinite term Y is superfluous (i.e., in the way that 'a certain Alexander the Great' and 'Alexander the Great' are the same), then B is an 'individual'.[1]

(73) But it is asked what 'existent' means: for an existent is an entity, i.e. a possible, and something else. All things considered, I do not see what is conceived in 'existent' other than some degree of entity, since it can be applied to various entities. Though I would not wish to say that 'that something exists' is possible, i.e. possible existence. For this is simply essence itself; we, on the other hand, understand actual existence, i.e. something added to possibility or essence, so that in that sense possible existence would be the same as actuality abstracting from actuality, which is absurd. I say, therefore, that an existent entity is that which is compatible with most things, i.e. is the most possible entity, and so all co-existents are equally possible. Or, what comes to the same, 'existent' is what pleases something intelligent and powerful; but in this way existence itself is presupposed. However, this definition at least can be given: 'existent' is what would please some mind, and would not please another more powerful mind, if minds of any kind were assumed to exist. So it comes to this,

C 376

[1] L.– If there is a term BA and B is an individual, A will be superfluous; or, if BA = C, then B = C.

that there is said to 'exist' that which would not displease the most powerful mind, if it should be assumed that a most powerful mind exists. But so that this definition shall be applicable to experience, it must rather be stated as follows: there 'exists' that which pleases some (existent) mind ('existent' must not be added if we seek a definition, and not a simple proposition), and does not displease (absolutely) the most powerful mind. But it is pleasing to a mind that there should be made that which has a reason rather than that which does not have a reason. So if there are several things, A, B, C and D, and one of these is to be chosen, and if B, C and D are alike in all respects, A alone being distinguished from the rest in some way, then A will please any mind which understands this. It is the same if a distinction does not at any rate *appear* between B, C and D, but does appear between them and A, and the mind decides to choose; it will choose A. But it chooses freely, for it can still ask whether there is not a distinction between B, C and D.

(74) All existential propositions, though true, are not necessary, for they cannot be proved unless an infinity of propositions is used, i.e. unless an analysis is carried to infinity. That is, they can be proved only from the complete concept of an individual, which involves infinite existents. Thus if I say, 'Peter denies', understanding this of a certain time, then there is presupposed also the nature of that time, which also involves all that exists during that time. If I say 'Peter denies' indefinitely, abstracting from time, then for this to be true—whether he has denied, or is about to deny—it must nevertheless be proved from the concept of Peter. But the concept of Peter is complete, and so involves infinite things; so one can never arrive at a perfect proof, but one always approaches it more and more, so that the difference is less than any given difference.

C 377

(75) If, as I hope, I can conceive all propositions as terms, and hypotheticals as categoricals, and if I can treat all propositions universally, this promises a wonderful ease in my symbolism and analysis of concepts, and will be a discovery of the greatest importance. Certainly, in general I call a term 'false' which in the case of incomplex terms is an impossible, or at any rate a meaningless term, and in the case of complex terms is an impossible proposition, or at any rate a proposition which cannot be proved; and so an analogy remains. So by A I understand either an incomplex term, or a proposition, or a collection, or a collection of collections, &c. So, in general, that term is 'true' which can be perfectly understood.

(76) Besides 'entity' we shall also use 'entities', from which there proceeds the whole and the part. In general, if A is not B and B

is not A, and the proposition 'A is L and B is L is the same as C is L' is primitive, then C is called a 'whole' and A (or B) a 'part'. It can be doubted whether and how far C is one real entity; whether one entity does not always result from several, even if they are scattered; and when this results or does not result.[1]

(76)[2] Not-A is not-(AB), or, not-A = Y not-AB. Every not-man is a not-(rational man). This follows from 77.

(77) In general, 'A is B' is the same as 'Not-B is not-A'. Whence the preceding proof; for AB is A, therefore not-A is not-AB.[3] It must be seen if this can be proved.

(This is proved below, 95 and 99.)

(78) A = B and not-A = not-B coincide.

(79) But if A is B, it does not follow that not-A is not-B; or, if man is an animal, it does not follow that a not-man is a not-animal. So although B can be substituted for A, one may not therefore substitute not-B for not-A, unless A in turn can be substituted for B.

(80) It must be seen whether it is possible to do without indefinite terms [*infinitis*]. Certainly, not-A seems to be the same as that which is not A, i.e. the subject of a negative proposition whose predicate is A; or, every thing which is not A. So if $\bar{Y}$ is not A, then $\bar{Y}$ = not-A; i.e. Y ≠ AX is the same as $\bar{Y}$ = not-A. $C\ 378$

(81) I use $\bar{Y}$, or the indefinite Y with a line, to mean 'anything' [*quilibet*]. Y is one indeterminate thing [*incertum*], $\bar{Y}$ is anything.

(82) It is also possible to say that 'B is not A' is the same as 'B is not-A'. So 'B ≠ AY' is the same as 'B = Y not-A'.

(83) Generally, 'A is B' is the same as 'A = AB'; for it is clear from this that B is contained in A, and that 'man' and 'man animal' are the same. I have already noted this in the margin of article 16 above; and though it might seem from this that man is a rational animal animal, an animal animal is the same as an animal, as I noted above in article 18.

(84) Hence if the proposition 'A is B' is said to be false, i.e. is denied, this is to say that A ≠ AB, i.e. that some A is not B.

(85) That A is not B is the same as to say that A = A (not-B). This is evident from 83. If you say that A = A not-B is false, or, that A ≠ A[4] not-B, this means that some A is B.

---

[1] L.– There is a continuum when the parts are indefinite.

Number arises if it is considered only that entities are several, and not that they are of certain kinds.

[2] *Sic.*

[3] Corrected by Couturat, from the 'est non B' of the text.

[4] Couturat notes that the second 'A' is missing from the MS.

(86) Again, not-B is the same as that which is not B, or, the genus whose species are A, C, D, etc., granted that A is not B, C is not B, and D is not B.

(87) Consequently, that no A is B is the same as that A is not-B, i.e. that any A is one of those things which are not B. Or, 'AY $\neq$ ABY' is the same as 'A = A not-B'. We have therefore a passage between indefinite affirmatives and negatives.

(88) A remark in passing: in general, that A is AB is the same as that A coincides with AB; i.e. if the proposition 'A is AB' is true, this will be reciprocal. I prove this as follows. A is AB by hypothesis, that is (by 83) A = AAB; i.e. (by 18) A = AB. The same is proved as follows: A is AB (by hypothesis) and AB is A (by 38); therefore (by 30) A = AB. These two proofs should be compared, for they will either end in the same, or they will afford a proof of some proposition which has been assumed without proof.[1]

C 379

(89) Let us consider the particular affirmative, 'Some animal is a man': BY = AZ. This can also be changed into BY = ABY; or, it can be said that that some animal is a man is the same as that some animal is a man-animal. This is evident from 83. It does not matter that Y is indeterminate—for whatever it is, let it be supposed to be known and to be present; then the reasoning would be valid.

(90) However, although in this way the indefinite Y can always be avoided in the predicate, it cannot be avoided in the subject; and it is better that it should be left even in the predicate, since inversion is clearer. In general, since indefinite letters cannot be eliminated absolutely, it is better for them to be left.[2]

(91) A is B, therefore A is not not-B. For let it be true that A is not-B, assuming that this is possible. Now, A is B (by hypothesis), therefore A is B not-B, which is absurd. (Add no. 100[3] below.)[4]

(92) The inference 'If A is not not-B, then A is B' is invalid. That is, it is indeed false that every animal is a not-man, but it does not follow from this that every animal is a man.

(93) If A is B, not-B is not-A. Let it be false (assuming that this is possible) that not-B is not-A, i.e. that not-B is not A; then it will be true that not-B is A. Therefore some A is not-B, and so it is false that every A is B, contrary to the hypothesis.

---

[1] Leibniz added 'NB' in the margin against this phrase.
[2] L.– Yet I think that they can be eliminated.
[3] Corrected by Couturat from the '99' of the text.
[4] L.– This method of reasoning, i.e. *reductio ad absurdum*, has already been established in what precedes.

(94) If not-B is not-A, A is B. Let it be false (assuming that this is possible) that A is B. Therefore A will be not-B, and so some not-B will be A (by conversion). Therefore it is false that some not-B is not-A (by 91);[1] much more, therefore, is it false that every not-B is not-A, contrary to the hypothesis.

(95) That A is B is the same as that not-B is not-A. This is evident from 93 and 94, with the addition of 30. It must be seen whether proposition 95 cannot be proved by itself, without 93 and 94.

(This is shown by article 99.)[2]

(96) Not-not-A = A.

(97) 'No A is B' is the same as 'A is not-B' (by 87).

(98) 'Every A is B' is the same as 'No A is not-B', i.e. 'Some A is not not-B'. This is evident from 97 or 87, simply putting not-B for B, and not-not-B, i.e. B, for not-B.   *C 380*

(99) 'A is B' is the same as 'A is not-not-B' (by 96), and the latter is the same (by 87) as 'No A is not-B';[3] that is, 'No not-B is A' (by conversion of the universal negative). That is (by 87), every not-B is not-A = A is B. Q.E.D.

(100) If A is B, it follows that A is not not-B, i.e. that it is false that every A is not-B. For if A is B, then no A is not-B, i.e. it is false that some A is not-B (by 87). Therefore (by 101) it is much more false that every A is not-B. Add no. 91.

(101) If it is false that some A is B, it is false that every A is B; or, what is the same, some A is not B, therefore every A is not B. For let it be granted (assuming that this is possible) that every A is B; therefore some A is B (by 29). But this is contrary to the hypothesis, and so is false; therefore the former is false also.

(102) If A is B and A is C, this is the same as 'A is BC'.

(103) If A is not-B and A is not-C, this is the same as 'A is not-B not-C'.

(104) Not-B is not-(BC) (this has been proved as no. 76), but it is not always the case that not-(BC)[4] is not-B. A formal or general mode of the proposition should have been devised, as if I were saying 'It is false that every composite negative is a simple negative, or, not-$\overline{YX}$ ≠ not-$\overline{Y}$', in such a way that $\overline{Y}$ and $\overline{X}$ signify any propositions which are similar.

(105) If A is not-(BC) it does not therefore follow either that A is not-B or that A is not-C; for it can happen that B = LM and C = NP, and that A is not-(LN),[4] so that A will be not-(LMNP), or,

---

[1] Corrected by Couturat from the '31' of the text.
[2] Corrected by Couturat from the '98' of the text.
[3] The text has another '87' here.
[4] The text does not bracket this expression; parentheses, however, seem required by the sense.

not-(BC). Meanwhile, it follows from this that it is false that, at the same time, A is B and A is C, i.e. that A is BC. This is evident from 91 or 100.[1]

(106) It is evident from this that 'not' must be separated as little as possible from the letter or formula to which it is prefixed in the calculus.

(107) Every $\overline{\overline{\text{combination}}}$ of propositions can be represented generally as $\overline{\text{A B C D}}$ &c. We can say that $\overline{\text{AB}} = \text{L}$, $\overline{\text{LC}} = \text{M}$, $\overline{\text{MD}} = \text{N}$, assuming that some of these, such as L or M or N, can be analysed similarly, and that the terms into which they are analysed can perhaps be analysed again, according to circumstances. The line drawn above, such as $\overline{\text{AB}}$, can indicate affirmation or negation, or rather coincidence or the lack of it; the line can have marks in the middle and at the ends—in the middle to indicate the mode of the proposition, whether it is affirmative or negative, &c., whilst the end of the line which is over A can have a mark which will show whether A is a universal or a particular term, &c., and similarly the end of the line which is over B will show the same of B. If we have

C 381

```
    4                    5     6
  ┌─────────────────┬──────┐ ┌───┐
    1       2        3
  ┌───────┬────────┬──┐
    A       B        C
```

place 1 will show the quantity or quality, &c., in accordance with which the term A is used here—i.e. the mode of use of the term A—place 2 will show the nature of the proposition AB, and place 3 the mode of the term B. Place 4 will show the mode of use of AB, or L, place 5 the nature of the proposition $\overline{\overline{\text{ABC}}}$ or $\overline{\text{LC}}$, and place 6 the mode of the term C.[2] It is possible to observe an order in the numbers such that we always begin from what is most subdivided, i.e. from the lowest grade of subdivision, or, from terms which are nearer to incomplex terms—as, e.g.,

```
 13                            14                       15
┌─────────────────────────────────────────────────┐ ┌──────┐
 10        11                  12
┌───────┬─────────┬──────────┐
     7        8           9
    ┌────┬──────┬──────────┐
         1    2      3      4    5    6
        ┌──┬───┬──────┐   ┌───┬────┐
 A    B      C    D         E    F
```

---

[1] Corrected by Couturat from the '99' of the text.
[2] Corrected by Couturat, from the '5' and 'B' of the text.

From this it can be understood in what astonishing ways the
relations and denominations of terms can be varied—both in
respect of order, if you consider only the disposition of the numbers, and in respect of the value of each number, if the topic is
quantity and quality alone.

(108) Every term, even an incomplex one, can be regarded as a
proposition, as if 'this entity' [τὸ hoc Ens] were added to it. Thus
'man' can be taken as if it were said that man is the same as this
entity, namely, is that which it is—that is (or rather, more generally)
as if 'fact' [τὸ verum] were added, e.g. 'Man is a fact', 'Man is an
animal is this fact'. 'This fact' functions here like unity in arithmetic, for filling up places or dimensions. That is to say, if it is
supposed that anything which is joined with something is subdivided in as many ways as that with which it is joined, so that a
term is assumed to be joined only to one which is equally complex
or incomplex, and if 'fact' or 'unity' is written as V, we shall get in
place of the preceding table the one which follows,[1] where the
places have been filled. For it can be said that 'A (is the same as   *C 382*
this fact)' is the same as 'This fact is this fact'. But it is to be noted
that the V which has been supplied must be changed everywhere:
A = A is a fact, i.e. A = a fact [?].[2]

43						44							45
37		38			39	40			41				42
25	26	27	28	29	30	31	32	33	34	35			36
1 2	3 4	5 6	7 8	9 10	11 12	13 14	15 16	17 18	19 20	21 22	23 24		
A V	V V	B V	C D	E V	V V	F V	V V						

(109) Just as any term can be conceived as a proposition, as we
have explained, so also any proposition can be conceived as a
term; thus, man's being an animal is a fact, is a proposition, is of
such a kind, is a cause, is a reason, &c. These serve to construct the
most universal statements about these combinations.

(110) New reflexive terms can also be formed, which can similarly
be treated as direct, since the subject of a proposition, 'such a
person' or 'such a thing', can be called by some name. One must
see how these, and the denominations themselves, can again be
mutually explained by means of letters. Thus, if the subject of a
universal affirmative proposition is the predicate of another affirmative proposition, whose subject is the predicate of the former,
then the subject is said to be the same as the predicate of the same
proposition. But if anyone wants this to be stated rigorously in the
common manner of logicians, or even of ordinary speech, he will

---

[1] Leibniz refers to these tables by conventional signs.
[2] The word is obscure in the MS.

find difficulty enough in his propositions—if, for example, he wants to say that the subject of a universal affirmative proposition, whose predicate is the subject of a universal affirmative proposition in which the subject is the predicate of the preceding proposition, is the same as the predicate of the said proposition of which it is the subject. And not even in this way can the relative terms 'the said' or 'the preceding' be avoided; how much more adequately, briefly and clearly shall we say, 'If A is B and B is A, A is the same as B'. Again, the proof of this can easily be given, as it has been given by us above, with, of course, the use of letters. But if it were expressed in words, the proof would doubtless be fairly intricate, and particular care would be needed to arrange them correctly. For if they were rightly arranged, I believe that they would give the same result, though I doubt if they would do so with equal clarity. Similarly, inferences are easily derived from letters; thus, it is immediately evident here that, as we have said that A is the same as A, so it can also be said that B is the same as B, which does not seem to appear so easily from words.

C 383

(111) It is to be noted that it is also possible, with regard to the whole chain of an analysis, for certain generalities about its progress to be discovered, even if the analysis is continued *ad infinitum*; and with regard to these, too, certain appropriate reflexive words can be invented, as well as certain general letters such as $\overline{\overline{Y}}$. But which of these is best will appear more clearly as we proceed.

(112) It must be seen whether, when it is said that AY is B (i.e. that some A is B), Y is not taken in some other sense than when it is denied that any A is B, in such a way that not only is it denied that some A is B—i.e. that *this* indeterminate A is B—but also that *any* A out of a number of indeterminates is B, so that when it is said that no A is B, the sense is that it is denied that A$\overline{Y}$ is B; for $\overline{Y}$ is Y, i.e. any Y will contain this Y. So when I say that some A is B, I say that *this* 'some A' is B; if I deny that some A is B, or, that *this* 'some A' is B, I seem only to state a particular negative. But when I deny that any A is B,[1] i.e. that not only this, but also this and this A is B, then I deny that $\overline{Y}$A is B. This is also why, when we speak, to deny that some A is B (or, to say 'Some A is not B') does not seem to sound like the assertion that no A is B; similarly, to say 'Every A is not B' does not seem to sound like the negation of 'Every A is B', but it seems to be said of any A that it is not B. However, it is established by what has gone before that the negation of a universal affirmative is a particular negative, and so the negation of a particular affirmative cannot also be a particular

---

[1] The 'B' is supplied by Couturat.

negative (for the negation of a particular affirmative and of a universal affirmative cannot be the same). It remains, therefore, that it is a universal negative; for it cannot be anything else.[1]

(113) This will usefully be shown by means of figures. A is B, i.e. A coincides with some B, i.e. A coincides with AB.

(114) Some A is B, i.e. some A coincides with some B.

(115) Hence A = A. In general, this must be imagined as if horizontal parallel lines, of which one is drawn below the other for the sake of distinguishing them, were drawn one on top of the other.   *C 384*

(116) AB = BY, where by Y I understand whatever there is in the entire line B which falls under A.

(117) A = BY is the same as that A = BA.

(118) A = BY, therefore BY = AY.

(119) A = BY and B = AY is the same as that A = B.

AB in general
A ————
B   ————

All these are evident from inspection of the figure.

(120) The negation of 'Some A is B', i.e. when it is denied that some A coincides with some B, will be expressed thus:

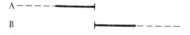

(121) But the negation of 'Every A is B' will be expressed thus:[2]

---

[1] Leibniz adds a marginal note, which is condensed and apparently incomplete: 'Univ. Aff. A aequatur B cum aliquo addito. Univ. Neg. negatur'. This may perhaps be rendered as 'In a universal affirmative, A is equated with B, with something added. In a universal negative, it is denied . . .'.
[2] In the margin of nos. 114–21 Leibniz has written:
    A perpendicular line signifies the limits beyond which terms cannot,

(122) Another consideration may be introduced, so that a genus is not assumed to be a part of a species—as we did a little above, on the grounds that the concept of a genus is a part of (or at least is included in) the concept of a species—but, on the contrary, a species is a part of a genus, on the grounds that the individuals of a species are a part of (or at least are included in) the individuals of a genus.

C 385   (123) So 'Every A is B' will be represented thus:

This representation is the inverse of the preceding one. In the same way the representation of a particular negative is the inverse of the preceding one. But a particular affirmative and a universal negative are represented in the same way as before, for it makes no difference whether you put something in front or behind,[1] and so it can be said generally that the former representation differs from the latter in this respect at any rate, that the lines in the figure are transposed.

(124) There is also another representation of propositions, namely, by numbers. If we put numbers for terms, the universal affirmative, 'A is B', means 'A (or at any rate the square or cube of A) can be divided by B'. For A and AB are here regarded as the same.

(125) The particular affirmative, 'Some A is B', means that A multiplied by B, or AB, can be divided by B. Understand that AB can always be divided by A, unless A is destroyed in AB—if, for example, A signifies $\frac{C}{B}$, and C cannot be divided by B.

---

and within which they can, be extended without affecting the proposition, i.e. the relation of the terms.

Just as a perpendicular line signifies a maximum, so a double horizontal line signifies a minimum, or, that which cannot be taken away without affecting the relation of the terms. A double line does not seem necessary in the subject, but only in the predicate; for I assume the subject arbitrarily. Instead of a double line I prefer a stronger one, so that when one line is drawn very closely below another it is understood that one term is composed, though it may always be understood as one in respect of the more distant lines drawn even further below.

[1] 'utrum praeponas aut postponas'.

(126) The particular negative is that it is false that A can be divided by B, though perhaps AB can be divided by B.

(127) The universal negative is that it is false that AB can be divided by B, the sole cause of which is that A contains $\frac{1}{B}$.

So strictly it is a universal negative if A contains not-B, from which it follows logically that a universal negative is the opposite of a particular affirmative; for if A is divided by B it cannot be the case that A is multiplied by B.[1]

(128) We have, therefore, these expressions: A = AB is the universal affirmative. AB = AB is the particular affirmative, for this also is false if a particular affirmative is false; for then AB is an impossible term, since A contains not-B. A = A not-B is the universal negative, from which it follows that the particular affirmative is false, i.e. that AB is an impossible, or rather a false, term (for if this cannot be proved completely except by analysing it *ad infinitum*,[2] it is false, not impossible). Finally, the particular negative is A not-B = A not-B. This I have learnt from a consideration of numbers. So at last we have wholly eliminated the indefinite Y; and this, too, we have learnt from numbers.

C 386

(129) Everything can be proved by numbers, if one complies with this sole condition—that AA and A are equivalent, and that $\frac{A}{A}$ is not admitted. For multiplication here represents a combination of concepts, but if any concept is added directly to itself, such as 'man man', all that is produced is 'man'. Division, when it does not proceed exactly, represents the fact that one term is denied of another. So when A can be divided exactly by B, i.e. when A contains B, the universal affirmative proposition 'A is B' is represented. When A can be divided exactly by not-B, i.e. by $\frac{1}{B}$ (i.e. when A contains the fraction $\frac{1}{B}$, which represents not-B), the universal negative is represented. But when A is not divided exactly by B, the particular negative arises, and when A is not divided exactly by $\frac{1}{B}$ there arises the particular affirmative. So

---

[1] Leibniz has added in the margin the beginning of par. 129: 'Everything can be proved by numbers, if only it is noted . . .'.

[2] The text has 'Si enim demonstrari hoc perfecte non possit resolvendo in infinitum', but in view of what is said below in par. 130 it seems likely that 'nisi' should be supplied in front of 'resolvendo'.

I have discovered that secret which I investigated vainly several years ago.[1]

C 387 (130) A true proposition is one which can be proved; a false proposition is one which is not true; an impossible proposition is one into which a contradictory term enters; a possible proposition is one which is not impossible. Is every universal negative, then, impossible? It seems that it is because it is understood of concepts, and not of existing things; thus, if I say that no man is an animal, I do not understand this of existing men alone. But from this it will follow that what is denied of some individual, such as Peter, is necessarily denied of him. Therefore it must be denied that every universal negative is impossible. In reply to the objection, it can be said that the fact that A contains not-B is proved either by a proof or analysis which is complete, or by nothing other than an analysis which can be continued *ad infinitum*, i.e. is always incomplete. Consequently it is certain, but not necessary, for it can never be reduced to an identical proposition, or its opposite to a contradictory proposition.

[1] Probably an allusion to the essays of April 1679. Leibniz has added (in a different ink) a long marginal note, in which he uses ':' as the sign for division. The note runs as follows:

Negation must be distinguished from division. For division is the omission of some term, but it is not therefore negation, except that in the case of an infinite number of things, what is not in them is denied. So in respect of the formula, division or taking-away [*ablatio*] is distinguished from negation, but in respect of the thing it will not be distinguished.

A = A is true	A = A:A is false
A = A	A ≠ A:A
A = AB Universal Affirmative	or A:B ≠ A:B
	i.e. A:B is false
A = A:B Universal Negative	or AB ≠ AB
	i.e. AB is false
AB = AB Particular Affirmative	or A ≠ A:B
A:B = A:B Particular Negative	or A ≠ AB

C 387 I understand here that some man is learned only if this is possible, for we are here considering abstract concepts, not the data of experience. For if it is possible that A = BY, then that BY is some B which is A. So if a particular affirmative is false, it is impossible that there should be such a concept.

It seems best that we should define particular propositions first; thus, AB is a true concept, or, AB = AB, is the particular affirmative.

Also, A:B is a true concept, or, A:B = A:B, is the particular negative.

However, when we say that AB is a false concept, i.e. when we deny a particular affirmative, a universal negative results. When we say that A:B is a false concept, i.e. that A:B ≠ A:B, a universal affirmative results. From this there is evident at once the conversion *simpliciter* of a universal negative and a particular affirmative. But it now has to be proved from these that A = AB if A:B ≠ A:B, and that A = A:B if AB ≠ AB.

(130)[1] That is true, therefore, which can be proved, i.e. of which a reason can be given by analysis; that is false of which the contrary holds. That is necessary which is reduced by analysis to an identical term [*identicum*], that is impossible which is reduced by analysis to a contradictory term [*contradictorium*]. A term or a proposition is false if it contains opposites, however they are proved; it is impossible if it contains opposites which are proved by reduction to a finite number of terms. Therefore A = AB, if the proof has been made by a finite analysis, must be distinguished from A = AB, if the proof has been made by an analysis *ad infinitum*, from which there arises what has been said about the necessary, possible, impossible and contingent.

C 388

(131) Analysis is of two kinds—either of mental concepts, without experience (except the reflexive experience of the fact that we are conceiving in such and such a way), or of perceptions or experiences. The former does not need proof, nor does it presuppose a new proposition, and to this extent it is true that whatever I perceive clearly and distinctly is true; the latter presupposes the truth of experience. In God, only the analysis of his own concepts is required, and in him, the whole of this occurs at once. So he knows even contingent truths, whose complete proof transcends every finite intellect.

(132) Every true proposition can be proved; for since (as Aristotle says) the predicate is in the subject, or, the concept of the predicate is involved in the concept of the subject when that concept is completely understood, then it must be possible for a truth to be shown by the analysis of terms into their values, i.e. those terms which they contain.

(133) A true necessary proposition can be proved by reduction to identical propositions, or by reduction of its opposite to contradictory propositions; hence its opposite is called 'impossible'.

(134) A true contingent proposition cannot be reduced to identical propositions, but is proved by showing that if the analysis is continued further and further, it constantly approaches identical propositions, but never reaches them. Therefore it is God alone, who grasps the entire infinite in his mind, who knows all contingent truths with certainty.

(135) So the distinction between necessary and contingent truths is the same as that between lines which meet and asmyptotes, or between commensurable and incommensurable numbers.

(136) But a difficulty stands before us. We can prove that some line—namely, an asymptote—constantly approaches another, and (also in the case of asymptotes) we can prove that two quantities

---

[1] *Sic.*

are equal, by showing what will be the case if the progression is continued as far as one pleases; so human beings also will be able to comprehend contingent truths with certainty. But it must be replied that there is indeed a likeness here, but there is not a complete agreement. Further, there can be relations which, however far an analysis is continued, will never reveal themselves sufficiently for certainty, and are seen perfectly only by him whose intellect is infinite. It is true that, as with asymptotes and incommensurables, so with contingent things we can see many things with certainty, from the very principle that every truth must be capable of proof. Consequently, if all things are alike on each side in our hypotheses, there can be no difference in the conclusions— and other things of this sort, which are true both in the case of necessary and of contingent propositions, since they are reflexive. But we can no more give the full reason for contingent things than we can constantly follow asymptotes and run through infinite progressions of numbers.

C 389

(137) We have, then, discovered many secrets of great importance for the analysis of all our thoughts and for the discovery and proof of truths. We have discovered how all truths can be explained by numbers, how contingent truths arise, and that they have in a way the nature of incommensurable numbers; how absolute and hypothetical truths have one and the same laws and are contained in the same general theorems, so that all syllogisms become categorical; and finally, what is the origin of abstract terms. It will be worth while to explain the last of these a little more distinctly.

(138) If the proposition 'A is B' is treated as a term, as we have explained that it can, there arises an abstract term, namely 'A's being B', and if from the proposition 'A is B' the proposition 'C is D' follows, then from this there is made a new proposition of this kind: 'A's being B is, or contains, C's being D'; i.e. 'The B-ness of A contains the D-ness of C',[1] i.e. 'The B-ness of A is the D-ness of C'.[1]

(139) In general, if it is said that something is B, then this 'something's being B' is simply 'B-ness'. Thus, 'something's being animal' is simply 'animality', whereas 'man's being an animal' is 'the animality of man'. From this we have the origin both of the abstract term and of the oblique of the abstract term.

(140) But through what abstract term will the fact that every man is an animal be expressed? Through 'the animality of every man'? This certainly differs widely from 'all the animality of man'. For provided that some man is learned, 'all the learning of man' is a true term; but unless every man is learned, 'the learning

C 390

---

[1] Corrected by Couturat, from the 'Ceitas ipsius D' of the text.

of every man' is a false term. (Unless someone understands the term exclusively, as geometers sometimes do, when they include under 'everything which has been moved' that whose speed is infinitely little, i.e. is at rest.) The erudition of every man also seems capable of being called 'the erudition of humanity'. But I should be unwilling to do this, if we insist on what has been said before—namely, that something's humanity is merely something's being a man.[1]

(140)[2] From the fact that some man is learned it follows that something learned is a man; is it therefore right to say, 'The learning of a man is the humanity of something learned'? I think that it is.

(141) How shall we explain quantity in abstract terms—for example, when A is twice as hot as B, i.e. when the heat of A is twice the heat of B? A's being hot is the heat of A; so if A's being hot is to B's being hot as 2 is to 1, then the heat of A will be twice that of B. But it must be seen further how A's being hot can be to B's being hot as one number to another. This happens owing to the fact that the cause which, with uniform action, makes A hot, makes B hot if the same action is continued; or the sign by which we recognize that something is hot is continuous, and in the one case is double the other. But much care is needed in this; consequently, although thermometers are signs of degrees of heat, they are not to be divided equally.

(142) But how shall we state negative propositions—e.g. 'Some man is not learned'—by means of abstract terms? Just as the negation of man is non-humanity, so the negation of the learning of man is the non-learning of man. And if it is said that no man is a stone, the abstract term which expresses this, i.e. 'no man's being a stone',[3] will have to be stated as 'the non-stoneness of every man'. Or will it be right to say, 'the stoneness of no man'—i.e. 'the stoneness of non-man'? I do not think so, for that does not express the fact that no man is a stone.

(143) We must now see whether this theory is consistent with the predication of abstract terms. Thus, 'Greenness is a colour' is a correct predication—but why is it? Is it because it follows that what is green is also coloured? But let us see if there are not examples to the contrary. A circle is uniform, and a circle is plane;   *C 391* but it cannot be said that uniformity is planeness, since planeness does not follow from uniformity. Should we say, however, 'The uniformity of a circle is planeness'? It does indeed seem that 'A

---

[1] Corrected by Couturat, from the 'animal' of the text.
[2] *Sic.*
[3] The text here has 'doctus', a mistake for 'lapis' (cf. Schmidt, p. 490).

circle is plane' follows from the proposition, 'A circle is uniform'.
But it is true that it does not follow from this proposition in particular, rather than from any other about the circle. Does it seem,
therefore, that predications of abstract terms demand not only an
inference but something else as well? What then—because every
circle is uniform (i.e. because, if A is a circle, it follows that A is
uniform) will it therefore be right to say that circularity is uniformity? Then 'Circularity is planeness' can be said with equal
right, and therefore one can say, 'Something which is uniformity
is planeness'. About this I am still considerably confused. Indeed,
if uniformity is the same as being uniform, and planeness as being
plane, is it true that sometimes A's being uniform is A's being
plane? From this it will be possible to say that uniformity in
respect of one centre is planeness, i.e. existence in a plane. Again,
just as in the case of concrete terms there are predications *per
accidens*, when a musician is a poet, I do not see why they should
not also be admitted in abstract terms, so that some uniformity is
planeness. So we shall be right in saying that the uniformity of a
circle is planeness, and shall therefore be able to follow a general
rule. But how shall we join these together in the case of circularity?
Because we say that circularity is uniformity, and circularity is
planeness, will it be right to say that uniformity is a circularity of
planeness?[1] And do not the functions of the categories seem to be
confused, as it can be said that a certain quality is a quantity? It
is a quantity since it sometimes follows from the fact that something is of a certain kind that it is of a certain size. But what of it?—
provided that it cannot be said that every quality is a quantity. It
must be seen whether, in the case of such a proposition stated in
abstract terms, necessity in concrete terms follows. I doubt if this
does follow, even if the conclusion is true;[2] for there are contingent
connexions, always true, which depend on free actions.

(144) Propositions are either essential or existential, and both are
either *secundi adjecti* or *tertii adjecti*.[3] An 'essential proposition
tertii adjecti' is, for example, 'A circle is a plane figure'. An 'essential
proposition *secundi adjecti*' is, for example, 'A plane figure having
a constant relation to some one point exists'. I say 'exists': that is,
it can be understood, it can be conceived, that among various
figures there is one which also has this nature, just as if I were to
say 'A plane figure having a constant relation to some one point
is an entity or thing'. An 'existential proposition *tertii adjecti*' is

C 392

---

[1] Reading 'planitiei' instead of Couturat's 'planities' (cf. Schmidt, p. 490).
[2] This seems to be the sense of Leibniz's phrase, which is not grammatical Latin: 'Puto ne hoc et si vera sequi'.
[3] Cf. Introduction, p. xlv, n.1.

'Every man exists liable to sin'. This is manifestly an existential or contingent proposition. An 'existential proposition *secundi adjecti*' is 'A man liable to sin exists, i.e. is actually an entity'.

(145) From every proposition *tertii adjecti* a proposition *secundi*[1] *adjecti* can be made, if the predicate is compounded with the subject into one term and this is said to exist, i.e. is said to be a thing, whether in any way whatsoever, or actually existing.

(146) The particular affirmative proposition 'Some A is B', transformed into a proposition *secundi adjecti*, will be 'AB exists, i.e. AB is a thing'—either possible or actual, depending on whether the proposition is essential or existential.

(147) The universal affirmative proposition is not, in this way, transformed with equal propriety into a proposition *secundi adjecti*; for from 'Every A is B' one may not properly make 'Every AB exists'. For since AB is the same as BA, it could with equal right be said 'Every BA exists', and therefore 'Every B is A'. So one must speak in this way: 'Every A containing B exists'. However, it will soon become evident how a universal affirmative proposition is reduced to a proposition *secundi adjecti* by another method.

(148) The particular negative proposition, 'Some A is not B', will be transformed into a proposition *secundi adjecti* as follows: 'A, not-B, exists'. That is, A which is not B is a certain thing—possible or actual, depending on whether the proposition is essential or existential.[2]

(149) The universal negative is transformed into a proposition *secundi adjecti* by the negation of the particular affirmative. So, for example, 'No A is B': that is, 'AB does not exist', i.e. 'AB is not a thing'. This could also be stated as follows—'No A is B': that is, 'Every A containing not-B exists'.

(150) The universal affirmative is transformed into a proposition *secundi adjecti* by the negation of the particular negative, so that 'Every A is B' is the same as 'A not-B does not exist, i.e. is not a thing', or (as I have said in no. 147) 'A containing B is a thing'. However, as I have already said, although the latter is true it is less apt, for it is superfluous. For B is already contained in A, but if not every A is B, a new thing is made of AB.

(151) We have, therefore, propositions *tertii adjecti* reduced as follows to propositions *secundi adjecti*:   *C 393*

'Some A is B' gives 'AB is a thing'.
'Some A is not B' gives 'A not-B is a thing'.
'Every A is B' gives 'A not-B is not a thing'.
'No A is B' gives 'AB is not a thing'.

---

[1] Corrected by Couturat from the 'tertii' of the text.
[2] Corrected by Couturat from the 'essentialis' of the text.

(152) As it is agreed that identical propositions themselves can be trusted only in the case of real concepts, so that no truth can be asserted without fear of the opposite except concerning the reality of those concepts themselves—at any rate their essential reality, though not their existential reality—it will therefore be permissible to express the four kinds of categorical proposition in this way:

Particular affirmative. AB = AB (i.e. AB and AB coincide, that is, AB is a thing).

Particular negative. A not-B = A not-B (i.e. A not-B is a thing).

Universal affirmative. A not-B ≠ A not-B (i.e. A not-B is not a thing).

Universal negative. AB ≠ AB (i.e. AB is not a thing).

(153) But this presupposes that every proposition which has as an ingredient a term which is not a thing is denied. So it remains that every proposition is either true or false, but that every proposition which lacks a consistent subject, i.e. a real term, is false. In the case of existential propositions this is far removed from the way we speak; but this is no reason for concern, since I am seeking appropriate signs, and I do not intend to apply generally accepted names to these.

(154) But if someone prefers signs to be used in such a way that AB = AB, whether AB is a thing or not, and that in the case in which AB is not a thing, B and not-B can coincide—namely, *per impossibile*—I do not object. This will have as a consequence the need to distinguish between a term and a thing or entity.

(155) All things considered, then, it will perhaps be better for us to say that, in symbols at least, we can always put A = A, though nothing is usefully concluded from this when A is not a thing. So if AB is a thing it will be possible to derive from this YA = ZB. For one can derive from this AB = R, and AB = RB; let B = Y and R = Z, we shall have YA = ZB. Conversely, YA = ZB, therefore YAB = ZB; now, A = R and B = (R) (i.e. A and B are things), therefore YAB = Z(R). Therefore AB = ((R)).

(156) A = A. A ≠ not-A. AA = A.

(157) A = B is a universal affirmative reciprocal proposition, which is the most simple. It coincides with not-A = not-B, and if it is negated it can be said that A ≠ B.

C 394

(158) D = ZC is the universal affirmative.

(159) YA = ZC is the particular affirmative.

(160) D = not-E is the universal negative.

(161) XE = not-F is the particular negative.

(162) There remain those terms into which there enters 'not-YA', that is, 'not such an A' (i.e. 'some A not'); these differ from 'not

some'. For it is one thing to say that it is false that some A is B, and another to say that it is false that such an A is B. As some equivocation arises from this, it will be better to eliminate the letter Y altogether; from this there will arise propositions of this sort.

(163) A = B, and not-A = not-B, are the most simple propositions.

(164) A = AB is the 'universal affirmative'.

(165) AB = AB, assuming that AB is a thing, is the 'particular affirmative'; or, YA = ZB.

(166) A = A^1 not-B is the 'universal negative'.

(167) A not-B = A not-B, assuming that A not-B is a thing, is the 'particular negative'.

(168) If A ≠ B, then either A not-B will be a thing, or B not-A will be a thing.

(169) 'AB is a thing' is equivalent to 'Some A is B' and 'Some B is A'.

'A not-B is a thing' is equivalent to 'Some A is not B' or 'Some A is not-B'.

'A not-B is not a thing' is equivalent to the universal affirmative, 'Every A is B'.

'AB is not a thing' is equivalent to the universal negative, 'No A is B', or 'No B is A'.

(170) Meanwhile, however, it is necessary for us to distinguish the proposition 'Some A is B' from the proposition 'Some B is A', and similarly 'No A is B' from the proposition 'No B is A'.

(171) Our principles are: first, A = A.

Second, not-A = not-A.

Third, AA = A.

Fourth, 'not not' = the omission of 'not', so that not-not-A = A.

Fifth, if A = B, AC = BC.

Sixth, if A = B, not-A = not-B.

Seventh, if A = B, A ≠ not-B.

Eighth, A not-A is not a thing.

(172) If A = B, AB = B. For A = B by hypothesis, therefore AA = BB by the fifth principle; that is, by principle 3, AB = B.

(173) If A = BC, AB = BC. For A = BC by hypothesis, therefore AB = BBC by the fifth principle; that is, by principle 3, AB = BC.

(174) If not-A = B, not-B = A. For let not-A = B, by hypothesis; then not-not-A ⇒ not-B, by the sixth principle. Now, not-not-A = A, by principle 4; therefore A = not-B.

C 395

This 'A' is supplied by Couturat, who also points out that the 'affirmativa' of the text should be replaced by 'negativa'.

(175) If A = not-B, A ≠ B. For let A = not-B, by hypothesis; then A ≠ not-not-B, by principle 7.[1] Therefore, by principle 4, A ≠ B.

(176) If A = BC, A = AC. For let A = BC (by hypothesis); then A = ABC = BCBC = BCC = AC.

(177) If A = YC, A = AC. As before.

(178) If A = YC, ZA = VC. For A = YC by hypothesis, therefore ZA = ZYC; let ZY = V, then ZA = VC.

(179) If A = YC, VC = ZA. This is evident from what precedes.

(180) If A = not-AC, A = not-C (if, that is to say, A is a thing). This must be proved accurately.

(181) Not-AC = Y not-C (= Z not-A).
(182) If Y not-C = Z not-A, this = not-AC.   } These must
(183) Not-A not-C = Y not-AC.   be proved.

(184) Every proposition which is commonly used in speech comes to this, that it is said what term contains what; also, the nature [?][2] of the containing term is examined, whether it is absolute, or with something added, and is said to contain an absolute content.

(185) 'Not every' and 'not some' may not properly occur in propositions; for they only negate the proposition affected by the sign 'every' or 'some', and do not make a new sign, 'not-every' or 'not-some'. Thus, if I say 'Not, some man is an animal',[3] this is the same as that it is false that some man is an animal.

C 396

(186) 'Some man is not a stone' means 'Some man is not-stone'. Again, 'Every man is not a stone' seems to mean 'Every man is not-stone'. In general, therefore, we shall interpret 'not' after 'is' as a negative predicate; but if 'not' is put in front of the sign of quantity,[4] we shall understand that the proposition is negated.

(187) I have pointed out above that what concerns propositions can be illustrated by and as it were reduced to numbers, so that we may conceive a term or concept as a fraction—for example, ab not-l not-m = H, which means that H contains a and b, but also contains not-l and not-m. In this we comply only with the rules that aa is the same as a, and not-a not-a is the same as not-a; that not-not-a is the same as a, and that the same term never contains a and not-a at the same time—i.e. that the term which contains a is not said to contain not-a, or conversely; and finally,

---

[1] Corrected by Couturat, from the '6' of the text.
[2] Leibniz has deleted the word 'quantitas' here, but has not replaced it by another word.
[3] 'Si dicam non, quidam homo est animal'.
[4] *Signum.* Cf. p. 17 n. 1.

that the term which contains *ab* also contains *a*, and the term which contains not-*a* also contains not-*al*.

(189)[1] Our principles, therefore, will be these: first, $aa = a$ (from which it is also evident that not-*b* = not-*b*, if we assume that not-*b* = *a*).

Second, not-not-*a* = *a*.

Third, the same term does not contain *a* and not-*a*; i.e. if the one is true the other is false, or at any rate the term itself, if of such a kind, would be said to be not true, but false.

Fourth, that A contains *l* is the same as that A = *xl*.

Fifth, not-*a* contains not-*ab*; i.e. if *l* contains *a*, not-*a* will contain not-*l*.

Sixth, whatever is said of a term which contains a term can also be said of a proposition from which another proposition follows.

Seventh, whatever cannot be proved from these principles does not follow by virtue of logical form [*vi formae*].

(190) The *universal affirmative*. 'Every A is L'[2] is the same as that A contains L, i.e. A = XL.

The *particular affirmative*. 'Some A is L' is the same as that A with something added contains L. For example, AB contains L, assuming that B = LX; or AN contains L, assuming that L = MN and A = BM, for in this way we have AN = BMN = BL. Consequently 'Some A is L' is the same as that AL contains L, i.e. AL = AL; assuming, of course, that AL is a thing, i.e. a true term which does not imply opposites, such as X not-X.

The *universal negative*. 'Every A is not-B'; i.e. A contains not-B, i.e. A = X not-B.

The *particular negative*. 'Some A is not-L'; i.e. AX contains not-L, or, AX = Z not-L, or, A not-L contains not-L, or, A not-L = A not-L, assuming that A not-L is a true term which does not imply opposites.

(191) If a universal affirmative is true, a particular affirmative is also true; i.e. if A contains B, some A contains B. For A = XB, by principle 4, therefore ZA = ZXB (from the nature of coincidentals). Let ZX = V (arbitrarily), then ZA = VB.

(192) In the case of true terms, a universal affirmative and a particular negative proposition cannot be true at the same time. For let A = XL and VA = Z not-L; then we shall have AVA, i.e. VA = AZ not-L = XLZ not-L; which term is false.

(193) These same propositions cannot be false at the same time.

C *397*

---

[1] Par. 188 is omitted by Leibniz.
[2] The text has 'Omn. A est B', but 'est L' must be meant. Cf. Schmidt, p. 490.

Let A ≠ AL and A not-L ≠ A not-L, then A not-L will be a false term; therefore A = AL.

(194) A false term is one which contains opposite terms, A not-A. A true term is not-false.

(195) A proposition is that which states what term is or is not contained in another. So a proposition can also state some term to be false, if it says that Y not-Y is contained in it, and to be true if it denies this. A proposition is also that which says whether or not some term coincides with another; for those terms which coincide are contained in each other reciprocally.

(196) A proposition is false if it contains opposite propositions, such as * and not-*.[1]

(197) The proposition itself can be conceived as a term: thus, 'Some A is B', i.e. 'AB is a true term' is a term—namely, 'AB true'. Again, we have 'Every A is B', i.e. 'A not-B is false', i.e. '"A not-B false" is a true term'; and again 'No A is B', i.e. 'AB is false, i.e. '"AB false" is a true term'.[2]

(198) Principles: first, coincidentals can be substituted for one another.

Second, AA = A.

Third, not-not-A = A.

Fourth, that term is false, i.e. not true, which contains A not-A; that term is true which does not contain it.

Fifth, a proposition is that which adds to a term that it is true or false; as, for example, if A is a term and there is ascribed to it A's being true or A's being not true. It is also often said simply that A exists or that A does not exist.

Sixth, the addition of 'true' or 'existence' leaves things as they were, but the addition of 'false' or 'non-existence' changes them into their opposite. So if it is said to be true that something is true or false, it remains true or false; but if it is said to be false that it is true or false, it becomes false from being true and true from being false.

Seventh, a proposition itself becomes a term if 'true' or 'false' is added to the term. Thus, let A be a term, and 'A exists' or 'A is

C 398

---

[1] This sign (in the MS, a dot in a circle) seems in this context to stand for 'any proposition'. The same sign is also used by Leibniz to indicate one proposition in particular, as in par. 1 of this paper.

[2] The text of the last part of this sentence is confused: 'Sic Nullum A esse B seu AB esse falsum est terminus novus'. In the translation, it has been assumed that what was meant was 'Sic Nullum A esse B, seu AB esse falsum, seu AB falsum est terminus verus'. This is consistent with what precedes; it assumes that 'novus' was written for 'verus', and that 'seu AB falsum' was omitted. The latter could easily be done, coming immediately after the very similar phrase 'seu AB esse falsum'.

true' be a proposition; then 'A true', or 'that A is true', or, 'that A exists' will be a new term, from which a new proposition can in turn be made.

Eighth, that a proposition follows from a proposition is simply that a consequent is contained in an antecedent, as a term in a term. By this method we reduce inferences to propositions, and propositions to terms.

Ninth, that A contains *l* is the same as that A = *xl*.[1]

(199) The *particular affirmative* proposition: AB exists.

The *particular negative:* A not-B exists.

The *universal affirmative:* A not-B does not exist (assuming that A and B exist).

The *universal negative:* AB does not exist.

From this it is evident at once that there are no more than these, and what are their oppositions and conversions. For a particular affirmative and a universal negative are opposed, as are a particular negative and a universal affirmative. It is also evident that in the proposition 'AB exists' or 'AB does not exist' each term is in the same relation, and so conversion *simpliciter* is valid. 'Not-A not-B exists' or 'Not-A not-B does not exist' could be added, but this is in no way different from 'LM exists' or 'LM does not exist', assuming that not-A is L and not-B is M. The universal affirmative, i.e. 'A not-B does not exist', is the same as that A contains B. *C 399* For that A does not contain B is the same as that A not-B is true; therefore that A contains B is the same as that A not-B is not true.

(200) If I say 'AB does not exist', this is the same as if I were to say 'A contains not-B, or B contains not-A, i.e. A and B are inconsistent'. Similarly, if I say 'A not-B does not exist', this is the same as if I were to say 'A contains not-not-B, i.e. A contains B, and similarly not-B contains not-A'. In these few propositions, therefore, the fundamentals of logical form [*formae*] are contained.

---

[1] L.– Every B is C.   B not-C does not exist.
Every A is B.   A not-B does not exist.
Every A is C.   A not-C does not exist.

This inference, although valid, does not appear from negatives alone, unless one makes a reduction to affirmatives. From this it appears that this reduction of universal to negative propositions is not so natural. Just as, if A contains B and B contains C, A contains C, so also, if A excludes not-B it includes B, and if B excludes not-C it includes C—so, finally, A includes C. If we use 'AB exists' and 'A not-B exists' for particular propositions, and if for universal propositions we use 'A contains B' or 'A contains not-B', we shall be able to dispense with negative propositions. Certainly, a negative term does not affect the copula except when a proposition is said to be false; otherwise it affects the predicate.

8. A specimen of a demonstrated inference from the direct to the oblique, sent by Leibniz to Vagetius[1] (January, 1687)

D vi. 1, 38   *First supposition,* derived from the part of logic which concerns inference from the direct to the direct.

To be a predicate in a universal affirmative proposition is the same as to be capable of being substituted without loss of truth for the subject in every other affirmative proposition where that subject plays the part of predicate; from a predication, therefore, this substitution follows, and conversely the predication follows from the substitution. For example, (*first part*) since painting is an art, if we have 'a thing which is painting' we shall be able to substitute 'a thing which is an art'. Conversely, (*second part*) if it should be shown that for 'he who learns painting' it is always possible to substitute in the way described, without loss of truth, 'he who learns an art', then the proposition 'He who learns painting, learns an art' will be true.

Second supposition, from the grammatical meaning of cases.

A general oblique case taken with a particular direct case is equivalent to a particular oblique case, and therefore they can be substituted mutually for one another. For example, (*first part*) 'he who learns a thing which is painting' can be substituted for the term 'he who learns painting'. Conversely, (*second part*) 'he who learns an art' can be substituted for the term 'he who learns a thing which is an art'.

D vi. 1, 39   *Third supposition.* If B can be substituted for A, and C for B, and D for C, then D can also be substituted for A.

Theorem

Inference from the direct to the oblique is valid.

Article 1. Grant, in the direct case, 'Painting is an art'.

Article 2. I assert that there follows from this, in the oblique case, 'He who learns painting, learns an art'.

Proof

Article 3. Let there be a term 'he who learns painting'.

Article 4. 'He who learns a thing which is painting' can always

---

[1] This title was supplied by the editor, Dutens.

be substituted for this (by the first part of the second supposition).

Article 5. Again, there can always be substituted for this, in the manner stated above, 'he who learns a thing which is an art' (by the first part of the first supposition). For painting (article 1) is an art.

Article 6. But for this, again, 'he who learns an art' can always be substituted (by the second part of supposition 2).

Article 7. By the third supposition, therefore, arguing from the first to the last (namely, from article 3 to article 6, through 4 and 5), for the term 'he who learns painting' there can always be substituted, in the manner stated above, 'he who learns an art'.

Article 8. From this, finally, there is inferred (by the second part of supposition 1) 'He who learns painting, learns an art'. Q.E.D., as was proposed in article 2.

Note

It must be understood that the converse inference, from the oblique to the direct, is not valid. For from 'He who strikes a human face strikes a man' it does not follow that therefore a human face is a man.

More briefly:

Suppositions. I. Inference from the direct to the direct. E.g. there is painting, therefore there is an art, since painting is an art.

II. The equivalence of a particular oblique case to a general oblique case and a particular direct case taken together—e.g. between 'painting' and 'a thing which is painting'.

III. The sorites.

Proposition: Painting is an art, therefore[1] he who learns painting, learns an art.

Proof[2]

1. For he who learns painting learns a thing which is painting (by supposition 2).

2. But painting is an art.

3. Therefore he who learns a thing which is painting learns a thing which is an art (by article 2, taken with supposition 1).

4. Further: he who learns a thing which is an art, learns an art (by supposition 2).

5. Therefore he who learns painting learns an art (by articles 1, 2 and 3, taken with supposition 1).

---

[1] 'Ergo' is omitted in the text, but is demanded by the sense.
[2] The word 'Demonstratio' is also written in front of the preceding sentence, but seems superfluous there.

9. *The Primary Bases of a Logical Calculus* (1 August 1690).

(1) 'A = B' is the same as 'A = B is true'.
(2) 'A ≠ B' is the same as 'A = B is false'.
(3) A = A.
(4) A ≠ B (not-A).
(5) A = (not-(not-A)).
(6) AA = A.
(7) AB = BA.
(8) 'A = B', 'not-A = not-B', 'A not ≠ B'[1] are the same.
(9) If A = B, it follows that A ≠ not-B. I prove this in this way. If it does not follow, let A = not-B (by assuming the contrary). Therefore (by hypothesis) B = not-B, which is absurd. It can also be proved in this way: B ≠ not-B (by 4), therefore A ≠ not-B.
(10) If A = AB, there can be assumed a Y such that A = YB. This is a postulate, but it can also be proved, for A itself at any rate can be designated by Y.

(11) If A = B, AC = BC. But A = B does not follow from AC = BC. For let A = BC, and the result will be AC = BC, by 10 and 6.
(12) 'A ⇌ AB' and 'not-B = not-B not-A' coincide.
(13) If A = YB, it follows that A = AB. I prove this as follows. A = YB (by hypothesis), therefore AB = YBB (by 10) = YB (by 6) = A (by hypothesis).

The universal affirmative can be expressed as follows:

$$A = AB \quad \text{or} \quad A = YB.$$

The particular affirmative can be expressed as follows: YA = YAB, or YA = ZB, or[2] also as AB = AB, or, AB is an entity, or A ≠ A not-B.

---

[1] 'A non non = B'.
[2] The phrase which follows renders a later insertion, the Latin of which is not wholly clear: 'vel etiam AB = AB, seu AB est Ens vel stare invicem possunt vel A non = A non B'. It may be that Leibniz originally meant to introduce two equivalent terms by 'stare invicem possunt' ('can stand for each other'), but then introduced a formula which states a non-identity; or it may be that 'stare invicem possunt' refers back to 'AB = AB' and 'AB est Ens'.

The universal negative, 'No A is B', can be expressed as follows: A = Y not-B, or, A = A not-B, or, AB is a non-entity.

The particular negative, 'Some A is not B' can be expressed as follows: A ≠ AB, or A not-B is an entity.

But let us see if the following are sufficient by themselves:

Universal affirmative, A = AB; particular negative, A ≠ AB; universal negative, A = A not-B; particular affirmative, A ≠ A not-B.

If A = AB, then A ≠ A not-B; i.e. from a universal affirmative a particular affirmative follows.

Proof: let A = A not-B (by assuming the contrary). Since A = AB (by hypothesis), the result will be A not-B = AB, which is absurd, by 4. Or, more briefly: A not-B ≠ AB (by 4); in this I substitute A for AB (for they are equivalent, by hypothesis), and the result will be A not-B ≠ A. Q.E.D.

If A = A not-B, then A ≠ AB; i.e. from a universal negative a particular negative follows.

Proof: A not-B ≠ AB (by 4). Substitute A for A not-B (for they are equivalent, by hypothesis), and the result is A ≠ AB.

'A ≠ A not-B' and 'B ≠ B not-A' are equivalent; i.e. a particular affirmative can be converted *simpliciter*.

Proof: from 'A ≠ A not-B' there follows (by 9) 'B ≠ B not-A'. Therefore the converse also is true; alternatively, 'A = A not-B' coincides immediately with 'B = B not-A' (by 9), therefore their contradictories also coincide. Q.E.D.

Let us see if we can deduce 'B = B not-A' from 'A = A not-B' in another way.

If A = A not-B, AB = AB not-B; therefore AB is a non-entity. But if we now deduce 'A = A not-B' from 'AB is a non-entity', we could with equal justice deduce its reciprocal, 'B = B not-A'.

Perhaps it can be proved as follows, without making any suppositions. Let AB be an entity; therefore A ≠ A not-B; for if A = A not-B, AB = AB not-B, and so AB would be a non-entity, which is contrary to the hypothesis. With equal justice, it can be said that B ≠ B not-A. When it is said that AB is an entity or a non-entity, it is understood that A and B are assumed to be entities. Let us see if it can be shown conversely that A ≠ A not-B, therefore AB is an entity—assuming that A and B are entities. Now if, assuming that A and B are entities, AB were not an entity, then one of them—A or B—must involve the contradictory of that which the other involves. Let us assume, therefore, that A involves C and B involves not-C (from which, again, it follows that B involves D and A involves not-D, it being assumed that

C 237

D = not-C). Let A = EC and B = F not-C. Now, EC = EC not-(F(not-C)), or, EC contains not-(F not-C) (or, whatever involves C involves the negation of that which negates C). That is, A = A not-B, which is contrary to the hypothesis. Therefore 'AB is an entity', 'A ≠ A not-B', and 'B ≠ B not-A' are equivalent, i.e. follow from each other mutually. Similarly 'AB is a non-entity', 'A = A not-B', and 'B = B not-A' are equivalent.

So we have found a key which permits us to use the reduction of complex to incomplex terms.

We have arranged matters better in the following paper, of 2 August 1690.

Not-(AB) is in not-B, i.e. not-B = not-B (not-AB).

If A = BC, does A:C[1] = B, so that it is understood that C is to be removed from A? Reducing this to primitive terms, let B = CE; the result is A = CEC, i.e. A = CE; therefore A:C does not always = B. So this is valid only in the case of primitive terms.

Wherever there is a general term EB, such that E is understood to mean 'any', B can be substituted; for assuming E for B, the result will be EB = BB = B.

If not-AB ≠ A not-B, then not-AB = B not-A, and conversely; i.e. 'not-AB ≠ A not-B' and 'not-AB = B not-A' are equivalent.

---

[1] Compare, for the use of this sign for division, the marginal note to *Generales Inquisitiones*, par. 129.

10. *The Bases of a Logical Calculus* (2 August 1690)

(1) 'A = B' is the same as '"A = B" is a *true* proposition'. C 421

(2) 'A ≠ B' is the same as '"A = B" is a *false* proposition'.

(3) A = AA; i.e. the multiplication of a letter by itself is here without effect.

(4) AB = BA, i.e. transposition makes no difference.

(5) 'A = B' means that one can be substituted for the other, B for A or A for B, i.e. that they are equivalent.[1]

(6) 'Not' immediately repeated destroys itself.

(7) Therefore A = not-not-A.

(8) Further, 'A = B' and 'A not ≠ B' are equivalent.

(9) That in which there is 'A not-A' is a 'non-entity', or, a 'false term'; e.g. if C = AB not-B, C would be a non-entity.

(10) 'A ≠ B' and 'B ≠ A' are equivalent. This follows from 5.

(11) 'A = B' and 'not-A = not-B' are equivalent; for since A can be substituted for B (by 5), by substituting in not-A the result will be not-B, i.e. not-B can be substituted for not-A. In the same way it is shown that not-A[2] can be substituted for not-B. Therefore, since A and B can be substituted mutually—i.e. since A = B —not-A and not-B can also be substituted mutually; i.e. the result C 422
is that not-A = not-B. Now, in the the same way that we have proved from A = B that not-A = not-B, it will also be proved from not-A = not-B that not-not-A = not-not-B, i.e. that A = B. Therefore these truths are proved from each other mutually, i.e. they are equivalent.

(12)[3] If A = B, AC = BC. This is proved from 5.

But it does not follow that, because AC = BC, therefore A = B; for if A = BC the result (by 3) would be AC = BC.

(13) B ≠ not-B; further, more generally, AB ≠ C not-EB.[4]

Proof. For (1) let AB = C not-EB. Now (2) AB = ABAB (by art. 3) and ABAB = ABC not-EB (by no. 1 of this article). Therefore, arguing from the first to the last, AB = ABC not-EB; which is absurd, by article 9, for AB would be a false term, i.e. implying a contradiction.

[1] L.– A proposition is false on the admission of which terms which have been assumed to be true give something false.

[2] Corrected by Couturat from the 'A' of the text.

[3] In Couturat's text, article 13 is printed before article 12.

[4] Leibniz has added the beginning of a phrase, 'et eodem modo (omissis . . .' ('and in the same way, omitting . . .').

(14) If A = B it follows that EA ≠ C not-FB. For EA ≠ C not-FA (by 13); therefore, substituting (by hypothesis) B for the last A, the result is EA ≠ C not-FB. It makes no difference when some proposition is negated.

(15) If A = FB, it follows that EA ≠ C not-FGB.

For EA ≠ C not-GA (by 13). Therefore, substituting FB for A, the result is EA ≠ C not-FGB.

(16) If A = A not-B, then A ≠ AB.

For A ≠ AB not-B (by 9). Therefore (substituting A not-B for A, by hypothesis) A not-B ≠ AB not-B. Therefore A ≠ AB.

(17) Not-B = not-B (not-AB); i.e. not-B contains not-AB, or, not-B is not-AB. This remains to be proved in our calculus.

(18) C = C not-(A not-C). This follows from 17, putting not-C for B.

(19) 'A = AB' and 'not-B = not-B (not-A)' are equivalent. This is conversion by contraposition.

For if (1) A = AB, since (2) not-B = not-B (not-AB) (by 17), putting A for AB in no.2 (by 1) the result is not-B = not-B(not-A). Again, if (1) not-B = not-B (not-A), since (by 17) (2) not-B = not-B (not-AB), by joining 1 and 2 the result is A = AB. *C 423* (However, the inference is somewhat dubious, by the note to 12. For we have, indeed, B not-A = B not-AB; but does A = AB follow from this? Certainly, if BC = BD, then indeed C = D, if C and B have nothing in common.)

(20) 'Not-AB ≠ Y not-B' and 'Not-AB = Z not-A' are equivalent; i.e. 'Not-AB ≠ (not-AB) not-B' and 'Not-AB = (not-AB) not-A' are equivalent. For 'not-AB' on one side put 'X'.[1]

For not-(AB) will contain one or other of not-A or not-B. So if it does not contain one, it will contain the other; which, however, does not prevent it from being able to contain both.

[1] Couturat notes that Leibniz has in fact written 'X' over 'not-AB' in the first member of the two preceding formulae.

11. *A Mathematics of Reason*[1]

(1) The laws of categorical syllogisms may best be proved by reduction to a consideration of the same and the different. For in a proposition or statement what we are doing is to state that two terms are the same as, or different from, one another. *C 193*
(2) In a proposition, a term (such as 'man') is either taken universally of any man, or particularly, of some man.
(3) When I say 'Every A is B', I understand that any one of those which are called A is the same as some one of those which are called B. This proposition is called a 'Universal Affirmative'.
(4) When I say 'Some A is B', I understand that some one of those which are called A is the same as some one of those which are called B; this is a 'Particular Affirmative' proposition.
(5) When I say 'No A is B', I understand that any one of those which are called A is different from any one of those which are called B; this is a 'Universal Negative' proposition.
(6) Finally, when I say 'Some A is not B', I understand that some one of those which are called A is different from any one of those which are called B; this is called a 'Particular Negative'. Hence, by virtue of logical form, the predicate is particular in affirmative propositions and universal in negative propositions.

It could also be that every A is every B; i.e. that all those which are called A are the same as all those which are called B; i.e. that the proposition is reciprocal. But this is not in accordance with our linguistic usage. In the same way, we do not say that some As are the same as all Bs, for we express that when we say that all Bs are A. But it would be superfluous [*inutile*] to say that no A is some B, i.e. that any one of those which are called A is different from some one of those which are called B; for this is self-evident, unless B is unique. Much more would it be superfluous to say that some one of those which are called A is different from some one of those which are called B. So we see that logical theory is perfected by transferring matters from predication to identity. *C 194*
(8)[2] In the examples given, A is called the 'subject' and B the 'predicate'. Propositions of this kind are called 'categorical'.

---

[1] L.– What is in this paper is sound, and so can satisfactorily be counted as finished.
[2] *Sic.*

(9) So, in the sense which we have stated, it is evident that every affirmative proposition (and only such a proposition) has a particular predicate, by articles 3 and 4,

(10) and that every negative proposition (and only such a proposition) has a universal predicate, by articles 5 and 6.

(11) Further, the proposition itself is called 'universal' or 'particular' by virtue of the universality or particularity of its subject.

(12) What are called 'simple categorical syllogisms' elicit a third proposition from two others. This is done by the use of two principles. One of these is that those terms which are the same as a single third term are the same as each other; thus, if L is the same as M and M is the same as N, L and N are the same.

(13) The other principle comes to this: that if two terms are different, and one of these is the same as a third, then the other is different from that third term. Thus, if L is the same as M, and M is different from N, L and N are also different.

(14) But if L is different from M and N is also different from M, it cannot be known from this whether or not L and N are the same; it can happen that L is the same as N, and also that L is different from N.

(15) It is at once inferred from this that a syllogism cannot be made out of two negative propositions; for in this way it would be stated that L is different from M, and that M is different from N.[1]

For example, if I say 'No dog is a stone' and 'No dog is a man', the sense is that any man is different from any stone, and any dog is different from any man. Here, therefore, there is no principle for comparing a dog and a man, and inferring which of them is the same or different. It is the same as if I were to say 'Some dog is not a man', for I am saying at any rate that some dog is different from any man.

C 195

(16) It is also evident that in the simple categorical syllogism there are three terms, as we are using some third term, and while we compare this equally with the one and the other of the extremes we are seeking a method of comparing these extremes with each other.

(17) Here, the proposition which we deduce from two assumed propositions is called the 'conclusion'; its subject is usually called the 'minor term' and its predicate the 'major term'. The third term which serves to compare these extreme terms is called the 'middle term'.

(18) The two propositions from which we infer the third, the conclusion, are called 'premisses'; in one of these the minor term, and in the other the major term is compared with the

---

[1] The text has 'N etiam esse diversum ab N'.

middle term. The premiss which contains the major term is called the 'major proposition', and the premiss which contains the minor term is called the 'minor proposition'. The middle term is in each of these.

(19) From this it is evident that the middle term must be universal in at least one premiss. For we are not using the determinate contents of a term, but either all or some of the contents indeterminately. So if the middle term in each premiss is particular, it is not certain that the contents of the middle term which are used in one premiss are the same as the contents of the middle term which are in the other premiss, and therefore nothing can be inferred from this about the identity and difference of the extremes. For example, if someone says

'Some man is happy.
Every learned man is a man.'

nothing can be inferred from this. For it is the same as if he were to say, 'Some man is the same as some happy man, but every learned man is the same as some man'. As 'some man' occurs twice here, it is clear that another man can be understood in the one premiss from the man who is understood in the other. Hence no argument can be derived for comparing the learned man and the happy man, such that one may infer from it, of some or every learned man, whether he is the same as or different from some or every happy man.

(20) It can also be seen easily that a particular term in the premiss does not imply a universal term in the conclusion, for it is not known to be the same or different in the conclusion unless it is known that it is the same as or different from the middle term in the premiss. So if we have compared only some of the content of a term, we may draw inferences only about what we have compared.

(21) It is none the less evident that if one premiss is negative, the conclusion also is negative, and conversely; for the reasoning used here is just the same as that whose principle was stated in article 13—namely, that if L is the same as M, and M is different from N, then L is different from N.   *C 196*

(22) There are four figures of simple categorical syllogisms, which are distinguished by the position of the middle term. Let the minor term be B, the middle term C, the major term D. The conclusion is always BD. In the premisses, the middle term can be the subject in the first premiss and the predicate in the second, or it can be the predicate in each, or the subject in each, or it can be the predicate in the first and the subject in the second. We

usually put the major proposition first, and the minor proposition second.

Fig. 1.	CD.	BC.	BD.
Fig. 2.	DC.	BC.	BD.
Fig. 3.	CD.	CB.	BD.
Fig. 4.	DC.	CB.	BD.

It will appear later which of these figures is valid, and by what laws.

(23) The vowels A, E, I, O stand for the 'quality' of propositions (that is, whether they are affirmative or negative) and for their 'quantity' (that is, whether they are universal or particular). Thus

A stands for the universal affirmative
E   the universal negative
I   the particular affirmative
O   the particular negative

(24) The quantity of the subject and the quantity of the proposition coincide; so do the quantity of the predicate and the quality of the proposition, by articles 9, 10, 11. S will stand for a universal, P for a particular, V, Y, ψ for an indefinite proposition. The quantity of a proposition will be designated by the sign of the subject, its quality by that of the predicate. Therefore the sign SBSD is a universal negative proposition, SBPD a universal affirmative, IBSD a particular negative, IBID a particular affirmative.[1]

C 197 (25) In every particular affirmative proposition, and only in such a proposition, each term is particular. For the subject is particular (art. 11) and the predicate is particular (art. 9).

Corollary. When a term is universal, therefore, the proposition is either universal or negative.

(26) In a universal negative proposition each term is universal, both the subject (art. 11) and the predicate (art. 10).

(27) If the minor term is particular in its premiss, the conclusion is particular. For an extreme term which is particular in a premiss is also particular in the conclusion (art. 20); but the minor term, being particular in the conclusion (since it is its subject: art. 17), makes the conclusion particular also (art. 11).

---

[1] L.– Any proposition, universal or particular, affirmative or negative, is expressed generally . . . as ψP. ψS.

(The dots in the sentence above represent a word which is illegible in the MS., and read by Couturat as 'unurarem'. Schmidt, p. 490, suggests 'universe', which seems otiose in view of the preceding 'generaliter'. Couturat's text also has 'ψF . ψS', but 'ψP . ψS' seems more likely (cf. Schmidt, p. 349).)

Corollary. If the conclusion is universal, the minor term is universal everywhere.

(28) If the major term is particular in its premiss, the conclusion is affirmative. For the major term will be particular in the conclusion (art. 20); but there it is the predicate (art. 17), therefore the conclusion is affirmative (art. 9).

Corollary. If the conclusion is negative, the major term is universal everywhere.

(29) If the conclusion is negative, the major proposition is either universal or negative. For if the conclusion is negative, the major term is universal everywhere (coroll. art. 28); therefore it is universal in the major proposition. So this proposition will either be universal, if the major term[1] in it is the subject (art. 11), or negative, if the major[1] term in it is the predicate (art. 10).

(30) If the minor proposition is negative, the major proposition is universal. For the major proposition is affirmative (art. 15), and furthermore the conclusion is negative (art. 21); therefore the major proposition (by art. 29) is universal.[2]

Corollary 1. Therefore if the major proposition is particular the minor proposition is affirmative, by conversion of the preceding proposition.

Corollary 2. There is no syllogism in which the major proposition is a particular affirmative and the minor proposition a universal negative; i.e. there is no mood IEO.

(31) If the conclusion is a universal affirmative, the syllogism must be in the first figure. For the conclusion is universal (by hypothesis), therefore the minor term in it is a universal term (by art. 11). Therefore the minor term is universal in the minor proposition (art. 20); but that is affirmative (art. 21), since the conclusion, by hypothesis, is affirmative. Therefore the universal term in it is not the predicate (art. 10); therefore the minor term is the subject in the minor proposition. So the middle term in that proposition is the predicate; therefore, as the proposition will be affirmative, the middle term (art. 9)[3] will be particular; therefore (art. 19) the middle term will be universal in the major proposition. But the major proposition is affirmative (art. 21), since the

C 198

---

[1] Couturat (*C 683*: Errata and Addenda) corrects the 'medius' of the text to 'major'.

[2] Sc. 'because it is not negative'. Because of erasions and insertions the text is confused here, but the general sense seems to be what is represented above.

[3] The text has 'art. 11', which seems to be a mistake of Leibniz's for 'art. 9', the relevant proposition here. This is one of a number of similar mistakes in this paper, probably due to the fact that Leibniz renumbered the articles (cf. note to art. 38).

conclusion is affirmative. Therefore the middle, universal term in the major proposition cannot be the predicate, but must be the subject. Since, therefore, the middle term will be the predicate in the minor proposition and the subject in the major, the syllogism will be in the first figure.

(32) Two particular propositions do not constitute a valid syllogism. For one of the premisses is always affirmative (art. 15); therefore, if the two premisses are particular, one of them is a particular affirmative. But this has both its terms particular (art. 25); therefore the extreme term and the middle term are particular. The middle term, therefore, is universal in the other premiss (art. 19); but as this is also particular (by hypothesis), the middle term cannot be the subject in that premiss (art. 11). Therefore it must be the predicate; therefore (art. 10) the premiss is negative. The extreme term is the subject, and since the proposition is particular, this extreme term will also be particular (art. 11). Both extreme terms, therefore, are particular; therefore (art. 20) they are also particular in the conclusion. Therefore the conclusion will be a particular affirmative (art. 25), which is absurd, since it has been shown that one of the premisses is negative, and therefore (art. 21) the conclusion also is negative.

(33) If one or other premiss is particular, the conclusion is particular; i.e. if the conclusion is universal, each premiss is universal. For if the conclusion is universal, the minor term is universal everywhere (coroll. art. 27), therefore it is universal in the minor proposition also. But since the conclusion also is affirmative,[1] the minor term is subject in the minor proposition (art. 31); therefore (art. 11) the minor proposition is universal. Again, the middle term in that proposition is the predicate, therefore the middle term there is particular (art. 9). Therefore the middle term is a universal term in the major proposition (art. 19); but there it is the subject (art. 31),[2] therefore (by art. 11) the major proposition also is universal. We have proved our point, therefore, if the conclusion is a universal affirmative. If the conclusion is a universal negative, each extreme term is universal (art. 26). Here, therefore, there is no particular affirmative premiss (art. 25); if there is a particular premiss, then, it can only be a particular negative. Therefore (by arts. 15 and 31) the other premiss is a universal affirmative. Since the extreme term in this premiss is universal (as has been shown), it will be the subject (arts. 9 and 11). Therefore the middle term in this premiss will

C 199

---

[1] Leibniz must mean '*If* the conclusion is affirmative'. He takes up later the case in which the conclusion is negative.
[2] Corrected by Couturat from the 'art. 3' of the text.

be the predicate, and particular (art. 9);[1] therefore (art. 19) in the other premiss, the particular negative, it will be universal, and will therefore be the predicate there (art. 10). Therefore the extreme term in it will be the subject; but it is universal, and so it is also absurd that the premiss should be a particular negative. So no premiss can be particular, whether the conclusion is a universal negative or a universal affirmative. Q.E.D.

Note. It does not follow that, if the conclusion is particular, a premiss also is particular; for every universal premiss is at the same time tacitly particular.[2] But it does follow that if the conclusion is negative, a premiss also is negative.

(34) When the major term is the subject in a premiss and the conclusion is negative, the major proposition is universal. For since the conclusion is negative, its predicate is universal (art. 10),[3] i.e. (art. 17) the major term is universal. Therefore this term is also universal in the major proposition (art. 20). But the major term is the subject in this proposition (by hypothesis), therefore (art. 11) the major proposition itself is universal. Q.E.D.

Corollary. It follows that when the major term is the subject in a premiss, the major proposition being particular, the conclusion is affirmative.

(35) When the major term is the predicate in a premiss, the conclusion being negative, the major proposition is negative. The proof proceeds as in the previous article, except that the last sentence reads, 'But the major term is the predicate in this proposition (by hypothesis), therefore (art. 10) the major proposition itself is negative'.

Corollary. It follows that when the major term is the predicate in a premiss, the major proposition being affirmative, the conclusion also is affirmative.

(36) When the minor term is the predicate in a premiss, the conclusion being universal, the minor proposition is negative. For if the conclusion is universal, the minor term in it is universal C 200 (art. 11), and therefore universal in the premiss (art. 20). But in that premiss it is the predicate (by hypothesis); therefore (art. 10) it is negative.

Corollary. Therefore, when the minor term is the predicate in a premiss, the minor proposition being affirmative, the conclusion is particular.

(37) When the middle term is always the predicate, i.e. in the second figure, the conclusion must be negative. For the middle

---

[1] The text has 'art. 11', but 'art. 9' seems to be meant.
[2] Couturat glosses, 'By virtue of subalternation'.
[3] The text has 'art. 11', but 'art. 10' seems to be meant.

term must be universal on one occasion (art. 19); but a universal predicate makes a proposition negative (art. 10), therefore one or other of the premisses is negative. Therefore (art. 21) the conclusion is negative.

Corollary. It follows that, if the conclusion is affirmative, the middle term is the subject somewhere.

(38) In this same figure, the major proposition is always universal. For since the conclusion is negative (art. 37),[1] the major term in it is universal (art. 10); therefore it is also universal in the major proposition (art. 20). But in that proposition it is the subject (by hypothesis), therefore (art. 11)[2] it also makes the proposition universal.

(39) When the middle term is always the subject, i.e. in the third figure, the conclusion must be particular.

Let the conclusion be universal: therefore the minor term in it is universal, therefore (art. 20) it is also universal in the minor proposition. But in the minor proposition it is the predicate (by hypothesis); therefore the minor proposition will be negative (art. 10). Therefore (art. 21) the conclusion also is negative, and therefore the major term in the conclusion is universal (art. 10). Therefore the major term in the major proposition is also universal (art. 20). But in that proposition it is the predicate (by hypothesis), therefore (art. 10) the major proposition will also be negative. Consequently, both premisses are negative, which is absurd, by art. 15. So when the middle term is always the subject, the conclusion must be particular. Q.E.D.

(40) When the middle term is now the subject and now the predicate, if the premiss in which it is the predicate is affirmative, the other premiss will be universal. For in the former the middle term will be particular (art. 9), and therefore it will be universal in the other premiss (art. 19). But in that proposition it is the subject (by hypothesis), therefore the proposition itself will be universal (art. 11).

C 201   *Corollary.* It follows that if, in the fourth figure, the major premiss is affirmative, the minor premiss is universal.

Note. In the case of the first figure, there is a useless corollary which could be drawn. This would run: if, in the first figure, the minor premiss is affirmative, the major is universal. This is indeed true, but it is not enough, since the minor premiss in that figure is always affirmative, and . . .[3]

[1] Couturat notes that Leibniz wrote '28', the original number of article 37.
[2] The text has 'art. 12', but 'art. 11' must be meant.
[3] Couturat notes that Leibniz was doubtless about to add that the major premiss is universal, but noticed that he had not yet proved this. He does so in art. 43.

(41) When the middle term is now the subject and now the predicate, if the premiss in which it is the subject is particular, the other will be negative. This is proved in the same way.

Corollary. It follows that if, in the fourth figure, the minor premiss is particular, the major will be negative.

Note. Each of these two propositions can be joined with the other, since one is merely the other's converse. That is, a premiss in which the middle term is the predicate cannot be affirmative at the same time as the premiss in which it is the subject is particular.[1]

(42) In the first and the third figure the minor proposition is affirmative. For if the minor proposition were negative, the conclusion would be negative (art. 21). Now when the conclusion is negative and the major term is the predicate in a premiss (as in the first and third figures, art. 22), the major proposition also is negative (art. 35). Therefore both the major and the minor premiss would be negative, contrary to art. 15.

(43) In the first figure, the major proposition is universal. For in this figure the minor proposition is affirmative (art. 42);[2] therefore the middle term is also the predicate of the minor proposition (art. 22); therefore the middle term is particular (art. 9).[3] Therefore the middle term in the major proposition is universal. But the middle term in the major proposition is the subject (art. 22), therefore (art. 11) the major proposition is universal. This also follows from propositions 40 and 42.

(44) If the middle term is the predicate[4] in the minor proposition, the major proposition is universal. For if the middle term is the predicate in the minor proposition, the figure is either the first or the second (art. 22). But in figure one the major proposition is universal (art. 43), and in figure two the major proposition is also universal (art. 38). This is what was to be proved.

(45) In the fourth figure, the major proposition is not particular at the same time as the minor proposition is negative. Let the particular major proposition in this figure (by 24) be PDψC, and the negative minor proposition be ψCSB;[5] then the negative conclusion will be PBSD. But this is absurd, since (art. 20) there cannot be PD in the major proposition and SD in the conclusion.[6]

(46) In the fourth figure, the minor proposition is not particular

C 202

---

[1] The text has 'universalis', but as this would contradict art. 40 it seems that 'particularis' should be read.

[2] Corrected by Couturat from the 'art. 40' of the text.

[3] The text has 'art. 11', but 'art. 9' seems to be meant here.

[4] Leibniz has here deleted successively 'praedicatum' and 'subjectum'; Couturat points out that 'praedicatum' should be read.

[5] Corrected by Couturat from the 'SCψB' of the text.

[6] Corrected by Couturat from the 'in minore' of the text.

at the same time as the major proposition is affirmative. For
suppose that they are: then the major proposition will be ψDPC,
and the minor proposition PCψB. But in this way the middle
term, C, is particular in each, which is contrary to art. 19. This
can also be derived as a corollary from proposition 40 or 41.

(47) Any figure, therefore, has two limitations. In the first figure,
the major proposition is universal and the minor affirmative; in
the second, the major proposition is universal and the conclusion
negative; in the third, the minor proposition is affirmative and the
conclusion is particular. The two limitations on the fourth figure
are more involved, as in articles 45 and 46.

(48) There is no universal affirmative conclusion except in the
first figure. The second and third figures are excluded by arts. 37
and 39.[1] Further, the minor term is universal in the conclusion[2]
(art. 11), and therefore in the minor proposition also (art. 20). But
that is affirmative (art. 21), therefore its predicate is particular
(art. 9); therefore the minor universal term is not its predicate but
its subject, and this does not hold in the fourth figure (art. 20).
Therefore only the first figure remains.

Were we now to come to an enumeration of moods, the first
figure must be proved, in four moods; from this, subalternation
will be proved, the identical proposition being assumed.[3] Thus we
shall have the remaining two moods of the first figure. From the
six moods of the first figure, the six moods of the second and the
six moods of the third are proved by regress,[4] and it is proved at
the same time that there are as many moods of the second or third
figure as of the first. Moods of the fourth figure are proved from
the first by means of conversion, and the ones which have been
proved give the remainder by regress. It must be maintained that
there are no more moods, and this must be done, not by an
enumeration of illegitimate moods, but from the laws of those
which are legitimate. For example, in the first figure the premisses
SCψD, ψBPD give:

SCPD	SBPD	AA	A	Barbara	1
			I	Barbari	2
	PBPD	AI	I	Darii	3
SCSD	SBPD	EA	E	Celarent	4
			O	Celaro	5
	PBPD	EI	O	Ferio	6

[1] Corrected by Couturat, from the '38' of the text.
[2] Sc. 'as the conclusion in question is a universal proposition'.
[3] See below, C 412 (p. 107).
[4] See below, C 412–15 (pp. 107–10).

12. Of the Mathematical Determination of Syllogistic Forms

I think that no one who understands these matters doubts that the part of logic which deals with the moods and figures of the syllogism can be reduced to geometrical rigour. Indeed, several gifted men have already applied themselves to the task of showing this; but it is a remarkable fact that the number of useful moods has still not been determined. This is what I shall now attempt to do, and it is a task which I think not unworthy of geometry. For if praise is given to the men who have determined the number of regular bodies—which is of no use, except in so far as it is pleasant to contemplate—and if it is thought to be an exercise worthy of a mathematical genius to have brought to light the more elegant properties of a conchoid or cissoid, or some other figure which rarely has any use, how much better will it be to bring under mathematical laws human reasoning, which is the most excellent and useful thing which we have. Logicians are not to be blamed because they have pursued these tasks, but because they have wearied boys with them. I shall not only show, for the sake of precision of thought, why there are only three direct figures, whereas the fourth figure is indirect, and why in each of the direct figures there are six moods and in the indirect there are nine; but to assist the learner I shall add a logical canon of extraordinary use. By means of this canon it will be possible to recognize instantly whether some proposed mood is valid without paying any attention to figures and logical rules, but simply by drawing three straight lines.[1]

The basis of the syllogism is this: if some whole, C, falls within some D, or if a whole, C, falls outside some D, then in the first case that which is in C will fall within D, and in the second case it will fall outside D. This is what is commonly called the *dictum de omni et nullo*.

From this there arise at once these primitive moods: 'Every C is D, every B is C, therefore every B is D', or, if you prefer, 'Every B is C, every C is D, therefore every B is D'. That is, the individuals belonging to B [*individua ipsius B*] are contained in the

---

[1] Cf. *Generales Inquisitiones*, pars. 113 ff., and *De Formae Logicae Comprobatione per Linearum Ductus*, C 292 ff.

individuals belonging to C, and the individuals belonging to C are contained in the individuals belonging to D, therefore the individuals belonging to B are contained in the individuals belonging to D. That is, the total aggregate of the individuals belonging to C is comprehended in the individuals belonging to D; now, all the individuals belonging to B are comprehended in the individuals belonging to C, and therefore in the individuals belonging to D.

'Every C is D, some B is C, therefore some B is D'; or 'Some B is C, every C is D, therefore some B is D'. That is, some individuals belonging to B are contained in the individuals belonging to C, all the individuals belonging to C are contained in the individuals belonging to D, therefore some individuals belonging to B are contained in the individuals belonging to D. More briefly, and including both moods: 'B, either wholly or in part (i.e. in respect of all or some of the individuals belonging to it) is in C; now, the whole of C is in D, therefore B also will be in D, either wholly or in part.'

'No C is D, every B is C, therefore no B is D'; also 'No C is D, some B is C, therefore some B is not D'.[1] That is, B, either wholly or in part, is in C; now, the whole of C falls outside D, therefore B also, either wholly or in part, falls outside D. These statements have no less geometrical certainty than if it were said that that which contains a whole contains a part of the whole, or that that from which a whole is removed has a part of that whole removed from it.

From these few moods I shall now prove all the others, using subalternation, regress and conversion. By subalternation (i.e. the argument from the universal to the particular) I shall show two derivative moods of the first figure which are not in common use; by regress I shall show, from the first figure,[2] all the moods of the second and third figures, and by these, conversion itself; finally, by adding conversion to the former methods (of subalternation and regress) I shall show the moods of the fourth, or indirect figure. C 412   For the sake of brevity I shall henceforth follow the custom of logicians and express the universal affirmative by A, the universal negative by E, the particular affirmative by I and the particular negative by O; I shall write ABC, EBC, IBC, OBC for the proposition to be expressed, and AAA, EEE &c. for the mood to be expressed.

Hence the four moods of the first figure which we have declared to be primitive, i.e. independent of the others, will be stated as follows—*Barbara*: ACD ABC ABD, *Celarent*: ECD ABC EBD,

---

[1] Corrected by Couturat, from the 'non est C' of the text.
[2] Reading 'prima' in place of Couturat's 'primis' (cf. Schmidt, p. 490).

Darii: ACD IBC IBD, *Ferio*: ECD IBC OBD. Here, A, E, I and O stand for the form, and B, C, D the matter—that is, B stands for the minor, C the middle and D the major term. For example, 'ACD' stands for 'Every C is D', 'ECD' stands for 'No C is D', 'IBC' stands for 'Some B is C', and 'OBD' stands for 'Some B[1] is not D'. *Subalternation* (by means of which the other two moods of the first figure are derived from these four moods) is proved as follows: every A is B, some A is A, therefore some A is B, which is an argument in *Darii*. Similarly: no A is B, some A is A, therefore some A is not B, which is an argument in *Ferio*. Hence *Barbari* is derived from *Barbara*, writing in place of ABD, the conclusion, IBD which follows from it; also *Celaro* is derived from *Celarent*, writing in place of EBD, the conclusion, OBD which follows from it. We have, therefore, two new moods—derivative moods—of the first figure: *Barbari* ACD ABC IBD, and *Celaro* ECD ABC OBD. The usefulness of these moods for the deduction from the first figure, by our uniform method, of all other moods of the other figures will appear as we proceed. It will also appear that the three direct figures (the first, second and third) have an equal number of moods, namely six, and that from each mood of the first (using the method of regress, which will now follow) one mood of the second and one mood of the third are proved. Hence I add two new moods to the second figure also; however, the third figure as usually stated is already complete.

In 'regress' I use this principle: that if a conclusion is false (that is, if its contradictory is true) and one of its premisses is true, then the other premiss must necessarily be false, i.e. its contradictory must be true. Regress, therefore, presupposes the principle of contradiction. A 'contradiction' holds between a universal affirmative and a particular negative, or, if A is false O is true, and conversely; it also holds between a universal negative *C 413* and a particular affirmative, or, if E is false I[2] will be true, and conversely.

I will now derive the moods of the second and third figures by regress from the six moods of the first figure, beginning with *Barbara*. Here I shall expound matters so clearly that I can be more brief in what follows. In *Barbara*, belonging to the first figure, we have, 'Every C is D, every B is C, therefore every B is D'. So if it is assumed that the major premiss is true (every C is D), and that the conclusion is false and therefore that its contradictory is true (some B is not D),[3] the minor premiss will be

---

[1] Corrected by Couturat from the 'quoddam O' of the text.
[2] Corrected by Couturat from the 'A' of the text.
[3] Corrected by Couturat from the 'C' of the text.

false (i.e. some B will not be C). Now, the argument 'Every C is D, some B is not D, therefore some B is not C' is in *Baroco*, belonging to the second figure. This mood, therefore, arises from and is proved by regress from *Barbara*, which belongs to the first figure, by supposing the conclusion of this mood of the first figure to be false, and the major premiss to be true. But if it is assumed that in *Barbara* the conclusion is false (i.e. that some B is not D) and that the minor premiss is true (i.e. that every B is C), then the major premiss will be false (i.e. some C will not be D), which is in *Bocardo*, belonging to the third figure. But to express all this in more concise symbols:

Barbara (1st fig.)	ACD	ABC	ABD	*Barbara* (1st fig.)	ACD	ABC	ABD
Regress	ACD		OBD	Regress		ABC	OBD
Therefore		OBC		Therefore	OCD		
Hence *Baroco*				Hence *Bocardo*			
(2nd fig.)	ACD	OBD	OBC	(3rd fig.)	OBD	ABC	OCD

Celarent (1st fig.)	ECD	ABC	EBD	*Celarent* (1st fig.)	ECD	ABC	EBD
Regress	ECD		IBD	Regress		ABC	IBD
Therefore		OBC		Therefore	ICD		
Hence *Festino*				Hence *Disamis*			
(2nd fig.)	ECD	IBD	OBC	(3rd fig.)	IBD	ABC	ICD

Darii (1st fig.)	ACD	IBC	IBD	*Darii* (1st fig.)	ACD	IBC	IBD
Regress	ACD		EBD	Regress		IBC	EBD
Therefore		EBC		Therefore	OCD		
Hence *Camestres*				Hence *Ferison*			
(2nd fig.)	ACD	EBD	EBC	(3rd fig.)	EBD	IBC	OCD

Ferio (1st fig.)	ECD	IBC	OBD	*Ferio* (1st fig.)	ECD	IBC	OBD
Regress	ECD		ABD	Regress		IBC	ABD
Therefore		EBC		Therefore	ICD		
Hence *Cesare*				Hence *Datisi*			
(2nd fig.)	ECD	ABD	EBC	(3rd fig.)	ABD	IBC	ICD

C 414

Barbari (1st fig.)	ACD	ABC	IBD	*Barbari* (1st fig.)	ACD	ABC	IBD
Regress	ACD		EBD	Regress		ABC	EBD
Therefore		OBC		Therefore	OCD		
Hence *Camestros*				Hence *Felapton*			
(2nd fig.)	ACD	EBD	OBC	(3rd fig.)	EBD	ABC	OCD

Celaro (1st fig.)	ECD	ABC	OBD	*Celaro* (1st fig.)	ECD	ABC	OBD
Regress	ECD		ABD	Regress		ABC	ABD
Therefore		OBC		Therefore	ICD		
Hence *Cesaro*				Hence *Darapti*			
(2nd fig.)	ECD	ABD	OBC	(3rd fig.)	ABD	ABC	ICD

It is evident from this table that whilst the corresponding mood of the second or third figure is derived by regress from the mood of the first figure, the major premiss in the first remains the major premiss in the second, but the minor premiss in the first remains the minor premiss in the third. The conclusion and the minor premiss in the first and second figure, and also the conclusion and the major premiss in the first and third, are permuted after having first been changed into their contradictories. That is, the conclusion of the first figure, by means of its contradictory, makes the minor premiss in the second, and the minor premiss of the first figure makes the conclusion in the second; or conversely. But the conclusion of the first figure makes the major premiss in the third, and the major premiss of the first figure makes the conclusion in the third. Further, the moods of the second and third figure which correspond (i.e. are derived from the same mood of the first figure) have the same proposition in common—the minor premiss in the second figure and the major premiss in the third; they also permute the others, first changed into their contradictories. Hence it follows that if anyone were to treat by regress, in the same way that I have treated the moods of the first figure, the moods of the second or third figure which have been discovered, there will appear no new moods, but the very same moods which I have just determined. For if we keep the major premiss in the second figure we return to the mood of the first, which has the same major premiss, from which that mood of the second figure had been derived. If we keep the minor premiss we return to the mood of the third figure (which has the minor premiss kept for its major), which had been derived from the same mood of the first figure. It is the same in the third figure, where, if we keep the minor premiss, we return to the mood of the first (of the same minor premiss), from which that mood of the third had been derived. If we keep the major premiss, we return to the mood of the third figure (which has the major premiss kept for its minor), which is derived from the same mood of the first. So from *Cesare* we get by regress its father *Ferio*, if we keep the major premiss; if we keep the minor premiss, we get its brother *Datisi*. Similarly, from *Datisi* we get by regress its father *Ferio* or its brother *Cesare*.

Hence it can easily be known to which mood of the first figure   *C 415* some given mood of the second or third is reduced, by following these two lines:

Figure two keeps the major, figure three the minor premiss
From the first figure, when there is a regress.

The result is that there is no longer any need for the barbarous terms *Cesare*, *Camestres*, &c., invented for the sake of reduction, provided that it is understood that 'regress' here simply means inferring the falsity of one premiss, assuming the falsity of the conclusion and the truth of the other premiss. In general, this is made evident as follows (suppressing quality and quantity):

In the first figure	CD	BC	BD
Regress	CD		BD
Therefore		BC	
Hence in the second figure	CD	BD	BC
In the first figure	CD	BC	BD
Regress		BC	BD
Therefore	CD		
Hence in the third figure	BD	BC	CD

This proof of the second and third figures contains at the same time their *a priori* origin, i.e. the method by which they could have been discovered. This is the best method of proof, for it is synthetic or combinatorial, and not analytic, which assumes that the figures are already given. By this method it can also be predicted how many moods and figures will arise, for one mood of the first figure gives one mood of the second and one of the third. The reason why this method has not been followed, I believe, has been the neglect of the new moods of the first and second figure which I have added; for otherwise its universality as a means of deriving the moods of the third figure from the first does not appear. This is why logicians commonly use conversions to prove the moods of the second and third figure; but in this way they have at the same time come upon the moods of the fourth. My method, however, derives the direct figures (namely, the second and third) from the first by regress; the indirect moods (those of the fourth figure) cannot be obtained by regress alone, but conversions have to be used. But these themselves must be proved by the second and third figures, as I shall now show. By this method, therefore, there appears the true reason why the fourth figure is excluded from the number of the direct figures and is to be placed after the second and third, since it is only through them that it is proved.

C 416   For us to reach the fourth figure, conversions must first be proved.

(1) In *Cesare* (second figure) it is proved that the universal negative can be converted *simpliciter*: No A is B, every B is B, therefore no B is A.

(2) In *Darapti* (third figure) it is proved that the universal affirmative can be converted *per accidens*: Every A is A, every A is B, therefore some B is A.

(3) In *Festino* (second figure) it is proved that the universal negative can be converted *per accidens*: No A is B, some B is B, therefore some B is not A.

(4) In *Datisi* (third figure) it is proved that the particular affirmative can be converted *simpliciter*: Every A is A, some A is B, therefore some B is A.

In this way (as also appeared in the proof of subalternation) inferences involving two terms provide us with syllogisms, which involve three terms, by the use of identical propositions, which state the same term twice. Conversion by contraposition is not applicable here, for in contraposition the terms themselves are changed by transferring the change from the copula, i.e. the form, to the term itself, i.e. the matter. Though identical propositions may be used in other moods, we shall not obtain any new conversions; for the most part we shall come upon a conclusion which repeats a premiss. There is the additional fact that only affirmative propositions can be identical, and contraposition has to be used for negative propositions. For just as I can say 'Every man is a man', so also I can say 'No not-man is a man'. But, as I have already said, contraposition does not belong here.[1]

---

[1] The paper does not contain the promised derivation of the moods of the fourth figure, though Leibniz added a reminder—'Figura Quarta'—at the bottom of the page of his MS.

13. An intensional account of immediate inference and the syllogism ('Logical Definitions')[1]

(1) That A includes B, or, that B is included in A, is that B, the predicate, is 'affirmed universally' of A, the subject. For example, 'The wise man includes the just man', that is, 'Every wise man is just'.

(2) That A excludes B, or, that B is excluded from A, is that B, the predicate, is 'denied universally' of A, the subject. For example, 'The just man excludes the unhappy man', that is, 'No just man is unhappy'.

(3) To deny that A includes B is to deny the predicate B of some subject, A; i.e. it is to state a 'particular negative'. I.e. to deny that the wealthy man is included in the just man is to state that some just man is not wealthy. For if every just man were wealthy (understand by this everyone who is, was, or will be) it could now be said that the wealthy man is in everyone who is just. So the just man would include the wealthy man, which is contrary to the hypothesis.

(4) To deny that A excludes B is to affirm a predicate, B, of some subject, A, i.e. it is to state a 'particular affirmative'. To deny that the wealthy man is excluded from the wise man is to say that some wise man is wealthy.

(5) If a new proposition follows from several propositions, and this new proposition is false, some one of the others will be false. This is inference by 'regress'.

(6) Contradictory propositions (i.e. propositions one of which affirms what the other denies) cannot be true at the same time, or false at the same time. This is called 'opposition'.

(7) From a universal proposition there follows a particular proposition of the same nature; this is called 'subalternation'. Thus, if A includes B, i.e. (by no. 1) if every A is B, it follows that A does not exclude B, i.e. (by no. 4) that some A is B. Again, if A excludes B, i.e. (by no. 2) if no A is B, it follows that A does not include B, i.e. (by no. 3) that some A is not B.

(8) If A excludes B, then conversely B excludes A. This is the basis of 'conversion *simpliciter*'. For it follows from this (by 2) that

---

[1] This title was supplied by Erdmann: *G.-G. Leibnitii opera philosophica* (Berlin, 1840), p. 100.

if no A is B, then no B is A, and (by 4) that if some A is B, then
some B is A.

G vii.
209

(9) If A includes B, then B does not exclude A. From this (by 1
and 4) there arises 'conversion *per accidens*': every A is B, therefore
some B is A.

(10) It is worth noting that both subalternation and conversion
can be proved by means of syllogisms.

(12)[1] A 'simple categorical syllogism' is one which draws some
inference about the mutual inclusion or exclusion of two terms
from what is given about the inclusion or exclusion of a third
term with regard to each of the other terms.

(13) An includer of an includer is an includer of what is included;
i.e. if A includes B and B includes C, A will also include C.

(14) An includer of an excluder is an excluder of what is excluded;
i.e. if A includes B and B excludes C, A will also exclude C.

(15) An includer of an excluder is excluded from what is excluded;
i.e. if A includes B and B excludes C, C also excludes A. This
follows from what precedes, with the addition of no. 8. Hence, by
changing C into A and conversely, what is excluded (A) from
what is included (B) is an excluder (A) of the includer (C). B
excludes A and C includes B, therefore A excludes C.

(16) An excluder of what is included is an excluder of the includer;
i.e. if A excludes B and C includes B, A excludes C. This is self-
evident.

(17) If A excludes B and C includes B, C also excludes A; i.e. the
excluder of what is included is excluded from the includer. This
follows from 16, with the help of 8. Hence if you permute C and A
you get: if A includes B and C excludes B, A also excludes C; i.e.
an includer of what is excluded is an excluder of the excluder.

(18) A first rule may be stated as follows: the inclusion of the
middle term in the subject also shows that the predicate which is
included in (or excluded from) the middle term is included in (or
excluded from) the subject. Hence, given an arrangement of
terms BC AB AC, we get from inclusion *aaa*,[2] from which we get
by subalternation *aai*. From exclusion we get *eae*, from which we
get by subalternation *eao*. But because *e*BC can be inferred from
*e*CB, from this we get *e*CB, *a*AB, *e*AC, and by subalternation
*e*CB, *a*AB, *o*AC.

(19) A second rule may be stated as follows: the exclusion of the
middle term from the subject also shows that the predicate which
includes the middle term is excluded from the subject. Hence we

---

[1] *Sic*.
[2] L.– *a* universal affirmative, *e* universal negative, *i* particular affirmative,
o particular negative.

get aCB, eAB, e (or o) AC. As this mood follows from aCB, eBA, e (or o) AC (by the conversion *simpliciter* of eAB into eBA), it will also be valid in this way.

(20) We have, therefore, ten moods from rules one and two. From any one of these, two moods are derived by regress, by denying the conclusion, affirming one of the premisses and denying[1] the other. Besides these ten, therefore, there will be another twenty, or thirty in all. There will be even more by taking for propositions which imply a consequence those from which they themselves follow—i.e. their conversions *simpliciter*. However, since there are in fact only twenty-four moods, as I have shown elsewhere, some must occur twice.

---

[1] The text has 'affirmatur', but 'negatur' must be meant.

14. A paper on 'some logical difficulties' (after 1690)

Some logical difficulties worth solution have occurred to me.
How is it that opposition is valid in the case of singular propositions—e.g. 'The Apostle Peter is a soldier' and 'The Apostle
Peter is not a soldier'—since elsewhere a universal affirmative and
a particular negative are opposed? Should we say that a singular
proposition is equivalent to a particular and to a universal proposition? Yes, we should. So also when it is objected that a singular
proposition is equivalent to a particular proposition, since the
conclusion in the third figure must be particular, and can nevertheless be singular; e.g. 'Every writer is a man, some writer is the
Apostle Peter, therefore the Apostle Peter is a man'. I reply that
here also the conclusion is really particular, and it is as if we had
drawn the conclusion 'Some Apostle Peter is a man'. For 'some
Apostle Peter' and 'every Apostle Peter' coincide, since the term
is singular.

A greater difficulty is this: that accepted conversion seems
sometimes to lead to what is false. I have in mind the conversion
per accidens of a universal affirmative proposition in a case such as
'Every laugher is a man, therefore some man is a laugher'. For the
former is true even if no man laughs, whereas the latter is not true
unless some man actually laughs; the former speaks of possibles,
the latter of actuals. However, a difficulty of this kind does not
occur if you remain within the limits of possibles: e.g. 'Every man
is an animal, therefore some animal is a man'. It must therefore
be said that the conclusion, 'Some man is a laugher', is true in the
region of ideas, i.e. if you take 'laugher' for some species of possible entity, just as 'soldier' is a species of man; or, just as man is
a species of animal, so some man is a laugher; the proposition will
be true, even if no laugher exists. Certainly, I have a proof of conversion, through a syllogism in the third figure: 'Every laugher is
a laugher, every laugher is a man, therefore some man is a laugher'.
I understand this to be in the region of ideas, if 'laugher' is taken
for a species of man, not for an actual laugher. This syllogism in
Darapti can be proved from the first figure by regress. In this, one
assumes only the laws of opposition, whilst taking for granted the
syllogism in the first figure and assuming the conclusion to be false
and one of the premisses to be true, from which it follows that the

other premiss is false; but the opposite of a false conclusion is true.

The laws of opposition, however, are primitive. For example, I say that the proposition 'Some man is not an animal' is opposed to 'Every man is an animal'. For 'Every man is an animal' is the same as 'Man A is an animal, man B is an animal, man C is an animal, and so on', and 'Some man is not an animal' simply says that B is not an animal, or something of this sort; consequently, 'Every man is an animal' and 'Some man is not an animal' are opposed. Similarly, 'No man is a stone' and 'Some man is a stone' are opposed. For 'No man is a stone' means 'Man A is not a stone, man B is not a stone, man C is not a stone, &c.'; therefore a proposition such as 'Man B is a stone', which is simply 'Some man is a stone', is false. This is properly the *dictum de omni et nullo*, as the foundation of the whole of syllogistic theory—namely, the theory of opposition and of the first figure. For instance, 'Every man is an animal, every soldier is a man, therefore every soldier is an animal' is inferred in this way. For every man is an animal, and a soldier man is an animal, by the *dictum de omni*. Now, 'soldier man' and 'soldier' coincide (since every soldier is a man); therefore 'A soldier man is an animal' and 'A soldier is an animal' coincide.

So we return to the basis of the analysis by which I have proved syllogistic laws elsewhere. I used to interpret 'Every man is an animal' as '"Man-animal" and "man" are equivalent'; i.e. if anyone says that you are a man, he says that you are an animal. There was once a man called Greenhill; a friend says to him, 'It would be enough if you were called "Hill"'. 'Why?' he replies, 'Do you think that all hills are green?' 'Yes—now, at any rate', says his friend; for it was summer. His natural good sense told him that 'Every hill is green' coincides with '"Green hill" and "hill" are equivalent'.

My old analysis was this. The universal affirmative: every A is B, that is, AB and A are equivalent, or, A not-B is a non-entity. The particular negative: some A is not B, i.e. AB and A are not equivalent, or, A not-B is an entity. The universal negative, no A is B, will be 'AB is a non-entity', and the particular affirmative, some A is B, will be 'AB is an entity'. From this interpretation there are evident at once the rules of opposition (by which I have proved the second and third figures from the first) and the laws of conversion (by which I have proved the fourth figure) as is clear from the terms themselves. For the universal affirmative and particular negative are opposed, since the equivalence between terms which the one affirms the other denies of the same terms; similarly,

G vii.
213

the universal negative and particular affirmative are opposed *simpliciter*, since the entity which the one affirms of a term the other denies of the same term. The universal negative and particular affirmative are converted *simpliciter*, for when I say that AB is a non-entity, or that AB is an entity, it makes no difference if I also say that BA is an entity or BA is a non-entity, for AB and BA are equivalent. But the universal affirmative and particular negative are not converted *simpliciter*, for the propositions 'AB is equivalent to A', or 'AB is not equivalent to A', do not treat A and B in the same way, nor does it follow that AB is or is not equivalent to B.

The conversion *per accidens* of an affirmative proposition which is treated in this way presupposes the conversion *simpliciter* of the particular affirmative, which has already been proved, and also the proof of subalternation (i.e. the proof of a particular affirmative from a universal affirmative: 'Every A is B, therefore some A is B'). The proof proceeds as follows: every A is B, i.e. AB is equivalent to A. But A is an entity (by hypothesis), therefore AB is an entity, i.e. some A is B. Since it could be said with equal justice that BA is an entity, i.e. that some B is A, from this you already have conversion *per accidens*, i.e. an inference of the type, 'Every A is B, therefore some B is A'.

A universal negative can also be converted *per accidens*, but this is proved in another way; for it can be converted *simpliciter*, and the subaltern of the converse taken. We have already proved that its conversion *simpliciter* is permitted, and it remains for us to prove subalternation in this case (i.e. 'No A is B, therefore some A is not B'). Now, no A is B; that is, AB is a non-entity. Therefore AB is not equivalent to A (since A is an entity); that is, some A is not B. However, since no A is B, that is, since AB is a non-entity, and therefore BA also is a non-entity, BA also is not equivalent to B, i.e. some B is not A. From this, therefore, we have both subalternation and conversion *per accidens* from a universal negative.

It has occurred to me besides that the universal negative and its opposite, the particular affirmative, can also be expressed in terms of equivalence[1] as follows. 'No A is B', that is, 'AB is a non-entity', can also be expressed as 'AB and AB-entity [AB *Ens*] are not equivalent'. Similarly, 'Some A is B', that is, 'AB is an entity', can also be expressed as 'AB and AB-entity are equivalent'. Therefore from this method of expression we also have the opposition of a universal negative and a particular affirmative, and their conversion *simpliciter*; we also have subalternation from a

[1] Literally, 'can be reduced to an equivalence' ('reduci posse ad aequipollentiam').

universal negative. For let it be granted that no A is B; it will result from this that AB and AB-entity are not equivalent. It is to be inferred from this that some A is not B, i.e. that A and AB are not equivalent. For A and A-entity are equivalent, by hypothesis; but if A and AB were equivalent, AB and AB-entity would be equivalent, which is contrary to what has been assumed. So we have reduced all the categorical propositions of logic to a calculus of equivalences.

Further, from this there appears even more clearly the root of the error in a conversion such as 'Every laugher is a man, therefore some man is a laugher', since it can happen and could have happened that no man really laughs now, or ever did laugh, or indeed that no man ever existed. Every laugher is a man: that is, 'laugher' and 'laugher-man' are equivalent. But a laugher is an entity, by hypothesis, therefore a laugher-man is an entity, therefore a man-laugher is an entity, i.e. some man is a laugher. Here, in the proposition 'A man-laugher is an entity', 'entity' must be taken in the same way as in the proposition 'A laugher is an entity'. If 'entity' is taken to refer to possibility, i.e. as meaning that there is a laugher in the region of ideas, then 'Some man is a laugher' must not be understood as other than 'A man-laugher is an entity', namely as possible, i.e. in the region of ideas. But if 'A laugher is an entity' is taken to refer to what really exists, 'A man-laugher is an entity' can also be taken to refer to this, and it will be true that some man actually laughs. It would be the same if we had proceeded by the way in which a particular affirmative is reduced to an equivalence: 'Every laugher is a man, that is, "laugher" and "laugher-man" are equivalent'. Now, 'laugher' and 'laugher-entity' are equivalent, therefore 'man-laugher' and 'man-laugher-entity' are equivalent; that is, some man is a laugher. This is in the region of ideas, and not outside it (whether it be that a man-laugher is an entity, or that 'man-laugher' and 'man-laugher-entity' are equivalent), and 'Some man is a laugher' does not mean that some man actually laughs. The words of our language, then, are ambiguous, but the ambiguity is removed by our analysis. When 'Some man is a laugher' is inferred, it is understood that some species of man coincides with the term 'laugher', i.e. that a laugher-man is a laugher. So . . .[1] a laugher-stone would not be a laugher, since a laugher-stone involves a contradiction.[2]

From this it is also evident that the universal affirmative, with its opposite, the particular negative, differs entirely from the universal negative with its opposite, for an entity is assumed in the

---

[1] One word illegible in the MS.
[2] Sc. 'and so is not an entity'.

latter but not in the former. In all of them, however, it is tacitly assumed that the ingredient term is an entity.

Every A is B, that is, AB = A.

Some A is not B, that is, AB ≠ A.

No A is B, that is, AB is not an entity, or, AB ≠ AB-entity.

G vii.
215

Some A is B, that is, AB is an entity, or, AB = AB-entity. It is evident from these that in every affirmative proposition the predicate is particular, but it is not equally evident that in every negative proposition the predicate is universal, i.e. is removed. In general, we can tell if a term A or B is universal if YA or YB can be substituted for A or B, where Y can be anything which is compatible with B, such as C, F &c. Now, from AB = A one may not infer AYB = A; for although B is contained in A, it does not follow that YB will be contained in A. Similarly, from AB = AB-entity it does not follow that AYB = AYB-entity; for although YB is an entity, by hypothesis, it does not therefore follow that AY is an entity. It is evident from this, therefore, that the predicate of an affirmative proposition is not universal. Let us now show by a similar method that the predicate of a negative proposition is universal. If AB ≠ A, then AYB ≠ A; for whether YB = B or AY = A or not, the inference is valid. For if YB = B, or AY = A, they can be substituted for B or for A. If, however, they are not equivalent, much more will AYB and A not be equivalent. The same holds in the case of AB ≠ AB-entity.

It remains for us to prove that the subject has the quantity of its proposition. In the universal affirmative, AB = A, therefore YAB = YA. But in the particular negative, if AB ≠ A, it does not follow that YAB ≠ YA; for if Y = B, we shall have YAB = YA. In the universal negative, again, if AB is not an entity, YAB also is not an entity; i.e. if AB ≠ AB-entity, YAB ≠ YAB-entity. But in the particular affirmative, if AB is an entity it does not follow that YAB is also an entity, for one can assume under Y something which is incompatible with A and B. So we have derived from our calculus all the rules of distribution.

Further, in that other method of proving logical forms, where we do not proceed by ideas but by instances [*exempla subjecta*], the invalid consequence 'Every laugher is a man, therefore some man is a laugher, or laughs', will also be refutable. The sense is, 'Every possible laugher is a man, therefore some man is a possible laugher', which is correct. That this is the sense is shown by our interpretation, which makes conversion *per accidens* legitimate. Laugher = laugher-man; now, laugher = laugher-entity, therefore laugher-man = laugher-man-entity, since laugher = laugher-entity.

This makes me fear that this cannot be established properly by an inductive interpretation.Aristotle himself seems to have followed the way of ideas [*viam idealem*], for he says that animal is in man, namely a concept in a concept; for otherwise men would be among animals [*insint animalibus*]. Let us see, however, what can be derived from collective reasoning. *Barbara:* all men are among animals, all soldiers are among men, therefore all soldiers are among animals. *Celarent:* all men are outside stones, all soldiers are among men, therefore all soldiers are outside stones. *Darii:* all men are among animals, some intelligent beings are among men, therefore some intelligent beings are among animals. *Ferio:* all men are outside stones, some substances are among men, therefore some substances are outside stones. In *Darapti* we argue thus: every man is intelligent, every man is an animal, therefore some animal is intelligent. By the collective interpretation: all men are among intelligent beings, all men are among animals, therefore some animals are among intelligent beings. Let us transfer to this syllogism, by which conversion *per accidens* is proved: 'Every laugher is a laugher, every laugher is a man, therefore some man is a laugher'. On the present interpretation we have, 'All laughers are among laughers, all laughers are among men, therefore some men are among laughers'. But what if no man actually laughs? I assert that the proposition 'All laughers are among men', i.e. 'All laughers are men' is also false, because for it to be true, the proposition 'Some laughers are among men', or, 'Some laughers are men', will also be true. But that proposition is false, if no man laughs. However, it is different if you say 'All (if any) who laugh are among men', since it does not follow from this that some who laugh are among men, but only that some (if any) who laugh, or, some supposed laughers, are among men. So the syllogism will be of this kind: 'All supposed laughers are supposed laughers' (for one may not say that all supposed laughers are actually laughers), 'all supposed laughers are men, therefore some men are supposed laughers'. Or, on the present interpretation, 'All supposed laughers are among supposed laughers, all supposed laughers are among men (namely, *supposed* men), therefore some supposed men (i.e. some who are among supposed men) are among supposed laughers'. From this it is also evident that the consequence of a subalternation—e.g. 'Every laugher is a man, therefore some laugher is a man'—is open to similar abuse, since if nobody really laughs, no laugher is a man. It is evident that in such an objection the universal proposition is usually understood of a supposed laugher, the particular proposition of an actual laugher. So when it is said, 'Every laugher is a man, therefore some laugher is a man', the sense will be, 'Every supposed laugher is a man, therefore some supposed laugher is a man', from which it is properly concluded that some man (namely, a supposed man) is a supposed laugher; but from this there does not follow 'Therefore some man is actually a laugher'. But if you say, 'Everyone now actually laughing is a man', you assume that there really is someone who is now actually laughing and that he is a man, and so that some man actually laughs. For it must always be assumed that a term is a genuine entity, but 'now actually laughing' will not even be an entity, if it is false that someone actually laughs; this is a hypothetical necessity which . . .[1] is enough.

G vii.
217

Finis.

---

[1] One word illegible in the MS. The point of the reference to hypothetical necessity is probably this: Leibniz has said that if it is false that someone is now actually laughing, then 'now actually laughing' is not an entity, which may suggest (cf. G vii. 214 (p. 118)) that it is not possible that someone should now be laughing, i.e. that it is necessary that no one is now laughing. Yet the proposition that it is false that someone is now laughing is surely not necessary, but is contingent. Leibniz would agree that this is so. In the Generales Inquisitiones (pars. 60–61, 130–6) he has distinguished between necessary and contingent truths by saying that the latter need an infinite analysis; in the present paper he uses a distinction which he draws between two kinds of necessity, and says in effect that the necessity which holds in the case of the proposition that no one is now laughing is 'hypothetical' as opposed to 'logical' necessity. To say that a proposition has logical necessity is to say that its denial would involve a contradiction (e.g. G vi. 441); to say that it has hypothetical necessity is to say that it is necessary, given that such and such is the case (e.g. G ii. 18; G iii. 400; G vii. 303; DM, par. 13)—in the present instance, that God has made certain decisions (cf. LR, pp. 109–10).

15. A Study in the Plus-Minus Calculus ('A not inelegant Specimen of Abstract Proof')[1]
(after 1690)

G vii.
228

Definition 1. Those terms are 'the same' of which one can be substituted for the other without loss of truth. Thus, suppose that there are A and B; that A is an ingredient of some true proposition, and that on substituting B for A in some occurrence of A there a new proposition is formed, which is also true. If this always holds good in the case of any such proposition, then A and B are said to be 'the same'; conversely, if A and B are the same, the substitution which I have mentioned will hold good. The same terms are also called 'coincident'; sometimes, however, A and A are called 'the same', whereas A and B, if they are the same, are called 'coincident'.

Definition 2. Those terms are 'different' which are not the same, i.e. in which a substitution sometimes does not hold good.

Corollary. Consequently, those terms which are not different are the same.

Symbol 1. 'A = B' means that A and B are the same, or coincident.

Symbol 2. 'A ≠ B', or 'B ≠ A', means that A and B are different.

Definition 3. If several terms taken together coincide with one, any one of those several terms is said to 'be in' or to 'be contained in' that one term, and the one term itself is said to be the 'container'. Conversely, if some term is in another, it will be among several which together coincide with that other term. Thus, if A and B taken together coincide with L, then A, and also B, is called an 'inexistent' or 'content'; but L is called a 'container'. However, it can happen that container and content coincide, e.g. if one should have A and B = L, and A and L coincide; for then B will contain nothing other than A . . .[2]

G vii.
229

Note. Not every inexistent is a part, nor is every container a whole. For example, a square inscribed in a circle and a diameter are in the circle; the square is a part of the circle, but the diameter is not

---

[1] This title—'Non inelegans specimen demonstrandi in abstractis'—was later struck through by Leibniz, but is retained by Erdmann.

[2] There is a lacuna in the text here, followed by the phrase 'significet A, significabit Nihil'. Perhaps the sense is that B will contain nothing apart from what A contains, and so will either stand for A (i.e. will be an equivalent term) or will stand for nothing.

a part of it. Something must therefore be added if the concept of whole and part is to be explained accurately; but this does not concern us here. Further, those inexistents which are not parts are not only in something, but can also be taken away. For example, the centre can be removed from a circle, in such a way that all the points except the centre remain. This remainder will be the locus of all points within the circle whose distance from the circumference is less than the radius; the difference between this locus and the circle is a point, namely the centre. In the same way you get the locus of all points which are moved if a sphere is moved whilst two separate points on its diameter are unmoved, if you take away from the sphere the axis, i.e. the diameter which goes through the two unmoved points.

On the same assumptions, A and B taken together are said to be 'constituents', and L 'that which is constituted'.

Symbol 3. 'A + B = L' means that A is in L, or is contained in it. *Note.* Even if A and B have something in common, so that both taken together are greater than L, what we have said or shall say here will still hold. It will be useful to clarify this by an example. Let L stand for the straight line RX; let A stand for a part of it, namely the straight line RS, and B for another part of it, namely the straight line XY. Let it be assumed that either of these parts,

RS or XY, is greater than half of the whole, RX; then it cannot be said that A + B equals L, i.e. that RS + XY equals RX. For since YS is a common part of RS and XY, then RS + XY equals RX + SY. Yet it can truly be said that the straight lines RS and XY together coincide with the straight line RX.

Definition 4. If some term, M, is in A, and the same term is in B, this term will be said to be 'common' to them, and they will be

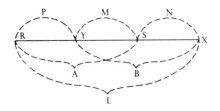

said to be 'communicating'. If, however, they have nothing in common, such as A and N (e.g. the straight lines RS and XS), they will be called 'uncommunicating'.

Definition 5. If A is in L, and some other term, N, should be produced, in which there remains everything which is in L except what is also in A (of which nothing must remain in N), A will be said to be 'subtracted' or removed from L, and N will be called the 'remainder'.

Symbol 4. If we have 'L — A = N', what is meant is that L is a container, of which the remainder is N if you subtract A from it.

G vii.
230
Definition 6. If some one term is assumed to coincide with several which are added or subtracted at the same time, those several terms are called 'constituents', and the one term, 'that which is constituted'.

Note. Hence all inexistents are constituents, but not conversely: thus, L — A = N, though L is not in A.

Definition 7. Constitution (that is, addition or subtraction) is either tacit or express. N or —M is the tacit constitution of M, just as A or —A in which N is. The express constitution of N itself is evident.

Definition 8. 'Compensation' is when the same term is added and subtracted in the same term, both the addition and the subtraction being express. 'Destruction' is when some term is thrown out on account of compensation, so that it is not expressed any further, and in place of M — M 'Nothing' is put.

Axiom 1. If the same term is taken with itself, nothing new is constituted; i.e. A + A = A.

Note. It is true that, in the case of numbers, 2 + 2 makes 4, or two coins added to two coins make four coins; but then the two which are added are other than the previous ones. If they were the same, nothing new would emerge, and it would be as if we wished for a joke to make six eggs out of three, by first counting three eggs, then removing one and counting the remainder, two, and then removing one again and counting the remainder, one.

Axiom 2. If the same term is added and subtracted, then whatever is constituted in another as a result of this coincides with Nothing. That is, A (however often it is added in the constitution of some thing)—A (however often it is subtracted from the same thing) = Nothing.

Note. Consequently A — A, or (A + A) — A, or A — (A + A), &c., = Nothing. For by Axiom 1, a return is always made to A — A.

Postulate 1. Several terms, whatever they may be, can be taken together to constitute one; thus, if there are A and B there can be formed from these A + B, which can be called L.

Postulate 2. Some term, e.g. A, can be subtracted from that in which it is—e.g. from A + B, i.e. L—if there are given the remaining terms, such as B, which together with A constitute the container L. Or, the same being assumed, it is possible to find the remainder, L — A.

Note. With the help of this postulate we shall later give a method of finding the difference between two terms of which one, A, is in the other, L, though the remaining terms which together with A constitute L are not given; that is, we shall give a method of discovering L — A, i.e. A + B — A, though only L and A are given, but not B.

THEOREM I

Terms which are the same as a third term are the same as one another.

If A = B and B = C, then A = C. For if, in the proposition 'A = B' (which is true by hypothesis) C is substituted in place of B (which may be done by def. 1, since B = C by hypothesis), the result is A = C. Q.E.D.

G vii.
231

THEOREM II

If, of two terms which are the same as each other, one is different from a third term, the other will also be different from that third term.

If A = B and B ≠ C, then A ≠ C. For if, in the proposition 'B ≠ C' (which is true, by hypothesis), A is substituted in place of B (which may be done by def. 1, since A = B, by hypothesis), the result is A ≠ C. Q.E.D.[1]

THEOREM III

If coincidents are added to the same term, coincidents are formed.

If A = B, A + C = B + C. For if, in the proposition 'A + C = A + C' (which is true in itself), you substitute B for A once (which may be done by def. 1, since A = B), the result is A + C = B + C. Q.E.D.

Corollary. If coincidents are added to coincidents, coincidents are formed. If A = B and L = M, then A + L = B + M. For (by the present theorem) since L = M, A + L = A + M; and if in this assertion B is put for A once (since A = B, by hypothesis), then A + L = B + M. Q.E.D.

---

[1] L.– Here could be inserted a theorem of this kind: *what is in one of two coincidents is also in the other.* If A is in B and B = C, A is also in C. For in the proposition 'A is in B' (which is true, by hypothesis) substitute C in place of B.

THEOREM IV

A content of a content is a content of the container; i.e. if that term in which there is another is in a third term, that which is in it will be in that third term; or if A is in B and B is in C, A will also be in C.

For A is in B (by hypothesis), therefore there is something to which we may give the name L, such that $A + L = B$ (by def. 3 or symbol 3). Similarly, since B is in C (by hypothesis), then $B + M = C$; and if in this assertion we put $A + L$ for B (which we have shown to coincide), we get $A + L + M = C$. Now, putting N for $L + M$ (by postulate 1) we get $A + N = C$. Therefore A is in C (by def. 3). Q.E.D.

THEOREM V

232

If each of a number of terms taken severally is in something, so also is that which is constituted by them.

If A is in C and B is in C, then $A + B$ (that which is constituted by A and B: def. 4) is in C. For since A is in C, there will be some M such that $A + M = C$ can be formed (by def. 3). Similarly, since B is in C, $B + N = C$ can be formed. Joining these (by the corollary of theorem 3) we get $A + M + B + N = C + C$. Now, $C + C = C$ (by axiom 1), therefore $A + M + B + N = C$. Therefore (by def. 3) $A + B$ is in C. Q.E.D.[1]

THEOREM VI

That which is constituted by contents is in that which is constituted by the containers.

If A is in M and B is in N, then $A + B$ will be in $M + N$. For A is in M (by hypothesis) and M is in $M + N$ (by def. 3), therefore A is in $M + N$ (by theor. 4). Similarly B is in N (by hypothesis) and N is in $M + N$ (by def. 3), therefore B is in $M + N$ (by theor. 4). Now if A is in $M + N$ and B is in $M + N$, then (by theor. 5) $A + B$ will also be in $M + N$. Q.E.D.

THEOREM VII

If some term is added to the term in which it is, no new term is constituted; i.e. if B is in A, then $A + B = A$.

For if B is in A, then $B + C = A$ can be formed (def. 3). Therefore (by theor. 3) $A + B = B + C + B = B + C$ (by axiom 1) $= A$ (by what has been said here). Q.E.D.

[1] L.– Familiar language must be intermingled, with which there must be mixed the familiar expressions of propositions, to be illustrated by examples.

Converse of the preceding theorem

If, by the addition of one term to another, no new term is constituted, that term is in the other.

If $A + B = A$, then B will be in A; for B is in $A + B$ (def. 3), and $A + B = A$ (by hypothesis). Therefore B is in A (by what is inserted between theorems 2 and 3). Q.E.D.

THEOREM VIII

If coincidents are subtracted from coincidents, the remainders are coincidents.[1]

If $A = L$ and $B = M$, then $A - B = L - M$. For $A - B$ *G vii.*
$= A - B$ (which is true in itself), and if in one or other of these   *233*
you substitute L for A and M for B, then (from the definition of
coincidents) you get $A - B = L - M$. Q.E.D.

THEOREM IX

(1) From an express compensation there follows the destruction of what is compensated, if nothing is to be destroyed in the compensation which is tacitly repeated and is an ingredient of some constitution outside the compensation; (2) so also if whatever is thus repeated is an ingredient of both an addition and a subtraction outside the compensation. (3) If neither of these holds, a destruction cannot be substituted for a compensation.

Case 1. If $A + N - M - N = A - M$, and A, N and M are uncommunicating; for then nothing is to be destroyed in the compensation $+ N - N$ which is in A or M outside the compensation; i.e. that which is added in $+N$ is contained in $+N$ as often as this is added, and that which is subtracted in $-N$ is contained in $-N$ as often as this is subtracted. Therefore (by axiom 2), for '$+N - N$' there can be put 'Nothing'.

Case 2. If $A + B - B - G = F$, and everything which $A + B$, G and B have in common is M, then $F = A - G$. Let us assume meanwhile that E is everything which A and G have in common—if they have something in common, so that if they have nothing in common, $E = $ Nothing. In this way $A = E + Q + M$,

---

[1] L.– In the case of concepts, subtraction is one thing, negation another. For example, a non-rational man is absurd, i.e. impossible; but one may say 'An ape is a man except in that he is not rational'. 'They are men except in so far as man differs from the beasts', as Grotius says in his iambic. 'Man'—'rational' is something other than 'non-rational man'; for 'man'—'rational' = 'brute', but a non-rational man is impossible. 'Man'—'animal'—'rational' is Nothing. Hence subtractions can make nothing, i.e. simple non-entity, or even less than nothing; but negations can make the impossible.

$B = N + M$, and $G = E + H + M$. From this we get $F = E + Q + M + N + M - N - M - E - H - M$, all of which terms (E, Q, M, N, H) are uncommunicating. So (by the preceding case) we get $F = Q - H = E + Q + M - E - H - M = A - G$.

Case 3. If $A + B - B - D = C$, and what is common to A and B does not coincide with what is common to $B + D$, it will not be the case that $C = A - D$. For let $B = E + F + G, A = H + E$, and $D = K + F$, in such a way that these ingredients do not communicate further and therefore there is no need for further analysis; then we get $C = H + E + E + F + G - E - F - G - K - F$. That is (by case 1) $C = H - K$; but $H - K \neq A - D$ (for $A - D = H + E - K - F$), unless it is assumed that $E = F$, i.e. that what is common to B and A is the same as what is common to B and D, contrary to the hypothesis. The same proof would hold even if A and D should have something which is common to them.

G vii.
234

THEOREM X

What has been subtracted and the remainder are uncommunicating.

If $L - A = N$, I assert that A and N have nothing in common. For from the definition of 'what has been subtracted' and of 'remainder', all the terms which are in L remain in N except those which are in A, of which nothing remains in N.

THEOREM XI

In two communicating terms, that in which there is whatever is common to each, and the two exclusive parts, are three terms which do not communicate with each other.

Let A and B be communicating, and $A = P + M$ and $B = N + M$, in such a way that whatever is in A and B is in M, but nothing of M is in P and N; I assert that P, M and N are uncommunicating. For both P and N are uncommunicating with M, since what is in M is at the same time in A and B, and nothing of this kind is in P or N. Consequently P and N are uncommunicating with each other, otherwise that which is common to them would be in A and B.

PROBLEM

To bring it about that, from the addition of non-coincidents to given coincidents, coincidents are constituted.

Let $A = A$; I assert that there can be found two terms, B and N, such that $B \neq N$, yet $A + B = A + N$.

Solution. Let there be assumed some term which is in A, such as M, and let N be assumed arbitrarily, but in such a way that neither M is in N, nor conversely N in M; then let B = M + N, and what is required will have been done. For since B = M + N, by hypothesis, and M and N are not in one another, by hypothesis, B ≠ N;[1] yet A + B = A + N, since A + B = A + M + N, and this (by theor. 7, since M is in A by hypothesis) = A + N.

THEOREM XII

In the case of uncommunicating terms, terms which make coincidents when added to coincidents are themselves coincident.

That is, if A + B = C + D and A = C, then B = D, provided that A and B, and also C and D, are uncommunicating. For A + B − C = C + D − C (by theor. 8); now, A + B − C = A + B − A (by hypothesis, since A = C), and A + B − A = B (by theorem 9, case 1, since A and B are uncommunicating), and (for the same reason) C + D − C = D. Therefore B = D. Q.E.D.

G vii. 235

THEOREM XIII

In general: if, by adding to coincidents other coincidents are formed, what are added are terms which communicate with each other.

Let the coincidents or the same terms be A and A, and let A + B = A + N; then I assert that B and N are communicating. For if A and B are uncommunicating, and A and N also, then B = N (by what precedes). Therefore B and N are communicating. But if A and B are communicating, let A = P + M and B = Q + M, by assuming that M is whatever is common to A and B and that there is nothing of M in P and Q. Therefore (by axiom 1) A + B = P + Q + M = P + M + N. Now, P, Q and M are uncommunicating (by theor. 11). Therefore if N also is uncommunicating with A, i.e. with P + M, from P + Q + M = P + M + N there will result (by what precedes) Q = N. Therefore N is in B; therefore N and B are communicating. If, however, on the same assumptions (namely, that P + Q + M = P + M + N, i.e. if A communicates with B) N also communicates with P + M, i.e. with A, then either N will communicate with M, in which case it will also communicate with B (in which M is), and our object will be attained, or N will communicate with P. In that case, therefore, let us similarly make

---

[1] 'B ≠ N' is not in the text, but is required to complete the sense; cf. K. Dürr, *Neue Beleuchtung einer Theorie von Leibniz* (Darmstadt, 1930), p. 144.

$P = G + H$ and $N = F + H$, in such a way that G, H and F are uncommunicating (in accordance with theor. 11), and from $P + Q + M = P + M + N$ we shall get $G + H + Q + M = G + H + M + F + H$. Therefore (by the preceding theorem) we get $Q = F$. Therefore N ($= F + H$) and B ($= Q + M$) have something in common. Q.E.D.

Corollary. From this proof we learn the following: if some terms are added to the same term or to coincidents and coincidents are formed, and both of the terms which are added are uncommunicating with that to which they are added, they themselves coincide (which is also evident from theor. 12). But if one should be communicating with that same term to which each is added, but the other is not, then the one which is uncommunicating will be in the one which is communicating; finally, if they are both communicating with that to which they are added, they will at least communicate with each other. (But otherwise it does not follow that those terms which communicate with the same third term communicate with each other.) In symbols: $A + B = A + N$. If A and B are uncommunicating, and A and N also are uncommunicating, then $B = N$. If A and B are communicating, but A and N are uncommunicating, then N will be in B; finally, if B communicates with A, and N also communicates with A, then B and N will at least communicate with each other.

16. A Study in the Calculus of Real Addition
(after 1690)

G vii.
236

Definition 1. Those terms are 'the same' or 'coincident' of which either can be substituted for the other wherever we please without loss of truth—for example, 'triangle' and 'trilateral'. For in all the propositions about the 'triangle' proved by Euclid, 'trilateral' can be substituted without loss of truth, and conversely.

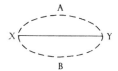

'A = B' means that A and B are the same. Thus, we may say of the straight line XY and the straight line YX that YX = XY; or, that the shortest paths of something moving from X to Y and from Y to X coincide.

Definition 2. Those terms are 'different' which are not the same, or, in which substitution sometimes does not hold. Such terms are 'circle' and 'triangle', also 'square' (namely, the perfect square; for so geometers always understand it) and 'equilateral quad-rangle'; for the latter can be said of a rhombus, of which, however, it cannot be said that it is a square.

'A ≠ B' means that A and B are different, such as the straight lines XY and RS.

Proposition 1. If A = B, then B = A. If any term is the same as another, then the other will be the same as it. For A = B (by hypothesis), therefore (by def. 1) in the proposition 'A = B', which is true by hypothesis, B can be substituted for A and A for B; therefore the result will be B = A.

Proposition 2. If A ≠ B, then B ≠ A. If any term is different from another, that other will be different from it; otherwise we should have B = A, and therefore (by the preceding proposition) A = B, which is contrary to the hypothesis.

Proposition 3. If A = B and B = C, then A = C. Those terms which are the same as a single third term are the same as each other. For if, in the proposition 'A = B' (true by hypothesis), C is substituted for B (by def. 1, since B = C), the resulting proposition will be true.

Corollary. If A = B and B = C and C = D, then A = D; and so on. For A = B = C, therefore A = C (by the above proposition); again, A = C = D; therefore (by the above proposition) A = D.

G vii.
237
Therefore, since equals are the same in magnitude, the consequence is that things which are equal to a third thing are equal to each other. To construct an equilateral triangle Euclid makes any side equal to the base, the consequence of which is that they are equal to each other. If anything is moved in a circle, it only has to be shown that the paths of two proximate periods, i.e. of returns to the same point, always coincide for it to be concluded that the paths of any periods coincide.

Proposition 4. If A = B and B ≠ C, then A ≠ C. If, of two terms which are the same as each other, one is different from a third term, then the other also will be different from that third term. For if, in the proposition 'B ≠ C' (true by hypothesis), A is substituted for B, the result will be (by def. 1, since A = B) that the proposition 'A ≠ C' is true.

Definition 3. That A 'is in' L, or, that L 'contains' A, is the same as that L is assumed to be coincident with several terms taken together, among which is A.

Definition 4. All those terms in which there is whatever is in L will together be called 'components' in respect of L, which is 'composed' or 'constituted'.

'B ⊕ N = L' means that B is in L, or, that L contains B, and that B and N together constitute or compose L. The same holds for a larger number of terms.

Definition 5. I call those terms 'subalternants' of which one is in the other, such as A and B, whether A is in B or B is in A.

Definition 6. I call those terms 'disparate' of which neither is in the other.

Axiom 1. B ⊕ N = N ⊕ B, or, transposition makes no difference here.

Postulate 1. Given any term, some term can be assumed which is different from it, and, if one pleases, disparate, i.e. such that the one is not in the other.

Postulate 2. Any plurality of terms, such as A and B, can be taken together to compose one term, A ⊕ B, or, L.

Axiom 2. A ⊕ A = A. If nothing new is added, nothing new is made; i.e. repetition changes nothing here. (For although four coins and another four are eight coins, four coins and the same four already counted are not.)

Proposition 5. If A is in B, and A = C, then C is in B. The coincident of an inexistent is an inexistent. For in the proposition 'A is in B' (true by hypothesis), the substitution of C for A (by the definition of coincidents, def. 1, since A = C by hypothesis) has the result that C is in B.

Proposition 6. If C is in B, and A = B, then C will be in A. What is in one of two coincidents is also in the other. For in the proposition 'C is in B', the substitution of A for C (since A = C) has the result that A is in B (this is the converse of the preceding proposition).[1]

Proposition 7. A is in A. Every term is in itself. For A is in A ⊕ A (by the definition of 'inexistent', i.e. by def. 3), and A ⊕ A = A (by axiom 2). Therefore (by prop. 6) A is in A.

G vii.
238

Proposition 8. A is in B, if A = B. One of two coincidents is in the other. This is evident from the preceding proposition. For A is in A (by the preceding proposition), that is (by hypothesis) it is in B.

Proposition 9. If A = B, A ⊕ C = B ⊕ C. If coincidents are added to the same term, coincidents result. For if, in the proposition 'A ⊕ C = A ⊕ C' (true in itself) you substitute for A in one place its coincident B (by def. 1), the result will be A ⊕ C = B ⊕ C.

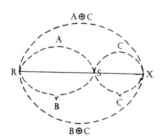

A 'triangle' ⎫
B 'trilateral' ⎭ coincide

A ⊕ C 'equilateral triangle' ⎫
B ⊕ C 'equilateral trilateral' ⎭ coincide

Note. This proposition cannot be converted, much less the two which follow. A method of finding an instance of this will be shown below, in the problem which constitutes proposition 23.

---

[1] The text has been followed here, but it will be noticed that Leibniz does not prove the proposition enunciated. In his proof he assumes, not that A = B, but that A = C, and he gives what is in effect another proof of proposition 5. The proof of proposition 6 should have run: 'In the proposition "C is in B", the substitution of A for B (since A = B) has the result that C is in A' (cf. Kneale, p. 341).

Proposition 10. If A = L and B = M, then A ⊕ B = L ⊕ M. If coincidents are added to coincidents, coincidents result. For since B = M, then (by the preceding proposition) A ⊕ B = A ⊕ M, and putting L for the second A (since A = L, by hypothesis) the result will be A ⊕ B = L ⊕ M.

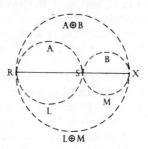

A 'triangle', L 'trilateral' coincide; B 'regular', M 'most capacious of equally many-sided figures with equal perimeters' coincide. 'Regular triangle' and 'most capacious of trilaterals making equal peripheries out of three sides' coincide.

Note. This proposition cannot be converted; for not even if A ⊕ B = L ⊕ M and A = L does it follow immediately that B = M. Much less can the following proposition be converted.

Proposition 11. If A = L and B = M and C = N, then A ⊕ B ⊕ C = L ⊕ M ⊕ N; and so on. Let there be assumed any number of terms, and as many other terms coincident with them, each corresponding to each; then the term composed of the former coincides with the term composed of the latter. For (from the preceding proposition, since A = L and B = M) the result will be A ⊕ B = L ⊕ M. Hence, because C = N, the result will be (again by the preceding proposition) A ⊕ B ⊕ C = L ⊕ M ⊕ N.

Proposition 12. If B is in L, then A ⊕ B will be in A ⊕ L. If the same term is added to content and to container, the result of the former operation is in the result of the latter. For let L = B ⊕ N (by the definition of 'inexistent'); A ⊕ B is also in B ⊕ N ⊕ A (by the same), that is, in L ⊕ A.

G vii.

239

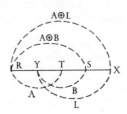

B 'equilateral', L 'regular', A 'quadrilateral'. 'Equilateral' is in, i.e. is ascribed to 'regular'. Therefore 'equilateral quadrilateral' is in 'regular quadrilateral', i.e. in 'perfect square'. YS is in RX. Therefore RT $\oplus$ YS, i.e. RS, is in RT $\oplus$ RX, i.e. in RX.

Note. This proposition cannot be converted; for not even if A $\oplus$ B is in A $\oplus$ L does it follow that B is in L.

Proposition 13. If L $\oplus$ B = L, then B will be in L. If any term does not become another when another is added to it, the added term is in it. For B is in L $\oplus$ B (by the definition of 'inexistent'), and L $\oplus$ B = L (by hypothesis), therefore (by prop. 6) B is in L.

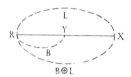

RY $\oplus$ RX = RX, therefore RY is in RX.

RY is in RX, therefore RY $\oplus$ RX = RX.

Let L be 'parallelogram' (of which any side is parallel to some side), B be 'quadrilateral'.

'Quadrilateral parallelogram' is the same as 'parallelogram', therefore 'being quadrilateral' is in 'parallelogram'.

Conversely, 'being quadrilateral' is in 'parallelogram', therefore 'quadrilateral parallelogram' is the same as 'parallelogram'.

Proposition 14. If B is in L, then L $\oplus$ B = L. Subalternants compose nothing new; i.e. if any term which is in another is added to it, it does not make anything which is different from that other. This is the converse of the preceding proposition. If B is in L, then (by the definition of 'inexistent') L = B $\oplus$ P; therefore (by prop. 9) L $\oplus$ B = B $\oplus$ P $\oplus$ B, that is (by axiom 2) = B $\oplus$ P, which (by hypothesis) = L.

Proposition 15. If A is in B and B is in C, then A is in C. A content of a content is a content of the container. For A is in B (by hypothesis), therefore A $\oplus$ L = B (by the definition of 'inexistent'). Similarly, because B is in C, B $\oplus$ M = C. Putting, in this assertion, A $\oplus$ L for B (which we have shown to coincide), the result will be A $\oplus$ L $\oplus$ M = C. Therefore (by the definition of 'inexistent') A is in C.

G vii. 240

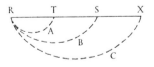

RT is in RS and RS is in RX, therefore RT is in RX.

A 'quadrilateral', B 'parallelogram', C 'rectangle'.

'Being quadrilateral' is in 'parallelogram', and 'being a parallelogram' is in 'rectangle' (i.e. a figure every angle of which is a right angle). Therefore 'being quadrilateral' is in 'rectangle'. These can be inverted, if instead of concepts considered in themselves we consider the individuals [*singularia*] comprehended under a concept; A can be a rectangle, B a parallelogram, C a quadrilateral. For all rectangles are comprehended in the number of parallelograms, and all parallelograms in the number of quadrilaterals; therefore all rectangles are contained in quadrilaterals. In the same way, all men are contained in all animals, and all animals in all corporeal substances; therefore all men are contained in corporeal substances. On the other hand, the concept of corporeal substance is in the concept of animal and the concept of animal is in the concept of man; for being a man contains being an animal.

Note. This proposition cannot be converted, much less the one which follows.

Corollary. If A ⊕ N is in B, then N is in B. For N is in A ⊕ N (by the definition of 'inexistent').

Proposition 16. If A is in B and B is in C and C is in D, then A is in D; and so on. A content of what is contained by a content is a content of the container. For if A is in B and B is in C, A is also in C (by the preceding proposition). Hence if C is in D, then (again by the preceding proposition) A will also be in D.

Proposition 17. If A is in B and B is in A, then A = B. Terms which contain each other coincide. For if A is in B, then A ⊕ N = B (by the definition of 'inexistent'). Now, B is in A (by hypothesis), therefore A ⊕ N is in A (by prop. 5). Therefore (by the corollary to prop. 15) N is also in A; therefore (by prop. 14) A = A ⊕ N, i.e. A = B.

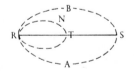

RT, N; RS, A; SR ⊕ RT, B.

G vii.
241 'Being trilateral' is in 'triangle', and 'being a triangle' is in 'trilateral'. Therefore 'triangle' and 'trilateral' coincide. So also with 'being omniscient' and 'being omnipotent'.

Proposition 18. If A is in L and B is in L, then A $\oplus$ B will be in L. What is composed of two terms which are inexistent in the same term, is in that same term. For because A is in L (by hypothesis), it can be seen that A $\oplus$ M = L (by the definition of 'inexistent'). Similarly, because B is in L it can be seen that B $\oplus$ N = L. Putting these together we have (by prop. 10) A $\oplus$ M $\oplus$ B $\oplus$ N = L $\oplus$ L. Therefore (by axiom 2)[1] A $\oplus$ M $\oplus$ B $\oplus$ N = L. Therefore (by the definition of 'inexistent') A $\oplus$ B is in L.

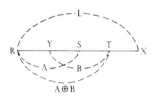

RYS is in RX.
YST is in RX.
Therefore RT is in RX.

A 'equiangular', B 'equilateral', A $\oplus$ B 'equiangular equilateral', i.e. 'regular', L 'square'. 'Equiangular' is in 'square', 'equilateral' is in 'square', therefore 'regular' is in 'square'.

Proposition 19. If A is in L and B is in L and C is in L, then A $\oplus$ B $\oplus$ C will be in L; and so on. Or, in general: if each of a number of terms taken severally is in something, so also is that which is composed of them. For A $\oplus$ B will be in L (by the preceding proposition); now, C is in L (by hypothesis), therefore (again by the preceding proposition) A $\oplus$ B $\oplus$ C is in L.

Note. It is evident that these two, and similar propositions, can be converted. For if A $\oplus$ B = L,[2] it is evident from the definition of 'inexistents'[3] that A is in L and B is in L. Also, if A $\oplus$ B $\oplus$ C = L, it is evident that A is in L, and B is in L, and C is in L; also that A $\oplus$ B is in L, that A $\oplus$ C is in L, and that B $\oplus$ C is in L; and so on.

Proposition 20. If A is in M and B is in N, then A $\oplus$ B will be in M $\oplus$ N. If the former term of one pair of terms is in the latter, and the former term of another pair of terms is in the latter term of that pair, then the term composed of the two former terms is in the term composed of the two latter terms. For A is in M (by

---

[1] The text has 'Axiom 5'.
[2] C. I. Lewis (p. 301) points out that Leibniz should in consistency have said that A $\oplus$ B is in L, and similarly that A $\oplus$ B $\oplus$ C is in L.
[3] The text has 'existentium'.

hypothesis), and M is in M $\oplus$ N (by the definition of 'inexistent'). Therefore (by prop. 15) A is in M $\oplus$ N. Similarly, because B is in N, and N is in M $\oplus$ N, B will be in M $\oplus$ N. Now, if A is in M $\oplus$ N and B is in M $\oplus$ N, then (by prop. 18) A $\oplus$ B will be in M $\oplus$ N.

G vii.
242

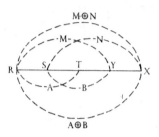

RT is in RY and SY in SX, therefore RT $\oplus$ SY, i.e. RY, is in RY $\oplus$ SX, i.e. in RX.[1]

Let A be 'quadrilateral', B be 'equiangular'; A $\oplus$ B will be 'rectangle'. Let M be 'parallelogram', N be 'regular'; M $\oplus$ N will be 'square'. Now, 'quadrilateral' is in 'parallelogram' and 'equiangular' is in 'regular'; therefore 'rectangle' (i.e. 'equiangular quadrilateral') is in 'regular parallelogram', i.e. 'square'.

Note. This proposition cannot be converted. Even granting that A is in M and that A $\oplus$ B is in M $\oplus$ N, yet it does not follow immediately that B is in N. For it can happen that both A and B are in M, and also that some terms which are in B are in M, but the rest are in N. Much less, therefore, can the following proposition and any like it be converted.

Proposition 21. If A is in M and B is in N and C is in P, A $\oplus$ B $\oplus$ C will be in M $\oplus$ N $\oplus$ P; and so on. That which is composed of contents is in that which is composed of the containers. For because A is in M and B is in N, A $\oplus$ B will be in M $\oplus$ N (by the preceding proposition). Now, C is in P, therefore (again by the preceding proposition) A $\oplus$ B $\oplus$ C is in M $\oplus$ N $\oplus$ P.

Proposition 22. Given two disparate terms, A and B, to find a third term, C, which is different from them and which together with them makes up the subalternants A $\oplus$ C and B $\oplus$ C: that is, that although neither of A and B is in the other, yet one of A $\oplus$ C and B $\oplus$ C is in the other.

Solution. If we want A $\oplus$ C to be in B $\oplus$ C, although A is not in B, this can be done as follows. Let there be assumed (by post. 1)

---

[1] The text has 'RT est in RY et ST in SX, ergo RT $\oplus$ ST seu RY est in RY $\oplus$ SY seu in RY'. In the translation, this has been corrected from the diagram and from the example which follows.

some term, D, of any kind provided that it is not in A, and (by post. 2) let $A \oplus D = C$; then we shall have done what is required.

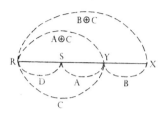

For $A \oplus C = A \oplus A \oplus D^1$ (by the construction) $= A \oplus D$ (by axiom 2). Similarly $B \oplus C = B \oplus A \oplus D$ (by the construction). Now $A \oplus D$ is in $B \oplus A \oplus D$ (by def. 3). Therefore $A \oplus C$ is in $B \oplus C$; which was to be done.

SY and YX are disparate. Let $RS \oplus SY = YR$, $SY \oplus YR$ will be in $XY \oplus YR$.

Let A be 'equilateral', B 'parallelogram', D 'equiangular', C 'equiangular equilateral', i.e. 'regular'; here it is evident that, although 'equilateral' and 'parallelogram' are disparate, such that the one is not in the other, yet 'regular equilateral' is in 'regular parallelogram', i.e. 'square'. But, you will say, the construction described above in the problem will not succeed in all cases. For example, let A be 'trilateral' and B 'quadrilateral'; a concept cannot be found in which there are at the same time both A and B, and therefore there is not a $B \oplus C$ in which there is $A \oplus C$, because A and B are incompatible. I reply that our general construction depends upon the second postulate, in which is contained the proposition that any term can be compounded with any term. Thus, God, soul, body, point and heat compose an aggregate of these five things. So 'quadrilateral' and 'triangle' can also be compounded, and the problem is solved. For let it be assumed that D is anything which is not contained in 'trilateral', such as 'circle'; $A \oplus D$ will be 'trilateral and circle', which may be called C. Now, $C \oplus A$ is nothing but 'trilateral and circle' again, and this is in $C \oplus B$, that is, in 'trilateral, circle and quadrilateral'. But if anyone wishes to apply this general calculus of compositions of any sort to a special manner of composition—e.g. if he wants 'trilateral', 'circle' and 'quadrilateral' not only to compose one aggregate, but also to be in the same subject, each concept at the same time—then he must see if they are compatible. Thus, unmoved straight lines at a distance from each other can be

G vii.
243

---

[1] The text has L in the proof where the diagram and the solution have D. D has been substituted in the translation.

taken together to compose one aggregate, but not to compose one continuum.

Proposition 23. Given two disparate terms, A and B, to find a third term, C, different from them and such that A $\oplus$ B = A $\oplus$ C.[1]

Solution. Let it be assumed (by postulate 2) that C = A $\oplus$ B, and what is desired will have been done. For A and B are disparate (by hypothesis), that is (by def. 6) one is not in the other, therefore (by prop. 13) it is not possible that C = A, or that C = B. These three terms, therefore, are different, as the problem requires. Further, A $\oplus$ C = A $\oplus$ A $\oplus$ B (by the construction), that is (by axiom 2) = A $\oplus$ B. Therefore A $\oplus$ C = A $\oplus$ B; which is what was to be done.

Proposition 24. To find several terms which are different, each to each, as many as shall be desired, such that from them there cannot be composed a term which is new, i.e. different from any of them.

Solution. Let there be assumed (by post. 1) any terms whatever and of any number, which are different from each other, A, B, C, D; of these (by post. 2) let A $\oplus$ B = M, M $\oplus$ C = N, N $\oplus$ D = P. I assert that A, B, M, N, P are the required terms. For M (by the construction) is made from A and B; further, A or B is in M, M is in N, and N is in P. Therefore (by prop. 16) any one of the former is in any one of the latter. Now, if you compound any two of these with each other, nothing new is constituted. For if you compound the same term with itself, nothing new is formed; L $\oplus$ L = L (by axiom 2).[2] If you compound one term with another, you compound the former with the latter, and therefore a term which is inexistent with the term which contains it, as L $\oplus$ N; but L $\oplus$ N = N (by proposition 14).[3] If you compound three terms, such as L $\oplus$ N $\oplus$ P, you compound the pair of terms L $\oplus$ N with the one term P. But the pair L $\oplus$ N of themselves constitute nothing new, but from them (as we have already shown) there comes one term, namely the latter term N. Therefore to compound the pair of terms L $\oplus$ N with the one term P is the same as compounding the one term N with the one term P, which we have already shown to constitute nothing new. Therefore the pair of terms together with the one term—i.e. the three together—constitute nothing new. And so on, in the case of more terms. Which is what was to be done.

G vii.
244

---

[1] The clause 'and such that . . .' is not in the text, but is demanded by the proof and by a reference in the note to prop. 9. Cf. Lewis, p. 302.
[2] The number of the axiom is not given in the text.
[3] The number of the proposition is not given in the text.

Note. It would have been sufficient to assume terms which exist successively in each other, as M, N, P, &c.; and indeed this will hold if in our construction we put A = Nothing, with the result that B = M. However, the solution which has been given extends somewhat more widely. Indeed, these problems can be solved in yet other ways; but to exhibit all possible solutions of the problems, i.e. to prove that no other methods are possible, needs the prior proof of several other propositions. For example, the five things A, B, C, D and E can be arranged so that nothing new can be compounded from them only in the following ways: first, if A is in B and B in C and C in D and D in E; second, if A $\oplus$ B = C and C is in D and D in E; third, if A $\oplus$ B = C and A is in D and B $\oplus$ D = E. The five concepts 'equiangular', A, 'equilateral', B, 'regular', C, 'rectangle', D, and 'square', E, are related in the third or last way. No new term can be compounded from these which does not coincide with them; for 'equiangular equilateral' coincides with 'regular', 'equiangular' is in 'rectangle', and 'equilateral rectangle' coincides with 'square'. Hence 'equiangular regular' is the same as 'regular' and 'equilateral regular' also, and 'equiangular rectangle' is 'rectangle' and 'regular rectangle' is 'square'.

Note to definitions 3, 4, 5 and 6. We say that the concept of the genus is in the concept of the species, the individuals of the species in the individuals of the genus; a part in the whole, and the indivisible in the continuum—such as a point in a line, even though a point is not a part of a line. Thus, the concept of an affection or predicate is in the concept of the subject. In general, this consideration extends very widely. We also say that inexistents are contained in those terms in which they are. Nor does it matter here, with regard to this general concept, how those terms which are in something are related to each other or to the container. So our proofs hold even of those terms which compose something distributively, as all species together compose the genus. Further, all the inexistents which are sufficient to constitute a container, or, in which there are all the terms which are in the container, are said to compose the container itself. For example, A $\oplus$ B will be said to 'compose' L if A, B and L stand for the straight lines RS, YX and RX, for RS $\oplus$ YX = RX. In the same way, RS $\oplus$ SX = RX. Such parts, which complete a whole, I customarily term 'co-integrants'[1], especially if they have no common part, such that they can be called 'co-members', like RS and RX. From this is it evident that the same term can be composed in

G vii.
245

---

[1] Cf. *Specimen Geometriae Luciferae*, G. M. vii. 284.

many ways, if the terms of which it is composed are again composite; and further, that if they can be analysed to infinity, then the variations of composition are infinite. Therefore the whole of synthesis and analysis depends on the principles laid down here. Further, if the terms which are in something are homogeneous with that in which they are contained, they are called 'parts' and the container is called a 'whole'. If any two parts are so related that a third thing can be found which has a part common to the one and a part common to the other, that which is composed of them is a continuum. From this it is evident in what way one consideration rises gradually from another. Further, I call 'subalternants' those of which one is in the other, as a species in a genus, or the straight line RS in the straight line RX. I call them 'disparate' when the case is different; such as the straight lines RS and YX, two species of the same genus, a perfect and an imperfect metal, and also the members of different divisions of the same whole, which have something in common. For example, if you divide 'metal' into 'perfect' and 'imperfect', and again into 'soluble in *aqua fortis*' and 'insoluble in *aqua fortis*', it is evident that 'metal insoluble in *aqua fortis*' and 'perfect metal' are two disparate terms, and that there is a perfect metal (i.e. which is fulminable, remaining in the cupel)[1] which is yet soluble in *aqua fortis*, such as silver; and that on the other hand there is an imperfect metal which is insoluble in *aqua fortis*, such as tin.

Note to axioms 1 and 2. As general algebra [*speciosa generalis*] is merely the representation and treatment of combinations by signs, and as various laws of combination can be discovered, the result of this is that various methods of computation arise. Here, however, no account is taken of the variation which consists in a change of order alone, and AB is the same for us as BA. Next, no account is taken here of repetition; i.e. AA is the same for us as A. Consequently, whenever these laws are observed, the present calculus can be applied. It is evident that this is observed in the composition of absolute concepts, where no account is taken of order or of repetition. Thus, it is the same to say 'hot and bright' as to say 'bright and hot', and to speak of 'hot fire' or 'white milk', with the poets, is a pleonasm; 'white milk' is simply 'milk', and 'rational man'—i.e. 'rational animal which is rational'—is simply 'rational

---

[1] Reading, with Lewis, 'cupella' for 'capella'. The reference is probably to 'cupellation', a process by which impurities are removed from impure precious metal, the purified metal remaining in the crucible (see, e.g., E. J. Holmyard, *Alchemy* (London, 1957), p. 41). 'Fulmination', as a metallurgical term, means 'becoming suddenly bright and uniform in colour'.

animal'. It is the same when certain determinate things are said to exist in things: real addition of the same thing is vain repetition. When two and two are said to make four, the latter two must be different from the former. If they were the same, nothing new would result; it would be just as if, for a joke, I wanted to make six eggs out of three by first counting three eggs, then taking away one and counting the remaining two, and finally taking one away again and counting the remaining one. But in the calculus of numbers and magnitudes, A, B or other signs do not stand for a certain thing, but for any thing of the same number of congruent parts. For any two feet are signified by 2, if a foot is the unit or measure, whence $2 + 2$ makes something new, 4, and 3 by 3 makes something new, 9; for it is presupposed that what are used are always different (though of the same magnitude). The situation is different in the case of certain things, for example lines. Let it be assumed that something moveable describes the straight line $RY \oplus YX = RYX$, or, $P \oplus B = L$, going from R to X. Then let us assume that the same thing goes back from X to Y and stays there; then, although it twice describes YX or B, it produces nothing else than if it had described YX once. So '$L \oplus B$' is the same as L, i.e. '$P \oplus B \oplus B$'; or, '$RY \oplus YX \oplus XY$' is the same as '$RY \oplus YX$'. This caution is of great importance in estimating the magnitude of things which are generated by the magnitude of the motion of those things which generate[1] or describe. For care must be taken that, in describing, one thing does not choose as its own path the track of another, or that one part of the describer does not succeed to the place of another; or there must be a subtraction, so that there is no reduplication. It is also evident from this that, according to the concept which we are using here, components can by their magnitudes constitute a magnitude which is greater than that of the thing which they compose. Hence the composition of things and of magnitudes differs widely. For example, if a straight line L, or RX, has two parts, A, or RS, and B, or YX, either of which is greater than half of RX—e.g. if RX is five feet, RS four feet and YX three feet—it is evident that the magnitudes of these parts will constitute a magnitude of seven feet, greater than the magnitude of the whole. Yet the straight lines RS and YX compose nothing other than RX, i.e. $RS \oplus YX = RX$. This is why I here designate this real addition by $\oplus$, as the addition of magnitudes is designated by $+$. Finally: when, in real addition, one is concerned with the actual generation of things, it makes a great difference what the order is—for the foundations are laid before the house is built. But in the mental formation of

G vii.
246

---

[1] Reading, with Lewis, 'generant' for 'generantur'.

things the result is the same, no matter which ingredient we consider first (although one method of consideration may be more useful than another), so the order does not make any change in the thing which is produced. In due course order also will be considered; for the moment, however, 'RY $\oplus$ YS $\oplus$ SX' is the same as 'YS $\oplus$ RY $\oplus$ SX'.

Note to proposition 24. Given that RS and YX are different, indeed disparate, so that neither is in the other, let RS $\oplus$ YX = RX; then 'RS $\oplus$ RX' will be the same as 'YX $\oplus$ RX'. For, in the case of concepts, it is always the straight line RX which is composed.

G vii.
247

Let A be 'parallelogram', B 'equiangular' (which are disparate) and let C be A $\oplus$ B, i.e. 'rectangle'. Then 'rectangular parallelogram' will be the same as 'equiangular rectangle', for each of the two is simply 'rectangle'. Generally, let Maevius be A, Titius B, and the pair of men composed of the two be C; then Maevius with this pair will be the same as Titius with this pair, for in neither case does anything result other than the pair itself. Still another solution can be given, which is more elegant but more restricted, if A and B have something in common, and this is given, and so what is peculiar to each is also given. Let it be, therefore, that M is peculiar to A and N is peculiar to B; let M $\oplus$ N = D, and let P be common to each; I assert that A $\oplus$ D = B $\oplus$ D. For since A = P $\oplus$ M and B = P $\oplus$ N, A $\oplus$ D = P $\oplus$ M $\oplus$ N, and again B $\oplus$ D = P $\oplus$ M $\oplus$ N.

INDEX